DOXA

Tamara—
I look forward to and anticipate
what God has on the horizon. I
am grateful for our growing partnership
in Jesus.   I Thess 2:11-12.

Jeremy

DOXA

Becoming a Church
Worthy of His Kingdom

JEREMY McKIM

Wipf & Stock
PUBLISHERS
Eugene, Oregon

To our Papa who loves us,

Our King who redeemed us,

And the Spirit who indwells us.

Contents

Foreword

YOU ARE HOLDING AN invitation in your hands. It doesn't look like a traditional invitation with scrolling letters and an RSVP at the end. It's a very different kind of invitation. The pages of this book offer an invitation to transformation and truth within a Christ-seeking heart. It's an invitation to the heart for the freedom to which Christ set us free.

It's possible that no one will ever know your story as you journey through these pages, but I encourage you to step with courage and invite others into the journey. It is within community that you will experience the most from this book. Just as the Trinity lives in perfect community, we as followers of Christ were not intended to reflect His glory in isolation.

This book may challenge you, confront you or confirm things you've been thinking about. The one certain thing is that this book will point you to Christ and the nearer you come to Him the more you will likely die to yourself and live in Him.

This book is obedience. It is not a story about obedience. It is an act of obedience. Jeremy heard the voice of God, paused and like Jeremiah he responded when God asked, "what do you see?"

The words on these pages are the outpouring of what Jeremy saw. Jeremy speaks as a prophet for our day as he calls out for the church to be still and listen to what the Spirit is saying.

I have great compassion for Jeremy and all those who are given a prophetic word for the church. Visions from God are awkward when placed in the plane of the world. They never seem to quite fit the comfort-hungry world. The messenger is often left scratching his head wondering if the whole experience was a blessing or a curse.

Jeremy has courageously, faithfully and obediently called out a warning when God revealed many are dangerously close to a cliff.

Every page of this book has been lived out by Jeremy. Before he could write one word, God took Jeremy through each step. The journey is sometimes painful and sometimes joyful, but always with hope. Jeremy has courageously allowed his own transformation to be publicly shared.

It would be difficult to avoid noticing that we are in a time of change within the church. From messages of post modernity to emerging church and dozens of other expressions of change, we are not without the signs that God is up to something in our day.

We can simplify the overload of messages and simply note that God is preparing the bride for her Bridegroom and the great day of the wedding banquet. Christ is not returning for a harlot. The One called Faithful and True is coming for His bride robed in the linen of His righteousness.

The preparation requires surrender and there . . . we will find joy.

I hope you will enter into the journey of this book and feel your heart tugged toward surrender and transformation via the Lord's gracious hand. I hope you will be inspired to open your bible and read it with a listening heart. I hope you will feel how much God loves you. I hope you feel moved to step out in faith and obedience to proclaim this Gospel of the Kingdom.

May God receive all the glory.

Jeanette Reed

Acknowledgements

I WROTE THIS BOOK during what has been the most difficult yet most fruitful time of my life. Nearly all that is written on these pages resulted from a desperate need to cling harder to God. Thus, I give thanks and credit to God for either engineering or allowing a series of difficult and painful circumstances to come our way. The only reason I have *anything* to say is because God has remained stubbornly faithful. I would also like to thank my wife, Sydel who heroically gave me her blessing to invest countless hours to write and willingly read and gave feedback on every portion of this work. This book also represents the faith, courage, and wisdom of numerous saints who are going before me and have generously shared with me the riches of Christ. This book has indeed been a group effort.

Introduction

"And now you Gentiles have also heard the truth, the Good News that God saves you. And when you believed in Christ, he identified you as his own by giving you the Holy Spirit, whom he promised long ago. The Spirit is God's guarantee that he will give us the inheritance he promised and that he has purchased us to be his own people. He did this so we would praise and glorify him" Ephesians 1:13–14.

WELCOME FRIENDS!

Doxa, a Greek word in the New Testament, is the word for *glory*. Doxa is the radiance and majesty that only God can possess due simply to His matchless and uncontested greatness. Nothing in all of creation comes close. Humanity reaches for perfection. God *is* perfection. Humanity reaches for superiority. God *is* superiority. His glory is so immense that were we to see Him fully unveiled, it would kill us—literally (See Exod 33:18–23). My heart's greatest desire is for us to live for God's glory to be displayed in a creation that is desperate for life. Even if I don't see it in my lifetime, I want to die knowing that I was faithful and true to God and all that He was doing in my lifetime. The Apostle Paul tells us "whenever someone turns to the Lord, the veil [that which hides the glory of the Lord] is taken away. For the Lord is the Spirit, and wherever the Spirit of the Lord is, there is freedom. So all of us who have had that veil removed can *see and reflect the glory of the Lord*. And the Lord—who is the Spirit—makes us more and more like him as we are changed into his glorious image" (2 Cor 3:16–18). This journey that we are entering is intended to help us become children of God—living like we are radically loved and cherished by our King. I want us to *see* that God is radically present and radically at work. And second, I want us to *become* vessels whereby He fills the world with His presence and glory and accomplishes His work. Outside of creation, God's glory remains constant and unchangeable. In the context of a fallen creation, God's glory is broadcasted through our humble obedience.

We will journey through the book of Acts throughout the next 10 weeks or so (you may need more than one week to complete a chapter). The book of Acts is a marvelous display of God working through ordinary underdogs. He seems to bypass those hung up on their professional credentials and instead uses weak and invisible pawns to display His glory. The book of Acts is also our tool for accountability as we see both the desires and capabilities of God transpire in human hearts and hands. We have no excuses to sit idly by. It is a storybook that should both enlighten and disturb us. It tells us what God is capable of and it gives us marvelous clues to learn how to step out of our man-centered religion and into a God-centered life. I hope the next 10 weeks are life-changing for you as you encounter a God without limits. Please bear in mind that this book is powerless to change your life. It is simply intended to be a tool that leads you to the One that can change your life and the world around you by infusing you and your community with His generous grace.

Of course I can't make you journey through this book with others, but I strongly encourage you to do so. Discipleship cannot exist in a vacuum of self or even self and God. Discipleship is a way of being in the world *with other people* that both delight us and bother us. If we are living in the isolation of 'me and Jesus,' we are not being discipled. Discipleship happens when we have a conflict with a friend or neighbor or when we get cutoff in traffic. God forms us when we journey with fellow believers. If we are journeying alone, we are not being discipled.

Let us help and guide one another towards becoming spiritual friends for one another—to draw out both our brokenness as well as the work and leading of the Holy Spirit as He goes about restoring, redeeming, and empowering us for the works God prepared for us long ago.

In order for this to work well, we all must dig deep and take some risks. I'm asking you to really *think* and maybe do things you've never done before. Every chapter will examine a story in the book of Acts that summons us to participate in the kingdom of a living King. Each chapter is divided into four sections. I recommend for you to walk through only one section per sitting in order to give your heart and mind adequate time to pray and reflect on things. I'm asking you to invest a significant block of time (30 minutes) four times throughout your week to mediate on the Scripture, pray, reflect on your life, and discern what God might be doing in your midst. The deeper you're willing to dig; the more fruit will come. Join the conversation with others around the world at http://jeremymckim.com/ and share how God is at work in your midst that we might all draw strength and courage as God calls us out.

Each chapter will uncover an aspect of what it means for us to be God's Church *in His kingdom*. This theme will be laid out on the week's first page like this:

The Kingdom of God is at Hand: God's kingdom is more truthful and more real than our kingdoms though often His kingdom will appear smaller and less significant than our kingdoms. And so we ask God for eyes of faith.

Repent: We must lay down our kingdoms, our plans, and our false identities. We acknowledge that our way causes harm and so we come to God asking Him for His Kingdom, His plans, and a true identity in Him.

Believe the Good News: God is inviting us into His kingdom. This indeed is good news! Once we have turned from our ways, we are free to receive the ways of God and follow His lead. Jesus said that the work God requires of us is simply to believe. Our life's work will be to believe that God's kingdom is more worthy of our allegiance than any and all worldly kingdoms.

Therefore, Go: Good and truthful news always calls us into action. Let's do something about it together.

Welcome aboard . . .

NOTE TO GROUP LEADER:

The questions interlaced throughout this study are intended to stimulate reflection, creativity, and forward momentum. This journey will be 100 times more valuable when it is a *shared* journey. Encourage group participation and as the subject matter at times becomes heavy, be prepared to offer additional counsel to those in your group. Every chapter contains an action item. Encourage those in your group to go after it and be sure that these experiences are discussed when you gather. This book is primarily intended to be a catalyst to discover the heart of God together. It aims to create disciplines such as prayer, reflection, conflict resolution, authenticity, study of the scriptures, etc. that grow into desires such as prayer, reflection, conflict resolution, authenticity, study of the scriptures, etc. that instill a trajectory and momentum to last for a lifetime. See it as 10 weeks of equipping for whatever God is going to initiate among and through you during and after the 10 weeks are over. Feel free to add or tweak the questions to fit the context of your group. Also feel free to go at a slower pace. I have taken a group through portions of the study and at times we needed two or three weeks to fully cover a chapter. May our God bless you as you seek His face together.

CHAPTER I

Becoming Less

"Christians are not naturally born in places like [your city] or anywhere else. Christians are intentionally made by an adventuresome church, which has again learned to ask the right questions to which Christ alone supplies the right answers."[1]

OVERVIEW:

Core Scripture: Acts 2:42–47 and 4:32–37

The Kingdom of God is at Hand: God has generously met all of our needs in Christ and we are therefore free to offer ourselves to Him and our neighbor uninhibited as nothing can harm us or separate us from Him.

Repent: Church involvement is gathering only at routine and planned events. Our lives are not truly shared. We only do spiritual or church things at official church events and gatherings. We do not see God in our daily lives or expect Him to show up there.

Believe the Good News: Because Jesus has triumphed over all things, even death; we trustingly abandon the lesser fairytales of self-improvement, self-actualization, and self-protection. We pledge our allegiance to Jesus knowing that we have nothing worthwhile to lose while all that He has to gain is both eternal and cherished. This is the God we boldly entrust our lives and livelihood to. We begin a journey that will call us to action and transformation. We do not journey alone but together and so we will learn to be vulnerable and help one another stay on the path Jesus has laid before us.

Therefore, Go: Identify what you believe defines your sense of worth (what makes you feel good and look good). Identify the audience that you are trying to impress (whose opinions matter to you?). Second, identify the habits, patterns, worries, fears, or behaviors that you must tend to in order to protect or maintain your sense of worth. Write this down and be prepared to share it the next time you meet with your community. If you get sweaty palms when you think about sharing this (like the rest of us do), let that be your starting point when you share this important piece of your life.

[1] Hauerwas and Willimon, *Resident Aliens*, 19.

Part 1: Free to Not Live Defensively;
Sent to Live Generously and Fearlessly.

Read Acts 2:42–47 and 4:32–37.
What is God showing you in this story?
Write down any thoughts, questions, or promptings.

_____

_____

_____

_____

_____

What do you think prompted all the sharing and generosity going on here?

_____

_____

_____

Imagine going before a panel of successful people on the pitcher's mound of Yankee Stadium. There is an audience of 30,000 watching—including friends, family, and co-workers. For an entire week this panel underwent briefing on your life. They are intimately acquainted with the worst and most shameful details of your life. To your horror they pull out a box of DVD's documenting things done in secret, thoughts, and embarrassing fantasies. They let it run on the re-play screen for over an hour. They then ask you to explain the apparent gap between the person you claim to be and the person you really are. Would you even attempt to muster a defense or would you run?

I'm convinced we spend most of our time and energy protecting and maintaining our identities. Jr. High was hell on earth for me. I had nothing as far as the world is concerned. I was virtually invisible; I could have walked the halls naked and no one would have noticed. In high school I began working out (and drinking milk). Soon I was noticed and counted for something as far as the world was concerned. I protected my athleticism with my life—it was my life because before I had that, I had no *felt* reason to live. Any identity we have that requires protection is an identity built on a lie. If our identity is susceptible to being lost, causing us to live in fear; our identity is built on lies. At some point in our lives, our culture fed us a list of qualities that if achieved, would give our lives value and meaning. Our culture tells us what it takes to be liked and tolerated. We grow up in fear that one day this identity will fall apart and in its place will be a an unlikable and undesirable person waiting to be mocked and spit out of the global marketplace of popularity.

We work hard to make sure that nothing remotely close to the situation described above at Yankee Stadium will ever happen to us.

Take a couple of minutes to think about your various identities—the pursuits or qualities that experience has taught you that if successfully achieved, will result in people liking you. Write them down below. Are any of these identities susceptible to being ruined? For example if my identity is in my career, my identity is in jeopardy because a bad economy or smarter coworker coming up the ranks to replace me could someday derail that career. Chances are, the things that threaten your identity are also the sources of your fears (unless you have arachnophobia). We most greatly fear that which threatens to steal or maim what we most treasure. Think on these things and write your responses below.

_____

_____

_____

_____

_____

_____

Who are the individuals or groups in your life that you allow to influence you because their opinions matter to you? These could be people you know (friend, co-worker) or don't know (Hollywood, a musician, etc.)

_____

_____

_____

God has promised His unconditional love to all of His children. Scripture is clear that the identity of a child of God is God Himself and the relationship that He offers us. *In Christ, we lack nothing; nothing can be taken from us; nothing can harm us; and nothing can separate us from him.* In short, as children of God, we have nothing to lose. Sometimes the love of God seems unimportant to me. What I *really* want is a guarantee that people will think what I want them to think of me—this more often seems like the most euphoric road in life. God seems distant and his words seem to be just that: words that never or rarely cross over into my heart or actual existence.

Take a minute to try and fathom what it would be like to carry the knowledge that the God who created the universe also harbors deep affection and longings for your life. If you suffer, He suffers. If you celebrate, He throws a party. What feelings or objections rise up within you as you picture this?

_____

_____

_____

_____

_____

_____

Part 2: Willing to Feel Afraid in Order to Become Real

Read Acts 2:42–47 and 4:32–37.
What is God showing you in this story?
Write down any thoughts, questions, or promptings.

_____

_____

_____

_____

_____

_____

Read the following commentary by Brennan Manning. As a follower of Christ, Brennan has endured excommunication from the Catholic Church; the stigma of being an alcoholic; the stigma of divorce; and being an internationally sought after author and speaker.

Brennan writes, "Christians who remain in hiding continue to live the lie. We deny the reality of our sin. In a futile attempt to erase our past, we deprive the community of our healing gift. If we conceal our wounds out of fear and shame, our inner darkness can neither be illuminated nor become a light for others. We cling to our bad feelings and beat ourselves with the past when what we should do is let go. As Dietrich Bonhoeffer said, guilt is an idol. But when we dare to live as forgiven men and women, we join the wounded healers and draw closer to Jesus."

Brennan identifies the false self; the part of us that clings to an image that others will be pleased by. He refers to the false self as The Imposter. Check out his description of the Imposter below and see if in anyway, it is a description of you.

"A glittering image must be kept at all costs. My imposter trembles at the prospect of incurring the displeasure and wrath of others. Incapable of direct speech, he hedges, waffles, procrastinates, and remains silent out of fear and rejection . . . Imposters are preoccupied with acceptance and approval. Because of their suffocating need to please others, they cannot say no with the same confidence with which they say yes. And so they overextend themselves in people, projects, and causes, motivated not by personal commitment but by the fear of not living up to others' expectations. The imposter is the classic codependent; 'A disease characterized by a loss of identity. To be codependent is to be out of touch with one's feelings, needs, and desires.' (John Bradshaw) To gain acceptance and approval, the false self suppresses or camouflages feelings, making emotional honesty impossible. Living out of the false self creates a compulsive desire to present a perfect image to the public so that everybody will admire us and nobody will know us. The imposter's life becomes a perpetual roller-coaster ride of elation and depression. The imposter cannot experience intimacy in any relationship. His narcissism excludes others. Incapable of intimacy with self and out of touch with his feelings, intuitions, and insight, the imposter is insensitive to the moods, needs, and dreams of others. Reciprocal sharing is impossible."[2]

Further, Brennan identifies the following:
- The imposter tries to blind us to the reality of our own brokenness
- We rationalize that if most people think well of us than we must be doing alright and thus we are able to think well of ourselves.
- The imposter is what he does. In other words, if I can do something I am worth something. If I cannot do something, I am worth less.

In what ways do you identify with Brennan's thoughts and conclusions about the false self, especially as they pertain to living up to others' expectations and maintaining an image?

_____

_____

_____

_____

_____

Would you rather be known or admired? Why?

_____

_____

_____

_____

I believe that deep down we all desire to be known for who we really are. We want to be known by someone who is fully aware of our worst qualities and yet is not scared away or ill equipped to continue to love us. It's easier to be admired because it makes us feel good. It's scary to be known. Our commitment to only be admired leaves us profoundly disconnected. "Disconnection can be regarded as a state of being, a condition of existence where the deepest part of who we are is vibrantly attached to no one, where we are profoundly unknown and therefore experience neither the thrill of being believed in nor the joy of loving or being loved. Disconnected people may often be unaware of the empty recesses in their souls that long to be filled. They often mistake lesser longings for greater

[2] Manning, *Abba's Child*, 30–31.

ones and settle for the satisfaction of popularity, influence, success, and intense but shallow relationships. Disconnected people are unaware of what God has placed within them that if poured into others could change lives. They feel either inadequate for questionable reasons or powerful for wrong reasons."[3] I fear that most of us live disconnected from God and one another. We may engage routinely in our friendships but that engagement is dominated by congeniality—politeness, niceness, what we bought, what we watched, etc.

Do you feel like there are people in your life that you can truly relate with in which the imposter goes away and the real you can emerge? If yes, what enabled you to relate with this person in this way? If no, what stands in the way of having relationships that are Imposter-free and what would help you overcome this? Discuss this with your community.

_____

_____

_____

_____

_____

_____

Think about the props in your life that you have successfully been able to hide behind. (I'm smart; I'm financially successful; I'm attractive; I'm athletic; I'm talented; I'm independent, etc.) Can you recall particular stories [your family, peers, movies, advertising, being teased in middle school, etc.] that told you these props would result in people liking you, admiring you, or at least leaving you safely alone to contentedly mind your own business? Write these down and expand on what you believed and how that belief has shaped your life as an adult. *For example, one of my props is performing well or earning recognition for accomplishments. The story that gave me this prop was being a successful athlete in high school as one of a few ways to achieve a social purpose. The resulting belief was that my life would only be significant when I was better at what I did than my competitors were. As an adult I am wired to compete for my position before God and with others. I live to prove that I am better than the next guy and thus more deserving of God's favor or the approval of those in my social context. To deny this tendency literally feels like suicide because it appears to be the only route to significance.*

_____

_____

[3] Crabb, *Connecting*, 45.

_____

_____

_____

_____

Read Ephesians 1:3–10 and Romans 3:23–24.

Are you bothered by the perplexity of being a sinner and being blessed with every spiritual blessing in Christ? What do you think it means to be both?

_____

_____

_____

_____

It's pretty easy to say, 'Yeah sure, I'm a sinner.' But it is a bit more frightening to say, 'I know I'm a sinner because yesterday I . . .' It's the *uniqueness or particularity* of our sin that scares us. We know that everyone is a sinner but only we know the darkness in our hearts so intimately. We thus reason that we are worse or somehow exist on some deeper echelon of darkness as far as sinners go. We are definitely above average when it comes to sin. So in our fear of being rejected or shown to the door—we hide our sin. This behavior might also indicate we are doubtful that we have been given a new nature and that this nature changes our identity and is potentially *more powerful than our sinful nature* (See Col 1:11).

If we are to function as one body, with Christ as the head, we need to be able to help one another see who we are becoming. We simply can't get around this without knowing one another well. The Imposter must go away so that the new self that God is creating can emerge as we relate with one another. God can do amazing things with what is actually happening. However there is little that can be done until the Imposter comes out.

It's my belief, and I could be wrong, that most Christians in America are primarily taught how to avoid the 'really bad' sins. We are shown a picture of what a model Christian (citizen of earth) looks like and we do our best to copy it. Smile a lot. Be warm and friendly. Don't look at porn. Be patient with difficult people. Don't fly off the handle. Don't cuss. Attend a church service every week and sing loudly. In doing, our lives become neutral. We are still sinners but we have hidden our distasteful qualities from the general public. Good days are determined by the absence of conflict; the absence of emotional turmoil; and the successful maintenance of our good reputations and tidy schedules.

Ephesians gives us a different picture. God has blessed us in Christ with *every* spiritual blessing. Our God can do *infinitely more* than we could ever imagine. Jesus said we would do *greater things than He did*, and He raised the dead. This tells me we have much more to give to one another than chronic niceness and an attractive lifestyle. "Without Jesus, Peter might have been a good fisherman, perhaps even a very good one. But he would never have gotten anywhere, would never have learned what a coward he really was, what a confused, then confessing, courageous person he was, even a good preacher (Acts 2) when he needed to be. Peter stands out as a true individual, or better, a true character, not because he had become 'free' or 'his own person' but because he had become attached to the Messiah and messianic community, which enabled him to lay hold of his life, to make so much more of his life than if he had been left to his own devices."[4]

Larry Crabb is a teacher who helps me see what it might look like for us to help each other discover what we have been given in order that we might live generously. "When people [relate] with each other on the basis of *a vision for who they are and what they could become*; when we see in others what little of Jesus has already begun to form beneath the insecurity, fear, and pride; when we long beyond anything else to see that little bit of Jesus develop and mature; then something is released from within us that has the power to form more of Jesus within them."[5]

What do you think Jesus is forming in you or moving you towards? Think of someone in your community. Write down what you see Jesus forming in them; who are they becoming because of Jesus? (Tell them what you see when you meet next)

_____

_____

_____

_____

_____

_____

The Apostle Paul said that we are like ordinary clay jars. There is nothing too exciting about clay pots. Paul also said that in each of these clay jars is a treasure (Jesus) that reveals the radiant glory of God (See 2 Cor 4). It's frightening to think that God's starting point for uncovering the Treasure is a confrontation with our very own unique sin and pain. As long as we hide and avoid our unique sinful composition, we deny God access to heal, restore, and transform us into his likeness.

---

[4] Hauerwas and Willimon, *Resident Aliens*, 65.
[5] Crabb, *Connecting*, 65.

What do you think it would take for us to be vulnerable about our sinfulness without dwelling on it or exploiting one another with what we know?

_____

_____

_____

_____

_____

Imagine if we could see that:
- Our new life in Christ means that the core of our being is no longer evil. (Christ is now potentially more substantive to our makeup than we ourselves are.)
- All change that is not centered in the transforming work of the Holy Spirit is cosmetic. (We cannot change ourselves in the way that God intends for us to be changed.)
- Our Christ-like desires will become stronger as we see how Christ wants to live in one another more clearly.
- Change depends on experiencing the character of God. (Simply knowing of God and his character fall short. Pharaoh knew of God.)

Based on these four truths, what new possibilities can you see in your relationships?

_____

_____

_____

_____

_____

And how might you begin to perceive yourself and those around you differently?

_____

_____

_____

_____

_____

Read and meditate on Acts 2:42–47; 4:32–37. What is God showing you in this story? Write down any thoughts, questions, or promptings.

_____

_____

_____

_____

Does the community in Acts seem to be more a collection of people with individual hopes and dreams or does it seem to be a collection of people with one hope and dream?

_____

Part 3: Beyond Small Talk

Read Acts 2:42–47 and 4:32–37.
What is God showing you in this story?
Write down any thoughts, questions, or promptings.

_____

_____

_____

_____

_____

small talk; *noun. polite conversation about unimportant or uncontroversial matters, esp. as engaged in on social occasions.*

Therefore, stripping off falsehood, "let each of us speak the truth to his neighbor," for we are members of one another (Eph 4:25). Paul compared God's people to the human body; we are one cohesive organism. If one part was suffering, all should suffer. Imagine breaking your leg and reasoning that it wasn't your problem but it was your *leg's* problem. When you found that you couldn't walk very well you became bitter and wished for your leg to be gone so you found a good surgeon to amputate your broken leg. Initially you feel good. "Yeah, I showed that leg whose boss . . . " Absurd isn't it? God's people seem to be (to continue Paul's analogy) made up of a pair of tonsils and an appendix. We are here, we require oxygenated blood to survive, but we serve no purpose and we have no consequential relationship to the rest of the body. If we were removed, we would simply be out of the way. On the other hand, if we saw ourselves as capable and integral members of one body we would understand that our cooperation and harmony were essential for the body to serve its purpose. If I'm a leg I better move when I'm directed to move or the whole body will suffer. Our purpose is to glorify God and this purpose is realized when we accept that we are a part of a whole and that we do not function as an isolated part but as a whole. Michael Jordan's left leg received no glory during his career in the NBA. His right thumb received no glory. Michael Jordan received glory and that glory was possible because every part of his body was submitted to one single agenda: bringing glory to Michael Jordan.

We live in a culture of vigilante consumerism meaning that we reject most options in the belief that we will find a better one if we keep looking. We are enticed with an array of choices tailored for our specific desires and thus we are more in the habit of rejecting than accepting. We have been taught to be choosy consumers. We have the right to receive exactly what we are looking for. I fear we have carried this mentality to our friendships with the result being that we do not see ourselves as a gift. We are first and foremost a consumer and since everyone else is a consumer entitled to exactly what they want, chances are they aren't interested in who I really am underneath the image I portray. We reason that we have either nothing to give or that what we do have to give is not good enough. This is the sort of believing that awakens the Imposter as we scramble to figure out what those around us are looking for. We devise ways to market ourselves so that we might become a product that others will want. In doing so, we destroy the very gift we are called to contribute—our true and vulnerable self.

If you won the lottery and suddenly your friends started calling and hanging around more often, would you be suspicious? Or if you attempted suicide and in the wake it seemed like your closest friends were avoiding you, would you wonder? In your own words, what is the true test of friendship and are you willing to undergo that test in your community? Why or why not? What fears stand in the way?

_____

_____

_____

_____

_____

_____

I believe one of the purest tests of friendship is conflict resolution. If we are close to someone, conflict is inevitable. If there is no conflict then I think it is safe to say that there is a fair amount of posing going on. I can't even count the number of friendships that I've seen split simply because a small conflict could not be safely acknowledged and resolved. A friend is someone that you know well enough to have been angered or hurt by but the relationship remains intact and actually grew because of the conflict.

Read the following Scriptures. Remember that we have been given the fullness of Christ. Remember that we have been given every spiritual blessing in Christ. We are much more than earth-bound citizens trying to do our best in our own strength. Our old nature has been turned upside down by a new nature that has supernatural power at its disposal. We are now capable of things that previously were impossible.

- "Owe nothing to anyone—except for your obligation to love one another. If you love your neighbor, you will fulfill the requirements of God's law" (Rom 13:8).
- "So then, let us aim for harmony in the church and try to build each other up" (Rom 14:19).
- "Instead, be kind to each other, tenderhearted, forgiving one another, just as God through Christ has forgiven you" (Eph 4:32).
- "So encourage each other and build each other up, just as you are already doing" (I Thess 5:11).

- "Let us think of ways to motivate one another to acts of love and good works. And let us not neglect our meeting together, as some people do, but encourage one another, especially now that the day of his return is drawing near" (Heb 10:24–25).
- "Confess your sins to each other and pray for each other so that you may be healed. The earnest prayer of a righteous person has great power and produces wonderful results" (Jas 5:16).
- "Dear friends, let us continue to love one another, for love comes from God. Anyone who loves is a child of God and knows God" (I John 4:7).
- "Therefore, accept each other just as Christ has accepted you so that God will be given glory" (Rom 15:7).
- "Always be humble and gentle. Be patient with each other, making allowance for each other's faults because of your love. Make every effort to keep yourselves united in the Spirit, binding yourselves together with peace. For there is one body and one Spirit, just as you have been called to one glorious hope for the future" (Eph 4:2–4).
- "If you have two shirts, give one to the poor. If you have food, share it with those who are hungry" (Luke 3:11).

As you read these scriptures, what new possibilities do you see for how you might relate to those around you? What new habits do you want to begin to cultivate in your community? What does God want the world to see when it looks at us?

_____

_____

_____

_____

_____

Emotionally and experientially speaking:
- Do you feel like others have been given more than you? (Talents, charm, good looks, money, etc.)

_____

- What things do you feel like you can't live without?

_____

_____

_____

All that we think we need that is not Jesus imprisons us. If I have what I think I need I live in constant fear that I will lose it; I am in prison *with* my stuff. If I don't have what I think I need I spend the rest of my life trying to get it; I am in prison *without* my stuff. Jesus said that the truth would set us free when we *know truth*. Nothing else has the power to set us free.

Part 4: Becoming a People Captured by God

Read Acts 2:42–47 and 4:32–37.
What is God showing you in this story?
Write down any thoughts, questions, or promptings.

_____

_____

_____

_____

_____

"In Jesus we meet not a presentation of basic ideas about God, world, and humanity but *an invitation to join up, to become part of a movement, a people.* By the very act of our modern theological attempts at translation, we have unconsciously distorted the gospel and transformed it into something it never claimed to be—ideas abstracted from Jesus, rather that Jesus with his people."[6]

Imagine being part of a community in which:
- We felt safe enough to be broken.
- We were sustained by a vision of what the Spirit of God wants to do in one another's' lives.
- Wisdom from God was present to make visible the activity of the Holy Spirit and remove what is getting in His way.
- Where the life of Christ pours out of us to energize the life of Christ in the other whereby the divine touch of God is offered and received.

Imagine if we diligently searched for in one another what is of God. Imagine if our relationships became characterized by:
- Recognizing what God is up to in each other's lives and joining the process.
- Knowing what God wanted to release in others right now.
- Uncovering evidence of God's Spirit at work in others' hearts.
- Calling out good urges that are dormant and hidden and nurturing them into fruitful obedience.[7]

---

[6] Hauerwas and Willimon, *Resident Aliens*, 21.
[7] Adapted from Crabb, *Safest Place*, Chapter 6.

Imagine if we consistently related with one another in this manner. Write down your fears, skepticism, and excitement as you ponder having relationships like this.

_____

_____

_____

_____

_____

I can clearly see how my pain leads me to attack others. As a child who could not participate in most things that other kids were doing, my sense of self-worth was attacked. I grew up believing that I didn't have a place of acceptance and belonging. As an adult, when I perceive that my belonging is in jeopardy, I feel the need to assert my place and defend my rights. It's like we've never stopped playing 'king of the mountain'. There is limited seating; the club can only legally allow 100 occupants. I assert my rights in fear that all seats are taken or that I am the 101st person requesting entrance. Therefore, I must find a way to kick someone else out so that I can have his or her spot.

Can you see how your own pain might create a similar coping mechanism for you? Write down any thoughts or reflections

_____

_____

_____

_____

Not only does our pain inflict pain in others but it also limits or prevents our lives from being a gift or offering to others. Is peace simply the absence of conflict? If I have learned how to avoid conflict am I truly at peace with my neighbor? "So many of us enjoy congenial friendships. We cooperate with likeminded folks to raise money for good causes and bring meals to the sick. We depend on a few reliable sources of comfort when things get rough, maybe a beer and a football game or a sexy movie or a nice church service. If things get too confusing and painful, there is always a counselor to give us perspective. And if our conscience points out areas of irresponsibility and failure, we might ask a few moral friends to help us conform to better standards."[8]

It's frightening to venture below the surface of our own life; not to mention going below the surface in someone else's life. Conflict is inevitable. Feeling the pain is inevitable and we fear hurting those around us as our pain surfaces. It just seems easier to hide it

---

[8] Crabb, *Safest Place*, 66.

and just go along with the program. I have a dream that the Church would cease being characterized as people who have learned how to be polite, smile most of the time, and tolerate one another. I dream that we would boldly and courageously ('I'm afraid but I do it anyway') become a people who are learning what it looks like to generously share with one another what God has given us.

The core of a Christ-follower's identity is found in Christ (See Col 2:12; 3:3). If our lives are not grounded in a growing understanding of Christ and the work He has yet to complete through us, we will be forced to adopt the best looking strategy to feel good and look good. "Jesus made it clear that a search for ourselves in all that is natural to us will always prove disappointing. Simon the fisherman could have explored every region of his ego prior to his encounter with Christ but he would not have found 'Peter' there. The true identity of Peter, the man created to replace Simon, was hidden in the mystery of Christ's soul."[9]

The Apostle Paul tells us that the best (and at times only) reason we have for being happy is our hope that God will be glorified (Rom 5:2b). As I reflect on life in America, I see the church following the general public as we place our hope in feeling good and looking good. We place our hope in what we believe will bring us life. The thing we hope for will determine every decision we make. If comfort, safety, or pleasure is the thing that gets me out of bed in the morning or causes me to stay there, my life will revolve around preserving a sense of comfort, safety, and pleasure. Jesus said that we would not be able to serve two masters; for either we will hate the one, and we will love the other, or else we will be devoted to the one, and we will despise the other. We cannot serve God and money (Matt 6:24).

"How does a person serve money? He does not assist money. He is not the bene-factor of money. Money exerts a certain control over us because it seems to hold out so much promise of happiness. It whispers with great force, 'Think and act so as to get into a position to enjoy my benefits.' Money promises happiness, and we serve it by believing the promise and living by that faith. So we don't serve money by putting our power at its disposal for its good. We serve money by doing what is necessary so that money's power will be at our disposal for our good. So if we are going to serve God and not money, then we are going to have to open our eyes to the vastly superior happiness which God offers. Then God will exert a greater control over us than money does. We will serve by believing His promise of fullest joy and walking by that faith. We will not serve by trying to put our power at his disposal for his good, but by doing what is necessary so that his power will be ever at our disposal for our good."[10]

The core scripture (Acts 2 and 4) for the week gives us a picture of a community that seems to have taken hold of the promise of God's glory. The hearts of those in these com-munities were set on it—it was the primary and perhaps only thing worth living for as far as they were concerned. Since everything else paled in comparison to God's glory revealed

[9] Crabb, *Connecting*, 38.
[10] Piper, *Brothers*, 43.

in their midst, they lived generously; they shared their things with those in need because their things became unimportant as God's glory shone in their midst. Miraculous signs were everyday occurrences because the apostles believed in and hoped for the glory of God and not their own reputations. I believe that this community understood they were part of a story that began hundreds of years before they were born and would continue on for hundreds of years after their death. With this truth in view, their lives were less important. They simply felt honored to play a small part in God's story of reconciling the world to Himself. In view of this bigger picture, they became less concerned about their own lives as their gratitude and affection for their Savior compelled them to seek His purposes and His glory during their short stay on earth. I believe God is still writing His story and He's inviting us to be characters in the drama.

Generous living cannot be made into a law; to require it ruins it. Generous living happens when we understand that we have been given everything, lack nothing, and can lose nothing. We can only see this truth by drawing near to Christ. He is all that we will ever need. He can never be taken from us. Nothing can separate us from Him. In this frame of heart and mind we see that God is bigger than our pain and can even use it for good. We see that all things come from God and what we have been given we have been given on loan to bless those in our midst. If we were to attempt to live generously apart from realizing that we are first beneficiaries of God's infinite generosity then we have fallen into a trap. We will either live legalistically; 'A good Christian must live generously and not selfishly,' or we will become burned out as we attempt to live within the limits of our own human potential; 'I keep giving and giving but it never seems to be enough'. The progression might look like this:

- *In Christ* I have all that I will ever need and want.
- *In Christ* I lack nothing.
- *In Christ* nothing can be taken from me.
- *In Christ* all that I have been generously given, I can generously give to others joyfully and without fear or reluctance.

"We cannot know Jesus without following Jesus. Engagement with Jesus . . . is necessary to understand Jesus. In a sense, we follow Jesus before we know Jesus."[11] How does this statement challenge you?

_____

_____

_____

---

[11] Hauerwas and Willimon, *Resident Aliens,* 55.

Read and meditate once again on Acts 2:42–47; 4:32–37. What is God showing you in this story? Write down any thoughts, questions, or promptings.

_____

_____

_____

What practical and tangible steps do you feel led to take this week? Write them down and be prepared to share them this week. Help one another take them, together and in the strength that God will supply for you to do so.

_____

_____

_____

_____

_____

CHAPTER 2

Becoming Authentic

"Knowing who we are by the story of the power and purposes of God makes a differ-ence in the lives of ordinary people. They are thereby given a power to be free from the strong social forces, prejudices, and conventions that determine the lives of so many who do not know such a story. Our enemies, our wider society, our past, cannot define us or determine the significance of who we are, since God in Christ has already done that for us."[1]

OVERVIEW:

Core Scripture: Acts 5:1–11

The Kingdom of God is at Hand: What makes us a community is when we live in the realization that we are God's children. It is Christ living in us that motivates our being together. Apart from Christ and the life He has given to us, we have no reason to gather or be involved in one another's lives.

Repent: Our relationships are marked by a commitment to get along and feel good about our selves and one another. This commitment pushes us to relate superficially; to avoid conflict; and avoid truthful relating and living. Essentially we pretend as we forfeit what is real for what is comfortable.

Believe the Good News: We can set our hearts and minds on the transforming work that God prepared for us long ago. Our lives together will have meaning and purpose because Christ is present and actively at work making us more like Him. If Christ is not in our conversations; if our prayers do not include one another; then we are stifling the brightness of His light and wasting our time.

Therefore Go: Identify a weakness or insecurity in your life that has caused you sig-nificant pain. Write down the ways that you have arranged your life in order to hide it and make up for it. Ask God to show you how He wants to release you from this grip of fear, shame, or paralysis. Prayerfully reflect on how God wants to use your weaknesses to cause you to rely on Him and not yourself. Share this in your community.

[1] Ibid., 67–68.

Part 1: Jesus Must Increase; We Must Decrease

Read Acts 5:1–11.
What is God showing you in this troubling story?
Write down any comments or questions that come to your mind.

_____

_____

_____

_____

_____

The TV show, *LOST* is a fascinating sociological snapshot that illustrates how we understand community in the U.S. The plot is pretty basic (well, season 1 anyhow). A plane crashes on a tropical island and a bewildered group of airline passengers with no prior history or common bonds must figure out how they will survive until they are rescued. Initially there is cooperation. People are in shock. People are wounded and there are dead bodies to burn or bury. The community is united in their quest for survival. Hours turn into days, which turn into weeks, and hopes of an immediate rescue slowly wane, a spirit of individualism emerges in the characters. There is still cooperation but it becomes limited and stifled by the emerging agendas of individuals. Over time, cooperation breaks down and it becomes clear that *the community is only valued by each individual to the degree that the community can assist each personal agenda.* Arguments lead to power plays which quickly escalate into acts of violence. The identity of the community is now lost. Relationships become strictly utilitarian. Unnecessary members are thought less of and ostracized or eliminated.

This community is unique in that they are stuck with each other. They have no choice but to figure out how to survive. Our situation is different. We are *not* stuck with one another. If someone threatens my agenda, I can simply abandon them and move on.

"A community is only valued to the degree that it assists the agenda of the individual." In what ways have you bought into this philosophy? Write down a few examples of how it leads you to treat people around you.

_____

_____

_____

_____

_____

Jesus calls His Church 'a bride'. This Church spans thousands of years encompassing people of faith in the living God from the beginning of time all the way through the end of days. It includes the likes of a king named David who had an affair with a woman and had her husband killed, a prostitute called Rahab, a former murderer named Paul, and tens of thousands of other ragamuffins with dark and twisted hearts. It is not our unworthiness that is in question but rather our willingness to journey with others in allowing Jesus to transform the darkness of our hearts into His radiant glory.

Jesus has an agenda and our agenda is meant to be His agenda. 'He must increase and I must decrease' (John 3:30). Even Christians compete with one another as they build their isolated fiefdoms and compete for influence and attendees in their local churches. This grieves God because He is advancing only one kingdom—His kingdom in which He rules with honor, glory, power, wisdom, wealth, strength, and blessing. Our picture of this Servant King is small in part because *we have not decreased*. Our lives continue to revolve around feeling good, safe, and comfortable. We gather with other Christians ready to protect our rights and agendas and to defend our wounds. The Spirit is capable of bringing unity yet we shatter that unity with our unwillingness to humble ourselves and exalt Jesus the King.

The community on the tropical island in *LOST* became dysfunctional because there lacked one single agenda that was powerful enough to capture everyone's hearts. There lacked one thing that was worthy of *increasing* at the *cost* of each individual *decreasing*. Our story is much different because we do have one thing worthy of increasing. We have been invited to participate in the one and only thing worthy of being magnified; the ongoing reign of Jesus, the King of kings. The cost of participation however is great. *We must decrease.*

We are largely out of touch with how serious God is in regard to His increasing and our decreasing. Acts 5 is a challenging text. I believe it illustrates to us how important it is to uphold the truth and resist the urge to pretend and avoid or ignore what is really happening. Things would seem much better if Ananias and Sapphira were just let off the hook. At least they gave *something*, right? Write down why this story is difficult for you to accept.

_____

_____

_____

_____

_____

"Christian community, life in the colony, is not primarily about togetherness. It is about the way of Jesus Christ with those whom He calls to himself. It is about disciplining our wants and needs in congruence with a true story, which gives us the resources to lead truthful lives. In living out the story together, togetherness happens, but only as a by-product of the main project of trying to be faithful to Jesus."[2]

A basketball team does many things together; they laugh, they talk, they ride in buses, and maybe they hang out after practice or on the weekends. But the primary thing they do together is basketball—if that one activity were removed they would cease to be a basketball team. What makes ordinary people 'the Church' is Jesus. If Jesus is not active and alive in our midst, we are just a bunch of religious people trying to get along with one another and peddle our beliefs to the world. It we cannot identify even one aspect of being 'about they way of Jesus Christ' with each other, we must stop everything and ask God to show us this.

Reflect on the ways in which you might just be going through motions and how you might begin to move towards engaging a God who is both alive and active. Discuss this with your community.

_____

_____

_____

What is the difference between seeking 'togetherness' and seeking 'the way of Jesus Christ'? Is there a difference between getting along and speaking the truth in love? Which is more difficult? Write down any fears you have about speaking and hearing the truth from one another in love.

_____

_____

_____

_____

Decreasing is frightening. It is the Holy Spirit's process of killing our flesh; the part of us that cries out to be self-reliant, self-sufficient, self-made, and self-actualized. It is a painful road to abandon the fulfillment we have achieved in our self and in faith chase after an invisible God. Letting go of false identities and accepting reality will inevitably involve pain and fear and it cannot be done alone. We journey together.

[2] Ibid., 78.

Fear happens when we believe false conclusions from a story that we believe to be ultimate. For example, I was teased relentlessly in jr. high. Because of these stories I came to the conclusion that I had no value as a free person. I was a target. Offering my self freely and openly to others as an adult is fearful. The stories from jr. high feel ultimate because they defined my existence. If someone were to offer me love and acceptance I would grow suspicious because *teasing and rejection were the stories that my heart was attached to and instinctively expected.* Accepting love from God or another person requires me to trust that God's story of love and reconciliation is ultimate while the story of my childhood is secondary and can even be transformed by God's ultimate story of love. Our fears reveal which story we believe to be true in our hearts regardless of what we profess with our mouths or even our actions. For example, *because I wasn't good at sports growing up, I was excluded and had no meaningful friendships. Therefore, in order to have friends, I must be good at the same things that my would-be-friends are good at. My life is devoted to mastering these things so that I am never excluded again. My life is an on-going pursuit to be smart, good-looking, successful, or in some way pleasing to those around me.* My experiences of rejection led me to believe that acceptance hinged on being attractive and successful. Thus the story of life became earning acceptance from those around me; including God.

Reflect on your own fears and insecurities. Based on these, write down in two or three sentences the story you presently believe to be true or partially true for your life

_____

_____

_____

_____

Part 2: Christin Us Means We Can Hope for His Glory.

Read Acts 5:1–11.
What is God showing you in this troubling story?
Write down any comments or questions that come to your mind.

_____

_____

_____

_____

_____

Faith is being sure of what we hope for and confident of what we do not see (Heb 11:1). We put our faith in the story that we believe to be true. The story we believe to be true defines our life and will determine what we think about, what we fear, what we love, what we hate, what we care about, and what we do with our time and resources. Fear has no place in the life of a Christian. God's perfect love casts out all fear. For in His love He has generously given us all things so that we lack nothing, can lose nothing, and can give everything. We need not fear because everything God promises you is guaranteed in Christ. Fear creeps in when we doubt God's willingness or ability to deliver what He has promised us. And this fear comes from a story. "If I have experienced pain and rejection in my life, how can God be so good and generous?" Maybe our story in Acts 5 makes you afraid. It's definitely unnerving. It says that the 'church was seized with great fear' after God struck Ananias and Sapphira to the ground. I'm sure that there were loved ones that mourned these deaths. God seems mean-spirited and cold-hearted in this story. Yet God's profile seems contrary. If He were on Myspace, His profile might read, "I am the Lord, the Lord, the compassionate and gracious God, slow to anger, abounding in love and faithfulness, maintaining love to thousands and forgiving wickedness, rebellion, and sin. Yet I do not leave the guilty unpunished; I punish the children and their children for the sin of the fathers to the third and fourth generation" (Exod 34:6–7).

God is not against happiness. Indeed, as John Piper says, 'God is most glorified when we are most satisfied in Him.' Our problem is that we want to control our happiness. We want it now and we want to achieve it in ways that deny God.

All good stories have a climax (a crisis—something is in jeopardy that must be restored or secured) and a resolution (what was in jeopardy during the climax has been successfully restored or secured). We can discover the condition of our hearts by understanding what we believe to be the climax and resolution in our lives. Most often our fears will reveal our foundational beliefs. Our fears show us what we are afraid of losing or not gaining. When I ran competitively, I feared losing because losing is a story with a disappointing resolution. Losing implied that I had failed to secure the thing that mattered; winning, improving, gaining recognition, and feeling good about myself.

We remain adamantly faithful to the story we believe defines us. Even when our efforts to secure what matters don't seem to be working, (I do things that normally make me happy but I am not yet happy) we continue on in determination that happiness is just around the corner (confident of what I do not see). We all live by faith. The question is not our *level* of faith but *the object* of our faith; the *thing* that we believe holds the greatest and surest promise of life.

A promise is some indicator of a gateway to a future that is better than what we are currently headed towards. Dieting fads are a good illustration of this. Each one promises to deliver a slimmer waistline and greater sex appeal. We quickly assume that a slimmer waistline and greater sex appeal must be a better future than a future with a broader waistline and diminished sex appeal. An athlete is passionate about their game because they believe the promises that come with winning. They assume that greater fame and fatter paychecks are a better future. Their passion to win is coupled with a fear of losing as losing threatens their hoped-for future. Passion operates independently and naturally. No reminders, disciplines, or exercises are needed to keep our hearts oriented towards what we believe to be the promise of ultimate fulfillment and purpose. No teenage boy needs to remind himself to look at attractive women. No one needs to remind me to jump when I see a spider. It simply happens.

What do your passions and fears tell you about the promises you believe to be true?

_____

_____

_____

_____

I often wonder, is it possible for my life to be oriented to the promises of God with the same intensity that my heart clings to false promises that seem good because they make me feel good or look good for a brief moment? Is it possible that my life could literally be consumed in a passion for Jesus as I see, know, and feel His promises in all their goodness?

Here's a picture of what the engine of our hearts might look like apart from Christ:
- *The person that drives me:* Me (feeling good; looking good)
- *The promise that drives me:* Experiences, achievements, or products that reinforce my identity and will provide the strongest level of pleasure or safety.
- *The passion that drives me:* Being able to feel the highest possible pleasure or assurance of safety.

- *The purpose that drives me:* Leveraging my time, talents, and resources towards acquiring the experiences, achievements, and products that hold the greatest promise.
- *Ultimate source of hope:* A secure identity and a happy life.

Where Christ wants my heart to be:
- *The person that drives me:* Jesus (Live in such a way that *He* is glorified)
- *The promise that drives me:* Life and hope for the future is found abundantly and only in Jesus Christ (there are over 7,000 promises in Scripture that are all fulfilled and guaranteed in Christ).
- *The passion that drives me:* Felt intimacy with Jesus Christ and awareness of His kingdom coming 'on earth as it is in Heaven'.
- *The purpose that drives me:* Positioning myself to be consumed by God's love and to be a participant in His reign.
- *Ultimate source of hope:* Eternity; when the reign of God will be fully realized and all things will be visibly and experientially fulfilled in Christ.[3]

An authentic community can only happen when Christ is the object of our faith. A community where everyone is getting their way and getting along is not authentic.

> *We are dealing with reality only when we are receiving the truthfulness of Jesus and acknowledging the destruction caused by a rebellious creation.*

If we remove the truthfulness of Jesus or deny the destruction caused from rebellion in our efforts to be authentic, we are chasing a fantasy. We have nothing else to hope in but Jesus. He is the only One who is able to help us and change us. If we cannot be helped or changed then there would be no supernatural or redemptive purpose behind our authentic gestures. We would simply be airing our dirty laundry. But because Christ has invaded our hearts; we live vulnerably with one another in faith that by doing so; God is changing our hearts through our love and prayers for one another. When Christ becomes the object of our faith, we are saying that His story is ultimate. Our hope is now set on God's glory and not our own felt happiness and gratification. The story of His glory takes over. In faith we journey as vulnerable friends, able to be authentically real because it is not about polishing our own images but rather it is about Jesus changing us and involving us in His Father's work.

> *The Holy Spirit's starting point is always reality; no matter how ugly it is.*

Only when we are vulnerable in faith can we seek to live in the one true and worthwhile story of Jesus Christ and his kingdom that began at creation and continues in its on-going climax on this day and in this place. By faith we allow Jesus to be the storyteller over and above all things in our lives. Graham Cooke says it this way. "Vulnerability is knowing that God is happy to send us out as lambs amongst wolves because He is hugely confident in His own ability to watch over us and work through our weaknesses. When

---

[3] Adapted from a lecture given by David Bryant.

we are vulnerable, we see our inadequacies in the light of God's sovereignty and power, and we discover hope and faith. Like Paul, we rejoice in our weaknesses that the power of Christ may rest upon us (See 2 Cor 12:9-10). The whole point of vulnerability is to bring us to a place of restful dependence in a powerful and overcoming God."[4]

Sometimes the church is a wolf. Sometimes a friend who betrays us is a wolf. Sometimes we ourselves are the wolves. Our culture is a wolf bent on exploiting us by telling us what we need (resources, minimal risk, manageable life-strategy, perfect body, entertainment) in order to matter. Wolves make us afraid so we either hide from the wolf or kill the wolf. Either way, our life begins to revolve around the wolf much like small children's lives revolve around the bullies they never see but work diligently to avoid.

What are the wolves in your life and how you have attempted to manage those wolves? Do experiences in your past keep you from being vulnerable today? What outcomes do you fear when you think about being vulnerable (e.g. I will be thought less of; people won't like me; people will think I'm a hypocrite, etc.)? Write these down below.

_____

_____

_____

_____

Jesus meets us where we are. Most people withhold their love from others until they come to them on their terms. Thankfully, Jesus does not do this. He starts with our pain, our coping mechanisms, our doubt, our rebellion, and our fear. His starting point is reality; regardless of how bleak, ugly, or complicated it might be. But we must come out of hiding and begin to fearfully trust that God is at work. If God were not at work then yes, it would be better for all of us to remain in hiding. Paul tells us that the mystery of the Gospel is that Christ lives in us and because He lives in us we can live in expectation and anticipation that God will be glorified (Col 1:27; Rom 5:2). Paul even tells us that we are to brag about our hope. Hope does not disappoint us; God's glory is assured.

When I look around me, I see people coping. We learn pretty early on that life is certainly not fair (at least from our corner). Complete satisfaction and perfection is a ridiculous pipe dream. So we suck it up and hope for the best possible satisfaction from moment to moment. We buy things. We get plastic surgery. We apply anti-wrinkle cream. We watch TV until we are too tired to think. We eat ice cream.

[4] Cooke, *Confrontation*, 2.

Larry Crabb identifies four agendas or coping lifestyles that we employ in order to make us feel better:

1. *Depend on your own resources to make life work.*
2. *Reduce the mysteries of life (the way God works) to manageable or visible strategies and follow them.*
3. *Make it a priority to minimize personal risk.*
4. *Find satisfaction wherever you can.*[5]

Our futures are dominated by our urgent need to relieve our suffering and feel better. Jesus offers us a better way via His promise to us that He is coming back. "The practical effect of this belief is to charge each moment of the present with hope. For if the future is dominated by the coming again of Jesus, there is little room left on the screen for projecting our anxieties and fantasies. It takes the clutter out of our lives. We're far more free to respond spontaneously to the freedom of God . . . [We are] to continue to live forward in taut and joyful expectancy for what God will do next in Jesus."[6] Anticipating the return of Jesus is much like a child who knows they are going to Disney Land in a week. Their daily existence has new hope and promise (even on a bad day) because their hearts are set on a joyful event that has not yet taken place. Without hope in the return and eternal reign of Jesus, we are left to conclude that "this life is our best shot at happiness . . . if this is as good as it gets, we will live as desperate, demanding, and eventually despairing men and women . . . All our addictions and depressions, the rage that simmers just beneath the surface of our Christian facade, and the deadness that characterizes so much of our lives has a common root: We think this is as good as it gets. Take away the hope of arrival and our journey becomes the Battan death march. The best human life is unspeakably sad."[7]

Knowing where God is taking history is extremely important. People who do not have a relationship with God can base their life on their past ("I am a victim") or on their idealized future ("I am in control"). Christians can reject both of these options. We are no longer victims and we have no need to control. Why? Because the future belongs to Jesus and not us. And we have been told how things will end up.

Do you think you are being shaped primarily by your past (believing that nothing will ever change), your ideal future (believing that you are in control), or God's future (God dwelling among his people forever)? How can you tell?

_____

_____

_____

_____

[5] Crabb, *Connecting*, 92.
[6] Eugene Peterson, quoted in Bryant, *Christ Is All!*, 225.
[7] Dr. John Eldredge, quoted in Bryant, *Christ Is All!*, 225.

Painful experiences in our past teach us that we can trust no one. We are led to seek life for ourselves. Take a deep look at the engine of your heart. What seems to hold the greatest promise of life based on what your time, resources, thoughts, fears, and desires are focused on?

_____

_____

_____

Part 3: Helping One Another Worship God and Not Ourselves.

Read Acts 5:1–11.

What is God showing you in this troubling story?

Write down any comments or questions that come to your mind.

_____

_____

_____

_____

_____

Shame is a powerful emotion that has the capability to shape how we relate and how we seek to project an image towards others. Shame lures us to fixate our attention on ourselves and coerces us to hide. "Shame is the traumatic exposure of nakedness—for example, when a person does something harmful (has an affair), commits a blunder (forgets a wallet), or is caught in some flaw of appearance (smudged mascara). This exposure occurs when we feel the lance of a gaze tearing open the various cultural, relational, or religious coverings we put on. What is revealed, we feel, is an inner ugliness . . . Shame is rooted in our inherent preference to trust false gods rather than depend on God for each and every moment of our existence."[8]

Shame reveals what we trust in to bring us life. If I am worshiping the idol of looking good or being smart or funny, I have placed my hope in a god who has no power to save me in a moment of ugliness or stupidity. This is not a problem until I actually need saving in a moment of looking bad or acting foolishly. The god that I have created sits silently mocking my cries for help. I grew up feeling disliked so my god became achieving a likable and attractive image. In third grade I peed my pants at recess because the recess monitor would not allow me to go inside to go to the bathroom. I distinctly remember standing behind a telephone pole on the playground as the wet spot on my pants grew larger and larger. I trembled in fear. 'How would I possibly hide *this*?' What will people think of me?' In this situation I had every right to blame the recess monitor. Apparently upholding a rule was more important than my dignity. Nasty recess monitor aside, my false god of fitting in and being liked was exposed.

In the movie 'Billy Madison,' a third grader named Ernie pees his pants and is standing in the corner ashamed and embarrassed. Adam Sandler notices what happened and splashes water on his own pants and proceeds to make a spectacle of himself by announcing to the entire class that 'Peeing your pants is the coolest.' Ernie then has the courage to turn around and face his peers revealing his own wet pants. A classmate exclaims, 'Hey

---

[8] Allender and Longman, *The Cry of the Soul*, 195.

look, Ernie peed his pants too!' By the end of the day, everyone has peed his or her pants. This illustrates well how we turn 'being liked or accepted' into a god. Adam Sandler simply changed the religious ceremony of accessing this god from 'don't pee your pants' to 'by all means, pee your pants because it's the coolest.'

Most of us probably grew up having to choose between living in constant fear of not being liked or living with the inconvenience of our cultural/religious ceremonies to keep our false gods propped up and looking alive (perfect makeup, perfect hair, the right clothes, the right stuff, good at sports, funny jokes, likable personality, whatever . . .). God wants to free us from all the wasted energy and bitter emotions that accompany the slavery of false idol worship. Scripture teaches us that shame arises because we are worshiping an idol and we feel foolish when our idol does not deliver the promise we perceived it capable of delivering. Shame exposes what we worship. "All who worship images are put to shame" (Ps 97:7, NIV).

Take a minute to ponder situations in your life that have caused you shame. Think about what embarrasses you or events that have exposed things that you didn't want exposed. Based on these sources of shame, what are your false gods? Write them below.

_____

_____

_____

> "Take a good look, friends, at who you were when you got called into this life. I don't see many of 'the brightest and the best' among you, not many influential, not many from high-society families. Isn't it obvious that God deliberately chose men and women that the culture overlooks and exploits and abuses, chose these 'nobodies' to expose the hollow pretensions of the 'some-bodies'? That makes it quite clear that none of you can get by with blowing your own horn before God. Everything that we have—right thinking and right living , a clean slate and a fresh start—comes from God by way of Jesus Christ. That's why we have the saying, 'If you're going to blow a horn, blow a trumpet for God. If I have to 'brag' about myself, I'll brag about the humiliations that make me like Jesus"
> —The Apostle Paul (I Cor 1:26–31; 2 Cor 11:30, MSG).

We have grown up believing that we must be strong, self-sufficient, independent, not a burden on those around us, needing nothing and no one. Paul seems to have delighted in his weaknesses. I once heard a lifeguard say that the most difficult person to rescue from drowning is the person who is still struggling to save themselves by their own strength. In their futile attempts to swim or keep themselves afloat, their flailing arms and legs prevent the lifeguard from being able to scoop them into the safety of their arms. In extreme cases the lifeguard must simply wait until the person becomes completely exhausted and limp at which point they can gracefully pull them from the water. We are a bit the same. We block intimacy with God and destroy the work He wants to do in us by attempting to be strong and capable people. God is waiting for us to admit that we are weak and in need of Him. Paul was given 'a thorn in his flesh'. We don't know what he meant by this but we can assume it was a weakness that he felt prevented God's ability to use Him. Paul appealed to God three times to take away this weakness. Jesus responded to his plea, "My grace is sufficient for you, for your power is brought to its end in weakness."[9] Paul then reasoned that he could boldly boast about his weaknesses in order that the power of Christ [not his!] may dwell in him. Further, Paul said that now he could "take delight in weaknesses, in insults, in necessities, in persecutions and calamities for the sake of Christ, for *when I am weak, then I am strong.*" (See 2 Cor 12:7–10). Paul informs us in First Corinthians 12:22 that the weaker members of the Church are actually the most important. That we think the strongest members are the most important tells us that our thinking is more influenced by our culture than it is the Spirit of God.

How can we turn from this way of thinking as a community and begin to admit our own weakness and expect God to do miracles in our midst *because of* our weaknesses? Share your ideas with your community.

_____

_____

_____

_____

When I was in high school and one of my friends started dating a girl we would always ask him, 'Hey man, have you passed the fart barrier yet?' It sounds goofy but I think it illustrates a powerful truth. Farting is gross. No one wants to smell the air that came out of somebody else's butt. But everyone farts. I guess that makes us all gross. My friends and I knew that if one of us couldn't fart around our girlfriends we were just posing. Remember all those first dates of holding the gas in for hours? The rumbling and cramping getting so bad that you swore you would start burping it up? All that pain and trouble just to not be gross! We are gross but we want to hide it. If one sneaks out we feel the world has come to an end because we just did something that is common to every person who has ever walked the planet. Our culture has a very powerful influence on us. Our real heroes are the rock stars and supermodels. They never fart; they have no imperfections according to our culture's standards of sex appeal. They are our gods and we want to be just like them. When we gather in the name of Jesus, this is where we can begin to stop idolizing celebrity culture and start idolizing the King of kings. The only real freedom is the freedom that comes from idolizing a God who is real, truthful, and immeasurably superior to all other imitations. All else is slavery!

---

[9] Marva Dawn offers this translation of verse 9 in *Powers*. See chapter 1.

"The only way for the world to know that it is being redeemed is for the church to point to the redeemer by being a redeemed people."[10]

Reflect on our story in Acts 5. Where do you see the four coping lifestyles below in the actions of Ananias and Sapphira? Why do you think God was so harsh with them? What was so important to Him that He thought it worthwhile to end their lives on the spot? And do you think God would ever do this sort of thing today? Why or why not? (Feel free to let your answer scare you.)

1. Depend on your own resources to make life work.
2. Reduce the mysteries of life (the way God works) to manageable or visible strategies and follow them.
3. Make it a priority to minimize personal risk.
4. Find satisfaction wherever you can.

Write your responses here:

_____

_____

_____

_____

_____

[10] Hauerwas and Willimon, *Resident Aliens*, 94.

Part 4: Feeling the Urgency of God.

"God overlooked people's ignorance about these things in earlier times, but now he commands everyone everywhere to repent of their sins and turn to him. For he has set a day for judging the world with justice by the man he has appointed, and he proved to everyone who this is by raising him from the dead" (Acts 17:29–31).

Read Acts 5:1–11.
What is God showing you in this troubling story?
Write down any comments or questions that come to your mind.

_____

_____

_____

_____

_____

We live in urgent times. Most of us are not aware that we live in urgent times. The TV series '24' illustrates this well. You can't really get any more urgent than Jack Bauer. He is intimately acquainted both with what is in jeopardy as well as what is required to safely secure what is in jeopardy. His urgency drives him to extreme measures. He is a man with little patience or tolerance for anyone who would oppose him or fail to match his speed and intensity. Meanwhile, the city of Los Angeles is sleeping, dining out, breaking it down in nightclubs, or watching television. They are oblivious and at ease simply because they do not know what Jack knows. If the city knew what Jack knew there would be widespread panic and chaos.

The Church is the new temple or dwelling place of God. Prior to Jesus, if you wanted to be in the presence of God, you had to go to the temple. In the temple there was a room called the Holy of Holies. Only the high priest could go in here and only once per year. Further, he would have to go through weeks of ceremonial cleansing before entering the Holy of Holies. The other priests would tie a rope to his foot in the event that God struck him dead. This way they could drag him out without anyone else having to enter. God is extremely powerful. When Moses spoke with God, his face glowed in the dark and he freaked everyone out. He wore a veil so that people wouldn't run away from him (See Exod 34). We are now the temple of God and God dwells in us. Isn't that amazing? God dwells in us and reveals himself to the world, not in a building, but in people.

God has a mission that only He can accomplish. He has graciously and mysteriously chosen to accomplish that mission in us; His bride, His temple, His church. God is good and we deserve nothing from Him.

Jack Bauer's mission has no guarantees. He faces an enemy that is his equal. Victory for Jack Bauer depends on his stamina, intelligence, and skill. There are no guarantees; he could be defeated at any turn. The citizens of Los Angeles could face death if Jack fails. The urgency we are called to is both similar and very different. It is different because:

1. The battle we fight is not won in our strength but in God's (Zech 4:6).
2. We are not equals with our enemy. We are more powerful than our enemy because Christ has conquered Satan and we are now hidden in Christ and possess His power to accomplish His purposes. When Satan encounters the presence of Jesus, he runs or hides (2 Pet 1:3; Jas 4:7).
3. We need not fear our enemy or wonder who will win. God has already won and our enemy knows it. He is like the knight in 'Monty Python' who has lost all his limbs yet continues to talk trash. 'Tis only a flesh wound!'
4. God is sovereign. Whatever He calls us to do (which will be impossible apart from His supernatural intervention) is guaranteed because nothing or no one is more powerful than Him. We are simply a vessel of His power (2 Cor 4:7).
5. Our responsibility is simply to listen and respond in faith that what He is beginning to do through us, He will complete (Phil 1:6).

I fear that most churchgoers are not even *on* this battlefield. We are on our own personal battlefields desperately trying to fit in or find happiness. Jesus died to free us from our own battles so that we could be released to work for eternal things. Jesus promised us that the Father is always at work and that He was in fact sent to do the work of the Father (John 5:17,19–20). We too are being sent to do the work of the Father (John 20:21). We can know the work of the Father because Jesus has sent the Holy Spirit to us (John 14:16–18). He will lead and guide us (John 16:13–15). *If you've not familiar with these verses in the book of John take a few minutes to look them over.* Our urgency then looks like this:

1. Moment by moment we are confronted with the decision to receive God's grace (allowing Him to work in and through us) or deny God's grace (figuring out how to make life work).
2. We know that God can do 'immeasurably more than we could ask or imagine' yet this does not excuse us from faithful action since God has chosen to reveal Himself to the world through us, His Church.
3. Our urgency is informed both by God's activity and His timeline. Since God is both always at work and always strategic in how He works, our urgency should primarily motivate us to listen to Him. Once we see, by faith, what God is up to and how He is doing it, we simply obey even when it appears foolish or pointless.

God calls us together because He wants us to help each other strip away our false gods that leave us fearful, insecure, isolated, shame-filled, and self-centered. His intention is to raise us into a mighty army, poised for battle at any moment. His desire is that we would become an expectant people waiting for His glory to be revealed in our midst. The route to seeing God's glory is personal vulnerability. I must become weak. I must humble myself. I must show my true colors in order for God's power to be displayed in my life.

Here is where we must be careful. We become vulnerable not to dwell on our sinfulness. We become vulnerable to become dependent on and to discover a God who is much bigger than we are. Vulnerability humbles us so that we might look to God for life and not ourselves or each other. Vulnerability gives us the courage to lay down our own agenda and to take up God's agenda. God wants to translate our acknowledged weakness into His power. We become vulnerable not to degrade one another or ourselves but so that God's nature and power might be revealed as we discover our need for it in the midst of our vulnerability.

I have seen many communities become vulnerable and then drown in a sea of morbid and prolonged sin-telling. Things go down hill fast as the group struggles to motivate itself out of sinful behaviors. Eventually the group falls apart. Why does this happen? Because there is no vision or hope provided by a bigger picture beyond 'not sinning anymore'. God's bigger picture is wonderful and exciting and He is calling us to join up. What could be better? "His divine power has given us everything we need for life and godliness through the full knowledge of the one who called us by his own glory and excellence. Through these he has given us his precious and wonderful promises, so that *through them you may participate in the divine nature*, seeing that you have escaped the corruption that is in the world caused by evil desires" (2 Pet 1:3–4). The point is to participate in God's nature and not simply stay out of trouble. For indeed, Jesus "died for everyone so that those who receive his new life will no longer live for themselves. Instead, they will live for Christ, who died and was raised for them" (2 Cor 5:15).

How do you see the connection between becoming vulnerable and participating in what God is doing?

_____

_____

If God is all-powerful, has already defeated Satan, destroyed the power of death, has promised His peace in place of our anxiety (See Phil 4:6–7) and has promised to complete in us what He started, why must we be urgent?

_____

_____

_____

I believe it is safe to say that when we invest our time, energy, and resources in protecting and maintaining our identity, hiding our insecurities, guarding our pain, or seeking fulfillment or escape through pleasurable experiences—we are simply wasting our lives. God is invisibly at work; doing what is necessary to free us with His grace and truth.

He will stop at nothing to get your attention. He is poised to accomplish immeasurable and inconceivable works in our lives but we are preoccupied by keeping unpleasant things at bay by engineering good times. We are settling for a safer, yet lesser form of life. We successfully distract ourselves from what we do not want to face yet we have also distracted ourselves from the tender voice of God calling us to receive Him. It sounds harsh to admit that we are wasting fat portions of our lives. Yet indeed, we are. Write down below the beliefs you hold that lead you to squander your life. Prayerfully ask God to give you the strength and will to turn from these old ways. Ask God to show you specifically what He wants to free you from (your personal and unique false and unreliable gods). And ask God to show you how He is calling you and your community to 'participate in His nature'. Share your findings with your community.

Becoming authentic is much more than uncovering things we wish could remain hidden. Stripping away what is false and hidden is the inevitable consequence of being drawn to the glory of God that comes from truthful and obedient living. A community that is becoming authentic mostly involves every individual being able to see and become who God has created that community to become in Jesus Christ by listening to Him carefully and responding faithfully.

"Let us not speak falsely now. The hour is getting late." —Bob Dylan

"Yes, I am coming soon."[11] —Jesus

What practical and tangible steps do you feel led to take this week? Write them down and be prepared to share them this week. Help each other take them together and in the strength that God will supply for you to do so.

---

[11] Rev 22:20.

CHAPTER 3

Becoming Prayerful

Religion is not a life without God, "but the God who is there tends to be mostly background and resource—a Quality of Being that produces the ideas and energy that I take charge of and arrange and use as I see fit."[1]

"The wind blows wherever it pleases. You hear its sound, but you cannot tell where it comes from or where it is going. So it is with everyone born of the spirit." — Jesus[2]

OVERVIEW:
Core Scripture: Acts 12:1–19

The Kingdom of God is at Hand: God has promised to meet our needs and do whatever we ask of Him for Christ's sake. Not only this, He has also promised to do immeasurably more than we could ask or imagine. He has promised to never leave us or turn His back on us. He has promised to show us all that He is doing and He has promised to supply all that we will need to participate in what He is doing.

Repent: We will do something cool for God because of our abilities and talents. I pray when I feel like something is missing from my life; I ask God to take away my pain and make things better. When God doesn't cooperate with my plans or desires, I feel like He must not care about me.

Believe the Good News: Believing that God loves us and guarantees his promises for us in Jesus Christ, we approach Him boldly and expectantly. We will trust that it is He that is calling us into His presence. We will listen like God has something to say to us. We will claim His promises as truth and ask Him for what He has already promised.

Therefore Go: Identify a few things that you believe God is doing or planning to do in your midst. Think about the people He has placed in your life. What is the work, (that is greater than the works Jesus did and immeasurably greater than what you could even ask for or imagine), that God wants to do in you and through you? Ask God to show this to you. Begin to pray for these things and be ready for action. Share these things with our community and we will help one another move forward.

---

[1] Wangerin, *Prayer*, 14.
[2] John 3:8.

Part 1: Fear-based Praying vs. Faith-based Praying.

Read Acts 12:1–19.
What does God show you in this story?
What stands out to you?
What questions does it raise for you?

_____

_____

_____

_____

_____

Have you ever thought about how precarious our planet is? As the earth spins on its access, the surface of the planet is barreling along at over 1,000 mph. At the same time, we are orbiting a flaming ball of Hydrogen at approximately 67,000 miles per hour. On top of that our galaxy which has a diameter of 100,000 light years and contains over 200 billion stars is hurtling through space at 370 miles per second towards two galaxies and over 600 miles per second towards a third galaxy. And let's not forget about all those black holes out there that are swallowing up entire galaxies like cosmic garbage disposals. And then there's the whole matter of chunks of rock the size of shopping malls screaming through space at breathtaking speeds. Chances are one of these days earth will line up with one of those flight patterns. Imagine if I told you that the majority of my praying centered around petitioning God to keep the earth safe in the midst of all this cosmic chaos. Hopefully you would think that was odd. I believe most of the praying that goes on among Christians in America is some form of this type of prayer. Prayer rooted in fear has become so commonplace in our churches that we believe it to be the standard way of praying. The pattern looks like this:

- Identify the most feared outcomes in your life.
- Present those feared outcomes to God and ask Him to prevent them from taking place.
- Do everything in your power to prevent your feared outcomes from taking place.
- Base your understanding of God on what happens in respect to those feared outcomes (blame Him or thank Him).

Are there times when your prayers reflect this sort of pattern? Reflect on things you have asked God for in the last week or month and write down how fear influences your praying.

_____

_____

_____

_____

Fear and anxiety are part of life. We were never meant to succumb to it though. Fear limits us. Even when we successfully avoid what we fear we are still limited by it as we arrange our life around it. I once took a scuba lesson in a swimming pool. I only lasted two minutes. I just couldn't get past the idea that I could be underwater and still inhale. I felt like I was taking water into my lungs so my breathing became panic driven. I would quickly exhale in fear that I was inhaling water. I finally gave up to the disappointment of my friend who was thoroughly enjoying watching my attempts to breathe under water. I was not able to breathe because I lacked faith in my regulator to deliver my air instead of water. During my scuba lesson my worldview was fear driven; "What if my regulator doesn't work properly?" My friend who was breathing easy was able to reason by faith, "My regulator will function properly; I am guaranteed air when I inhale." Thus, he was able to focus on swimming and was eventually able to become a certified diver and see the Great Barrier Reef.

If we are praying in fear it means that we have failed to see the all-sufficiency of God or perhaps we are trying to get something from Him that He has not promised to give. Scripture is clear how we are to posture ourselves when we are confronted with fear.

- "We have been rescued from our enemies so we can serve God without fear" (Luke 1:74).
- "So you have not received a spirit that makes you fearful slaves. Instead, you received God's Spirit when he adopted you as his own children. Now we call him, "Abba, Father" (Rom 8:15).
- "Such love has no fear, because perfect love expels all fear. If we are afraid, it is for fear of punishment, and this shows that we have not fully experienced his perfect love" (I John 4:18).
- "So we can say with confidence, "The Lord is my helper, so I will have no fear. What can mere people do to me?" (Heb 13:6).
- "But even if you suffer for doing what is right, God will reward you for it. So don't worry or be afraid of their threats" (I Pet 3:14).
- "When I saw him, I fell at his feet as if I were dead. But he laid his right hand on me and said, "Don't be afraid! I am the First and the Last" (Rev 1:17).
- "Give all your worries and cares to God, for he cares about you" (I Pet 5:7).

- "I praise God for what he has promised. I trust in God, so why should I be afraid? What can mere mortals do to me?" (Ps 56:4).
- "The Lord is for me, so I will have no fear. What can mere people do to me?" (Ps 118:6).
- "For I can do everything through Christ, who gives me strength" (Phil 4:13).
- "And this same God who takes care of me will supply all your needs from his glorious riches, which have been given to us in Christ Jesus" (Phil 4:19).
- "Now all glory to God, who is able, through his mighty power at work within us, to accomplish infinitely more than we might ask or think" (Eph 3:20).
- "Don't be afraid, for I am with you. Don't be discouraged, for I am your God. I will strengthen you and help you. I will hold you up with my victorious right hand" (Isa 41:10).

Many of our prayers are formed by a fear-driven worldview. The platform or our prayers are worry and fear. 'What if God forgets me?' 'What if God doesn't come through?' 'What if God allows something bad to happen to me?' We believe that we are not cared for or thought of by God. We believe that our possibilities are limited by our own human nature or capability. We have more faith in statistical probabilities and coincidences then we do in God's promise to invade and change what is happening in our hearts and in the physical world around us. Many times fear will be our starting point in prayer. If we are seeing God rightly, our fears will subside as we sit in God's presence.

Early on in my relationship with God, my prayers were driven by *me*. I wanted to believe prayer 'worked' because I wanted to get what I wanted. I would bring Jesus my fears of losing what mattered and my hopes of gaining what I longed for. My words and prayer-filled wishes revolved around contentment, comfort, safety, and acquiring greater happiness. It all seemed logical to me. God wants me to be happy right? Well, a new car, a bigger house, or a 51 inch flat screen would make me very happy so clearly God wants to give me these things. I just need to learn how to get on God's good side and pray right so that He will give me these things. In doing, we appoint ourselves to be judges of God's character based on what He does and does not grant us. For example, if I believed God wanted me to be happy above anything else and I was not happy I might conclude that God did not love me. Or if I were happy, I would falsely conclude that my happiness was evidence of God's love for me. God loves us regardless of how happy we feel.

> Happiness has become our god when God simply becomes the means to achieving that happiness.

If happiness is our god we have reason to be fearful and anxious because there is no guarantee of happiness and seamless pleasant circumstances. Fear is the direct result of an uncertain future. Faith is the direct result of a foreseen certain future. We are future-oriented beings. The Living God gives us the power to face the future in confidence. When our lives are oriented to personal happiness, the feelings we want to achieve are not guaranteed so we face the future fearfully.

Happiness is an idol. When we idolize God by longing for what He longs for, we can begin to live without fear since nothing is more powerful than God (He will always accomplish what He ordains). His promises contain the life that He offers us. This life is guaranteed and nothing and no one can take that away from us. Does God act on our behalf? Absolutely. The important distinction to note is that He only and always acts on behalf of us *for His glory*. God will not be shy to bring you suffering if for the purpose of bringing glory to His name. James wrote, "Where do you think all these appalling wars and quarrels come from? Do you think they just happen? Think again. They come about because you want your own way, and fight for it deep inside yourselves. You lust for what you don't have and are willing to kill to get it. You want what isn't yours and will risk violence to get your hands on it. You wouldn't think of just asking God for it, would you? And why not? Because you know you'd be asking for what you have no right to. You're spoiled children, each wanting your own way. You're cheating on God. If all you want is your own way, flirting with the world every chance you get, you end up enemies of God and his way" (Jas 4:1–4).

How has your quest for happiness influenced how you view God and fear the future?

_____

_____

_____

_____

_____

Immature relationships are based on good feelings. I spent several years serving junior high school students in a youth ministry. I knew a few boys who would cycle through as many as 3 or 4 girlfriends per week. This always seemed odd and amusing to me so I usually inquired further. 'Brian, why did you break up with Melinda?' 'Ahhhh . . . she got all mad about something and started crying so I broke up with her.' In a state of immaturity, we only place our faith in what makes us feel good and we ditch out on people or situations that cause us discomfort. Could this have something to do with our present day church hopping phenomena?

One of my heroes in high school was my cross-country coach. He spotted me when I was a 100 lb, 6 foot, awkward freshman with no depth perception who just wanted to hide from the big people. When I met him he told me I would be a fast runner and that I should be on his cross-country team. Since no one aside from my parents had told me I would ever be good at anything, I showed up. For a long time that 'fast runner' never materialized. Coach Matthews however, saw something that no one else had the ability to see. He saw a runner with promise. He had to endure many races watching me lean across the finish line only to claim second-to-last. He never gave up though. He never stopped encouraging and sharing his faith that he had in me. Eventually it paid off (four years later) when I held a spot on his state championship team. 'Berto,' as we affectionately called him, had faith in something greater than his own happiness and immediate gratification. His faith in me required him to endure unpleasant feelings, sacrifice his reputation, and be okay with the possibility of looking like a fool.

Happiness is our oxygen and 30 seconds without it sends us into panic. Our happiness is being strangled before our eyes so we grab it from whoever or whatever is threatening it and quickly revive it. When we are confronted with the likelihood of an unpleasant future, we respond by doing whatever is in our power to change that future and if we are incapable of changing our circumstances then we will change our beliefs in order to feel better about things beyond our control. How many of us have been hurt by someone and afterwards reasoned that they were just an asshole? We reason that we are better off without them. What is *really* going on here is that we have been told that we are not loved and in our insecurity we diminish the person so that their opinion of us might also be diminished. We diminish our picture of God when we live in fear and insecurity. Our perpetual fear insults Him. Our prayers are centered on us. We come to God thinking we are large and that He is small. We have been told that God wants us to be happy so we bring to Him our fears of encountering unhappiness and expect Him to bow to our request.

Take a few minutes to confess to God how you have made you and your happiness the center of your life (we all have and do). Scripture tells us that it is God's kindness that changes our hearts (Rom 2:4). Picture yourself being tenderly and affectionately embraced by God. Let go of any need to impress God or polish your image before Him. You were not placed on this earth to impress God. You were placed on this earth to be impressed by God. Let His love and kindness for you impress you. Write down below how you believe God wants to change your fear-driven words into faith-driven words.

_____

_____

_____

_____

_____

Read our story in Acts 12:1–19.
Why do you think God rescued Peter from prison?

_____

_____

Do you think that the prayers of a handful of people directly resulted in some Roman soldiers dying a cruel and unjust death? Does God love Peter more than the guards? If God loved the guards as much as He loved Peter, why did God allow them to die so that Peter could go free?

_____

_____

Are your prayers wish-driven or belief-driven? How can you tell?

_____

_____

_____

Part 2: Prayer: The Pathway to a Disrupted Life

"People cannot stand too much reality." —Carl Jung

"The Lord tears down the house of the proud, but he protects the property of widows" (Prov 15:25).

Read Acts 12:1–19.
What does God show you in this story?
What stands out to you?
What questions does it raise for you?

_____

_____

_____

_____

_____

In my sophomore year of college I tried out for crew. I was invited by the coach to try out because I'm tall and skinny. I couldn't say 'no' because I was so desperate to establish myself in a new pecking order. To my surprise, I became good. I eagerly invested 40 hours of my week, learned to function on 4 hours of sleep per night, and adapted to constant oozing blisters on my hands. The head varsity coach took notice of me from the beginning and wanted to move me from the novice boat (first year rowers) up to the varsity boat. I quickly became one of the most skilled rowers and had the fastest time for 2,000 meters on a rowing machine. I quickly excelled beyond my fellow rowers that had been in the sport for years. This experience was brand new for me. Nineteen years of experience had told me that the speed in which I acquired a new skill was always slower than my cohorts. For the first time in my life I felt truly hopeful about my future. I believed God had finally given me favor after a long drought of adolescent unpopularity and dead-ends. Coincidentally, near the end of my sophomore term, I also for the first time began sincerely seeking God. Maybe I sought Him because I now believed that He was good and cared about me by helping me to be good at something and be recognized. That summer, I turned my life over to Jesus after several years of just doing religion. Days after I turned it all over to Jesus, I was in the gym doing leg presses. My eyes were set on my future. I would sit in seat 7 or 8, which are reserved for the most skilled rowers. I would lead my boat to a victory at the Pacific Coast Rowing Championships in Sacramento. It would be great. These were my thoughts as I was heaving hundreds of pounds into the air with my legs when suddenly a crisp popping noise escaped from both knees. My legs gave out and the weight collapsed and came to rest.

For the next two years, even casual walking would be difficult. Simply bending my legs involved excruciating pain. Four years later I was still not able to run even 50 yards. Twelve years later I am still reminded by occasional deep and sharp pains below my knee-caps.

God opposed *me* so that I would stop opposing *Him*. He had to destroy the source of my false hope so that I would long for the only source of true hope. A false hope (ascribing to a promise that is not from God) is always in indicator of a false god.

What we place our hope in reveals who or what we worship.

I was not *intentionally* fighting God; I just wasn't surrendered to His future. I wanted my future. If I'm living for my future, I am picking a fight with God and He won't be fooled by our neat gestures of religion. "I know all the things you do, that you are neither hot nor cold. I wish that you were one or the other! But since you are like lukewarm water, neither hot nor cold, I will spit you out of my mouth! You say, 'I am rich. I have everything I want. I don't need a thing!' And you don't realize that you are wretched and miserable and poor and blind and naked. So I advise you to buy gold from me—gold that has been purified by fire. Then you will be rich. Also buy white garments from me so you will not be shamed by your nakedness, and ointment for your eyes so you will be able to see." (Rev 3:15–18) These words of Jesus are a warning for us to see that He is tired of us riding the fence. I look back on my experience in college and can see that it was not wrath that God was inflicting on me but it was His grace. I was angry with God for months because I felt like He wasn't on my side. In truth, He *wasn't* on my side. But He was calling me to be on *His* side. Once I understood this, I saw my destroyed knees as evidence of God's commitment to draw me into the center of His life. He destroyed my agenda because He knew that it was so important to me that I wouldn't have the strength to lay it down; so He took it from me. Jesus came to me when I swore I was rich and satisfied. He showed me my wretchedness, my poverty, my nakedness, and my blindness. He called me to repent; to surrender my future and to subscribe to His future.

I once felt led while praying through Psalm 23, to ask God for a valley. I wanted to know what it would be like to walk through the valley of the shadow of death and not fear evil because of God's presence. So I did just that. I asked God to give me a valley. Be careful what you ask God for. God faithfully provided a valley. Spiritual valleys are dark confrontations with evil; the evil in our hearts and the evil in the world around us. They are lonely, confusing, and painful. God does not delight in evil yet evil shows us how severely we need God. This is why it was weird to ask God for an encounter with evil and to then see it happen as if He personally delivered it Himself. This was the first time that I intentionally and sincerely asked God to disrupt my life. I knew that my life was comfortable and easy. I was tired of being apathetic to my own laziness. I was in need of a spiritual defibrillator. The only person who needs a defibrillator is a person with no pulse. No one says, 'Hey I think I'm going to head down to the hospital for a little de-fib; anyone else want to come?'

Two months after my prayer, an ex-boyfriend of my wife-to-be committed suicide. I was going to ask her to marry me in one week. The loss of his life and the manner in which it ended were devastating. I sat on the couch with Sydel for two days straight. Few words were spoken; I just held her. My fiancé was made to believe that she was the cause of her friend's suicide. He asked her to provide something that she or anyone could not. Immediately after her last conversation with him, he went home and hung himself. It was the kind of tragedy that seems to permanently alter your physiology and your personality. It has been six years since that suicide. Many days I feel I am still in the valley. Not because of his suicide, but because God has not released us from the valley. For years I asked God to lead us out of the valley. In hindsight I wanted a valley like a child wants to hold a snake or a beetle. They clasp their hands around it and immediately toss it back to the ground once they feel it move. A taste was all they wanted. A taste was all I wanted. God would not remove us from the valley. By asking God to remove me from the valley was a clear indicator that my circumstances or my happiness was still my god; I just wanted God to give me access to my false god. God is very persistent and patient. He watched us suffer many days. He watched our marriage grow thin and weary. He watched us trying to salvage pieces of our shattered bliss.

It should make us very uncomfortable that God wants to renovate our hearts. We are stubborn and very committed to our happiness. We will not go down without a long and bloody fight. God has kept me in the valley to direct my eyes not to the hills (the loneliness, despair, and pain) on either side of me but to Himself. God seems to ask me everyday, "Am I enough? Am I truly your god or would you still rather chase after fantasies and illusions?" These are hard questions. We are devoted to many things; things that we believe will provide us with happiness. God is not interested in sharing your devotion with your assorted gods that occupy space in your heart. He is interested in all of your devotion.

Is God enough for you? Complete this sentence: I need God and _____.

It is alarmingly easy and safe to be a practicing atheist. This doesn't mean that we aren't religious; we can still attend worship services, recite morning prayers, and occasionally read our Bible. All of these routines can give us some sense of comfort that there's another world of happiness on the other side of the clouds. Our atheism has to do with this life; not the next. We think we are worshiping God but we are really worshiping *what we want* from God. I drive an '86 Toyota. It has nearly 300,000 miles on it and faithfully gets me where I want to go. I often have feelings of gratitude towards my vehicle; my life would certainly be different without it. The reason I have a vehicle though is because there is something else I want that my vehicle can give me access to. I want a vehicle because I need to get to the store to buy food or go see friends. If I did not need to buy food and had no friends, I would have no practical need for my truck. Don't we often have the same understanding of God? Maybe I often have feelings of gratitude towards God because I believe in hell and God gives me my 'get out of hell free' card. I want out of hell and only God can give me access to this wish. Maybe if I did not believe in the existence of hell,

I would feel no practical need for God. I feel convicted when I see that I am a practical atheist.

What is it that you want God to give you access to?

_____

_____

This brings us back to our future-oriented DNA. God meets us when we are steeped in seeking *our* future on *our* terms. Christians have done a good job of communicating to the world what they should not do in the future (don't swear, don't sleep around, don't get drunk, don't cheat, don't lie, etc.). We have done a lousy job of joyfully discovering God's new future of hope for humanity. I have had countless conversations with high school students who voice their disinterest in being a Christian because all God does is destroy their hope of reaching happiness. God must be anti-happy, they surmise. Heaven must be the most boring place not-on-earth. They have not been pointed to a living source of hope that transforms and transcends life as we know it. God is not anti-happy. There will be no tears in eternity. Joy will become a constant and unwavering emotion for all of us. C. S. Lewis tells us that it is the duty of every Christian to be as happy as possible. Indeed God wants us to be happy. The Apostle Paul tells us to rejoice always. God is most glorified when we most enjoy Him. We are clear that we are not to feast on the pleasures of the world. We fail to feast on the pleasures of God. Perhaps because we are not aware that we serve a God who is the fullness of perfect joy? We scold one another for extramarital sex, greed, and drunkenness yet we neglect to remind one another of the life and future that has been prepared for us. We settle for asking God to keep us out of trouble and for things to 'go okay'. Our prayers lack vision. We know what we are *not* intended to have but we do not see what God is waiting to give us in place of these things. Christianity easily becomes a list of things that we are no longer allowed to do. Our Christian life becomes a lifelong struggle to stop doing things on this list.

It is the joy of an anticipated better future that captures our hearts. Several times a day my heart will burst for eternity. Ponder it for a moment. Revelation 21 vividly describes life after Jesus comes again. The New Jerusalem descends on earth from the sky. God thunderously and jubilantly announces that His new dwelling place is with us! He gently wipes away all tears, banishes death, destruction, mourning, crying, and pain from this city forever! Everything is made new. Creation is restored. The New Jerusalem is big, very big. Its borders measure 1,400 miles on each side! The walls and foundations of this city are built with gold and precious stones—what a sight! There is not a single church building in this city because Jesus walks freely among us. In this city, the sun's light is not required because God's glory shines; radiantly swallowing up all darkness. A multi-cultural street festival ensues with feasting and dancing. The celebration literally never ends, never gets old, and always gets better. We reign with God forever! We enjoy complete relationship with the God who thought of us and carefully brought us into existence. We enjoy complete relationships with those around us. Aged wine. Choice meats. Eternity with God will be life as it is intended to be lived! Jesus prayed that His Father's will would be done, that His Kingdom (the celebration scene above) would arrive here on earth *as it already is in Heaven*. Our picture of eternity, God's better future, informs our prayers. I used to think that Heaven was going to be a church service that never ended. Organ music, standing up, sitting down, standing up, sitting down, trying to stay awake, crossing out items on the order of service as they happened like I was counting down the days 'til Christmas. If that's eternity, count me out! God is beckoning your heart towards eternity. To do this, He will strip you of your false gods and hopes. For three generations, Americans have convinced themselves that they are able to buy that better future on their own terms. God is breaking us of this. God wants to disrupt your life to break you of the false gods you cling to in order that your hope might be in Jesus, our Warrior King.

Based on vv. 2 and 3 in Acts 19. What was the fate of Peter?

_____

For many throughout history, a life disrupted by God has meant premature death and suffering. (Check out Hebrews 11:35–38. Seriously, read it!) James, whose execution is mentioned in verse 2, more than likely had family and friends that were part of the company of believers praying for Peter's deliverance. If James were your brother or husband, what emotions would have run through your mind during that prayer meeting?

_____

_____

Part 3: Pray in Order to See

Read Acts 12:1–19.
What does God show you in this story?
What stands out to you?
What questions does it raise for you?

_____

_____

_____

_____

_____

"The [Christian] lives like everybody else, works like everybody else, thinks like everybody else and reacts like everybody else. He is seduced by technology. He shares the same hopes and fear with everyone. He feels crushed by the [latest] tragedy, lives through eventualities emotionally and follows the news feverishly. Thus he participates in the hopes and terrors of all. If that is the way it is, let's not fool ourselves. It means that this Christian is of the world. He is fed the same information and is subject to the same influences. He belongs to the same organizations, is troubled in the same ways and obeys the same reflexes as other people."[3]

Words are losing their meaning in America. Take the word 'love'. I love pizza. I love my wife. I love sleeping in. I love it when you call me 'big papa'. I love Jesus. I love rock-and-roll. Or how about 'awesome'? My dictionary says, 'extremely impressive or daunting; inspiring great admiration, apprehension, or fear.' We think everything is 'awesome'. We ask our friends, 'hey you want go get lunch?' And we say, 'Yeah, that sounds daunting and it even makes me a little apprehensive and fearful just thinking about it—sure.'

Words and concepts get their meaning from people and events. 'Crap' no longer primarily means a losing throw of 2, 3, or 12 in the game of craps. It's a socially acceptable replacement for 'shit'. The Bible says that God is love. Therefore, if we want to know anything about love, we must know who God is and what He has done and continues to do for His children. When we look at His character and actions then we can say, *that's what love is; now I know what it means to be loved and to love another.*

> *Prior to an encounter with God, our understanding of love will come from movies and advertisers and hormones.*

When Americans speak about 'justice' we are usually talking about kicking some ass with our bombs and guns. Christians have bought into this definition even though bibli-

___

[3] Ellul, *False Presence*, 46.

cal justice has nothing to do with revenge or retaliation. Biblical justice has nothing to do with protecting rights, freedoms, or economies. In His longest sermon, Jesus paints a picture of a community that confronts evil yet loves their enemies and refuses to seek retaliation or revenge. Justice is in God's hands; not in our hands or our nation's.

What we most deeply hope for will determine what we pray for (if we are honest). We may speak other words with our mouths out of guilt, duty, or ceremony but God wants us to pray with our hearts. God's mission is to capture your heart with His character and His work. Further, the content of our prayers will be determined by what we believe should happen in the future. We have some future in mind and so we pray according to that future. If our hope is that life will work out the way we want it to then our prayers will revolve around trying to convince God that He should do things our way. The future is in God's hands, not ours. Yet we try and claim it from Him when we insist that we must have control over it or have a say in the outcomes of tomorrow. We simply have no grounds to do so. It's quite easy to become swept up into feeling like God is always against us. Sometimes He must oppose us in order for us to see that He is calling us to want what He wants and feel what He feels.

In what ways do you feel like God is opposing you right now? What do you think He is trying to show you?

_____

_____

_____

Even when God opposes us in our pride He is still for us. His heart's desire is that all would be called to repentance and turn to Him for life. He is always seeking to turn us away from the poverty of our own riches and the ignorance of our blindness so that we might receive His richness and hope for His future. It is by grace that God opposes us. We are in need of conquering.

Any trouble that God might cause for us or allow for us while pursuing *our* agenda can and will line up with His commitment to turn us towards *His* agenda. And any trouble we might encounter while in His agenda can and will be overcome through the glory of our Risen King. This is the foundation of a prayerful life. God, through intimate personal relationship, continually calls us out of ourselves and into His infinite goodness and grace. This journey will not end in your lifetime. Apart from prayer, trouble is simply trouble. We become frustrated and refuse to accept trouble for what it is; God's attempts to win us to His heart. "Above all else the [human] heart is stubborn, prideful, and deceitful." We are bent on our own destruction while we simultaneously numb our selves. The result is that we believe we are okay as we drug ourselves with our culture's latest offering. Prayer is the painful and grueling bus ride out of the life we have made and into the life of God.

Sometimes the best starting point in prayer is to ask God to render you incapable of pursuing your own agenda or future. Take a few moments to ponder your own agenda. Think of the vast amounts of time, energy, and resources you commit to your agenda. Think about how your agenda is truly important to your heart. What are you hoping for that has little or nothing to do with what God has promised us?

Could you sincerely ask God to derail your agenda? Are you willing to endure the pain of letting go of what you currently treasure in your heart? What might it look like if God derailed your agenda? What would He need to take from you?

Prayer is the primary venue where God will begin the life-long work of healing your vision. If we could see God in all His glory, we would take pleasure in nothing but Him! The beginning of this journey is difficult because as God increases, we decrease, and decreasing is painful. Prayer used to be mostly boring for me because deep in my heart I wanted to 'get back to what was really important to me'. Prayer was a discipline and a duty—something I knew I *should* do. Years later my friend Jeanette taught me to pray in response to a vision of God and how He was bringing glory to His name on *this* day and in *this* place. Prayer became exciting, like playing capture the flag in the middle of the night. I began to see that God wanted to do something supernatural and I believed that He was capable of doing it.

One of my favorite TV shows growing up was 'Knight Rider' which told the adventures of a crime-busting hotshot whose partner was a black Camero named Kit that could think, talk, perform impossible stunts and came equipped with plenty of James Bond-like extras. My favorite part in every episode was when Michael Knight was in a jam and he would call his superhero car via his watch, "Kit, I need help!" Kit would roar to life, corral all the bad guys and rescue Michael from his dire straits. This was my favorite part because throughout the entire episode I would anticipate this inevitable scene and I knew that Kit was unstoppable. I couldn't wait to see how Kit would do it. I would yell at the TV when death became further and further eminent for Michael, "Call Kit! Call Kit! What are you waiting for?!" This is what prayer has become for me. God backs His people further and further into trouble; they call upon Him, He delivers them and His fame spreads. He gets the applause, not us.

Part of the problem is that we fail to see the whole picture. We live most of our days unaware that history is in a revolving climax and crisis all around us. Most of us in America can buy our way out of trouble and discomfort.

A well-rounded picture of reality will beckon us to call upon God in these days of trouble.

The reality that really does bite . . .
- One half of the world's six billion citizens live on less than $2 per day. 1.3 billion live on less than $1 per day. Over 1 billion have no access to clean water; 3 billion have no access to sanitation.
- The three wealthiest people in the world exceed the combined Gross Domestic Product of the 48 least developed countries.
- The 200 wealthiest people in the world have a combined wealth of $1 trillion. This is equal to the combined wealth of the world's 2.5 billion poorest citizens.
- The disproportion of wealth between the richest and poorest countries has risen from 3 to 1 in 1820 to 72 to 1 in 1992.
- The world's wealthiest 20% (annual income of $1,820 USD or more) consume 86% of all goods and services in the world. The world's poorest 20% consume approximately 1% of all goods and services in the world.[4]
- Worldwide, 250 million children are working and 600 million live in extreme poverty. Over 30 million children are currently being bought and sold into abuse and exploitation. Roughly half a million children have died of AIDS.
- Most US citizens believe that the US government spends between 16 and 18% of its budget on foreign aid. In reality, they spend close to 1% on foreign aid.
- One in ten US households lives with hunger or is at risk of hunger.
- In 1998 the average CEO in the US was paid as much as 419 factory workers.
- A higher percentage of blacks than whites live in poverty at every level of educational attainment.
- In Africa, 17 million have died from AIDS, 26 million are infected with HIV, and 12 million children have been orphaned.
- Worldwide, 1,800 babies are born with HIV each day; 42,000 children die of AIDS each month; and 3,000,000 children lose one or both parents to AIDS each year.
- US arms sales have resulted in 45 to 50 post—Cold war conflicts where 70 to 90% of all casualties were civilian.
- September 11, 2001 was unquestioningly a dark day for many Americans (roughly 2,800 deaths resulted from the terrorist attacks). I do not downplay or make light of the tragedy. I want to call our attention to the many other things that took place

---

[4] If you want to know where you stand on the global pay scale, checkout http://globalrichlist.com.

on that day and *have continued each day since then*. The number of children killed from preventable causes around the world on 9/11/01: 35,615. Minutes of silence: 0. National days of remembrance: 0. National monuments erected: 0. US funds allocated to prevent a reoccurrence: 0.[5]

The reality that bites back harder . . .
Jesus was sent by the Father and given power to:
- Announce that God's better future was now trumping man's future. Jesus was not bringing advice. He was bringing *news*; a divine revelation that is changing the course of our history as you read these words. Specifically, He brought this news to the poor.
- Announce freedom to those imprisoned by physical and spiritual forces.
- Announce that those living in blindness are recovering their sight. Jesus stated this as a reality and not a possibility or likelihood. Just as God said, 'let there be light' and there was light, Jesus' announcement brought and is bringing recovery of sight into existence.
- Release those living in physical, mental, moral and spiritual oppression.
- Declare a season of God's favor (See Luke 4:16–20).

Jesus is pointing us to a better future. My hope is that we might see these words both for us as well as our suffering neighbors. Yes in some way we are all oppressed and imprisoned. We who are rich are imprisoned by our riches and oppressed by our ability to relieve our suffering with those riches. However, can we please stop using our own oppression and bondage as reason to continue neglecting the poor? For their oppression and bondage is far worse than ours. The Bible contains over 1,000 references regarding God's desires for the poor—not the rich who are 'made poor' by their lust for money—but for those who have no options because they have no means by which to live.

Jesus is pointing us to a better future that includes freedom for the rich and the poor. My hunch is that this freedom will have something to do with the rich sharing their riches and the poor acquiring food and shelter. God can and does equip us to participate in this vision. God owns this future and it transpires only in His authority. Wealth and poverty then are spiritual matters that require divine intervention.[6] If Jesus is simply giving good advice here, we have no reason to hope. Lots of people possess wisdom, knowledge, or ideas but are powerless to wage war against the forces that aggressively plot the destruction of all human life. If Jesus has no power, if He has not the ability to transform us through our obedience, it would be pointless to pray for the rich and act on behalf of the poor. It would be more beneficial to share our hopes and troubles with a counselor who will do nothing more than acknowledge our pain and comfort us with the fact that we are not alone.

---

[5] These statistics were compiled from various sources by Dawn, *Unfettered Hope*, 32–39.
[6] For an informative and provocative discussion on poverty, see Meyers, *Walking With the Poor*, and Maxwell, *It's Not Okay With Me*.

It is not advice or exhortation that truly encourages us. It is news and reminders of a future that is both good and guaranteed that encourages us.

Jesus is not calmly sitting in a room waiting for you to talk to Him. He is a victorious and mighty warrior routing your enemies, gathering those who have been scattered, restoring your fortunes, removing your punishment, and banishing your fear of ever incurring harm. In addition, this Mighty Warrior tenderly loves you, quieting you with His love, delighting in you, giving you praise and honor, and rejoicing over you in song (Zeph 3:14-20). What humanity is in need of is the felt presence of *this* King and *His* present and future kingdom. William Wallace convinced his people that to bow to England was the equivalent of slavery. We are inspired to rise up in prayer when we become convinced that God has no equal and that no matter how hopeless things appear, Jesus' victory is not diminished or undone.

A conversation with William Wallace would not be boring. You would most likely walk away with some level of gumption to take up the cause of Scotland. Sharing your 'shopping list' with Jesus would be like asking William Wallace to trim your fingernails. How does a warrior picture of Jesus as described in Zephaniah 3:14–20 inspire you to petition this Warrior to advance His kingdom in your community?

_____

_____

_____

What does the reign of Christ actually mean? It literally means *everything*. Without His kingship, there would be no life. Because He reigns,

- We are made alive in Christ (I Cor 15:22).
- All dominion, authority, and power will be destroyed (I Cor 15:24).
- Death will be destroyed (I Cor 15:25).

God's better future is certain. The reign of Christ guarantees it. Therefore we can pray boldly for God to bring to pass what He has promised and is capable of delivering ('your kingdom come, your will be done . . .'). It's important that we continually remind ourselves that Jesus is the King of kings and that His reign spells the destruction of death. The Bible contains prayers, that when read through the lens of Christ's supremacy, shake the foundations of the earth. For example, look at Ephesians 3:14–21. I will paraphrase and substitute 'the One who has destroyed death forever' for the name of Jesus.

> "I pray that out of the Father's glorious and abundant riches that He would strengthen you with power through the giving of His Spirit into the depths of your hearts so that the One who has destroyed death forever may do what He does best in your hearts through faith. And I pray that you, being rooted and established in love, may have power, together with all the saints, to grasp how

wide and long and high and deep is the love of the One who has destroyed death forever, and to know this love that surpasses knowledge—that you may be filled to the measure of all the fullness of God. Now to Him who is able to do immeasurably more than all we ask or imagine, according to His power that is at work within us, to Him be glory in the church and in the One who has destroyed death forever throughout all generations, for ever and ever! Amen."

Or check out Ephesians 1 in Eugene Peterson's translation, *The Message.*

"How blessed is God! And what a blessing he is. He's the Father of our Master, [the One who has destroyed death forever], and takes us to the high places of blessing in him. Long before he laid down earth's foundations, he had us in mind, had settled on us as the focus of his love, to be made whole and holy by his love. Long, long ago he decided to adopt us into his family through [the One who has destroyed death forever. (what pleasure he took planning this!) He wanted us to enter into the celebration of his lavish gift-giving by the hand of his beloved Son, [the One who destroyed death forever]. Because of the sacrifice of [the One who destroyed death forever], his blood poured out on the alter of the Cross, we're a free people—free of penalties and punishments chalked up by all our misdeeds. And not just barely free, either. Abundantly free! He thought of everything, provided for everything we could possibly need, letting us in on the plans he took such delight in making. He set it all out before us in [the One who destroyed death forever], a long-range plan in which everything would be brought together and summed up in him, everything in deepest heaven, everything on planet earth. It's in [the One who has destroyed death forever] that we find out who we are and what we're living for. Long before we first heard of [the One who had destroyed death forever] and got our hopes up, he had his eye on us, had designs on us for glorious living, part of the overall purpose he is working out in everything and everyone."

And because of this, we pray that . . .

"The God of our Master, [the One who has destroyed death forever], the God of glory—to make you intelligent and discerning in knowing him personally, your eyes focused and clear, so that you can see exactly what it is he is calling you to do, grasp the immensity of this glorious way of life he has for Christians, oh, the utter extravagance of his work in us who trust him—endless energy, boundless strength! All this energy issues from [the One who has destroyed death forever]: God raised him from death and set him on a throne in deep heaven, in charge of running the universe, everything from galaxies to governments, no name and no power exempt from his rule. And not just for the time being, but forever. He is in charge of it all, has the final word on everything. At the center of all this, [the One who has destroyed death forever] rules the church. The church, you see, is not peripheral to the world; the world is peripheral to the church. The church is the body of [the One who has destroyed death forever], in which he speaks and acts, by which he fills everything with his presence . . . He creates each of us by [the One who has destroyed death forever] to join him in the work he does, the good work he has gotten ready for us to do, work we had better be doing."

How do these words inspire you? Write down any hopes or dreams that surface in your heart as a result of the truth in these words.

_____

_____

_____

_____

_____

In Acts 12, Peter's friends prayed in boldness and confidence. There was no fear in their prayers. They understood that Jesus reigned over the government that was holding Him. They understood that Jesus created the properties of the iron that was fashioned into the chains around his wrists and ankles. Neither the laws of physics nor the laws of the land intimidated them into believing that this was a situation beyond the hand of God. *Their picture of God determined how they prayed for Peter that night.*

Think of a situation in your life that you have believed is beyond God's ability to reverse or transform. Briefly state it below.

_____

_____

_____

Reread our story in Acts 12 and meditate on Ephesians 1 and 3 above. Picture God's future. Picture what God is capable of. Ask God to show you how to pray for the above situation. Write this prayer below.

_____

_____

_____

Part 4: Pray So That Nothing Else Matters

"For I fully expect and hope that I will never be ashamed, but that I will continue to be bold for Christ, as I have been in the past. And I trust that my life will bring honor to Christ, whether I live or die. For to me, living means living for Christ, and dying is even better. But if I live, I can do more fruitful work for Christ. So I really don't know which is better. I'm torn between two desires: I long to go and be with Christ, which would be far better for me. But for your sakes, it is better that I continue to live" (Phil 1:20–24).

I love this Scripture! It shows me a man who was so impacted by Christ that the prospect of death was welcomed as it meant instant reunion with God. While Paul grew giddy at the thought of being with Christ he also knew that it was necessary for him to remain in his body or 'earthly tent' as he called it in a letter to the church in Corinth. His heart's longing for the eternal feast didn't distract him from the here and now; this longing actually motivated him to dig deeper; to see clearer; to work harder; to pray bigger. When I was growing up I thought that things had to get really bad in order for Jesus to come back. I've heard sincere Christians say things like, 'the *world* has to go to hell before *we* can go to heaven'. In this sentiment, they welcomed destruction of human life (primarily in the form of war) as a sign that Jesus would be returning soon. War was thus a welcomed and endorsed measure because it was necessary to usher in the second coming of Jesus. This is not how Jesus taught us to pray and think. He asked His Father that the character of life on earth move towards the character of life as it was currently being lived in Heaven (Matt 6:10). In heaven there is joy, peace, and love because God's presence is clearly seen and felt by all.

Only God can, as Belinda Carlisle sang, 'make heaven a place on earth'. God has commissioned the Church to be a glimpse for the world of what eternity will be like. He accomplishes this through His own creative ideas and strategies that He graciously gives to us. He accomplishes this through His sovereign power at work in us; nothing and no one can oppose Him. The ridiculous part of this is that He has chosen to work through us. In no way does God need us. "The Gospel is not a help-wanted ad. It is a help-available ad. Nor is the call to Christian service a help-wanted ad. God is not looking for people to work for him but people who let him work mightily in and through them: 'The eyes of the Lord search the whole earth in order to strengthen those whose hearts are fully committed to him.' (2 Chr 16:9). God is not a scout looking for the first draft choices to help his team win. He is an unstoppable fullback ready to take the ball and run touchdowns for anyone who trusts him to win the game."[7]

God is both the mastermind and the power source for His work. I often have ideas that I don't know what to do with. They seem beyond my capability—involving millions of dollars and countries in multiple continents. I'm doing well if I can pay my bills each month. I write down all my ideas—they're all saved in a document on my computer. It's

---

[7] Piper, *Brothers*, 40.

a dusty document. I lack the power to make the ideas happen. If God has an idea and has the power to make it happen and He has chosen to make that idea happen through us, we need to listen and be ready to respond.

Have you ever thought that God was looking for bright and talented people? God's work does not depend on you. We are like a glove that is used to work with sharp and abrasive objects. God is the hand that goes inside the glove. The glove cannot take credit for picking up the object. Or consider a puppet. A puppet is lifeless without a living hand inside it to personify it. God's work involves things that you cannot do; yet God still wants you to be part of what He is doing. Why do you think this is?

_____

_____

_____

Read Acts 12:1–19. What does God show you in this story? What stands out to you? What questions does it raise for you?

_____

_____

_____

_____

_____

Peter's friends prayed for an outcome that they themselves had no power to create. Only God could free Peter from prison. God led the people to pray for Peter. The people did not initiate their prayer. God did. As a result, this entire community of Christ-followers was intimately joined to God as a result of their praying. God told them to pray for Peter's release. They listened and prayed for Peter's release. God released Peter. Peter showed up at their house and they were all astonished and in awe of God's powerful presence among them. Do you think God is leading us towards this sort of prayerfulness? Maybe you want to believe that this is how God wants to relate and work with us but you are skeptical. Peter's friends were skeptical. They thought that an angel that *looked* like Peter was the more likely explanation. Jesus wants to heal our unbelief. Take a few moments and talk to God about your unbelief. Write anything down that He shows you.

_____

_____

_____

_____

_____

If God works strategically, there are no coincidences. "The lot is cast into the lap, but its every decision is from the Lord."[8] Even in the midst of evil, God works for the good of those who love Him (Rom 8:28). God wants to strategically and uniquely use you and your community of faith to reveal Himself and reconcile the world to Himself. The fullness of Christ dwells in us. It is through us that God has chosen to 'fill everything in every way' (Eph 1:23). Together we are being made into a dwelling place for God. He has placed His Spirit within us (Eph 2:21–22); the same Spirit that raised Jesus to life three days after his crucifixion. The same Spirit that counsels us, guides us, leads us into truth, speaks the words of Jesus to us, and shows us things that have not yet happened (John 16:13–15). This is no small thing. Even if you feel like you're guessing, how do you see God working strategically in your midst? Ponder how God has made you and where He has placed you. What about other believers in your midst? Write your thoughts below.

_____

_____

_____

_____

God is the most egocentric person in the universe. He adamantly declares: "My glory I will not give to another!" (Isa 48:11) We can always count on God glorifying Himself; it is at the core of why He created us—so that He would have an audience of worshipers. God loves His own glory more than He loves us. This concept might scare you. Maybe it conjures up images of powerful people in your life that abuse their power. They are self-centered and they abuse others to promote their own name. God is vastly different. The bible tells us that God has saved us, not for our sake but for the sake of His glory (Ezek 20:14; 36:22; Eph 1:6,12,14; Isa 43:7; Rom 9:22–23; I Sam 12:22; 2 Cor 5:15). Bullies pick on little people for their own sake. Their bullying makes them feel powerful. Their bullying increases the fame of their own name. My freshman year of high school, a bully put me in a garbage can butt first. My arms, feet, and head protruded from the top of the can. I was completely immobilized. He then dragged the can outside into the rain and positioned the can in the middle of a courtyard where I was clearly made visible to seven classrooms. Eventually windows opened and jeering began. My bully was giddy with laughter as he high-five'd his friends. My only means of rescuing myself was to begin rocking back and forth until the can fell over enabling me to crawl out. This taught me

[8] Prov 16:33.

that when I encounter someone seeking his or her own glory, I will probably have to forfeit my own dignity.

God's zealous pursuit of His own glory via increasing the fame of His name should bring us great comfort. God is glorified through your salvation (transferred from a kingdom of evil to a kingdom of eternal life) and sanctification (the life-long process of becoming more like Christ). Maybe you feel like God might abandon you or give up on you because you are stubborn and rebellious. Rest assured that God's commitment to you rests on His commitment to his own ego. God's ego is biggest and brightest when He freely gives you His grace, mercy, love, peace, and the fruits of His Spirit living in you.

When we pray for God to glorify Himself and to show us how He wants to make Himself famous through us, we are in a good place. This is God's greatest desire and it is the goal of all of our activity; to be positioned to live for God's glory. When this is our posture, we cannot fail because God will not compromise His glory. Even if our life ends (See Phil 1:20) and we are reunited with Christ, we can die knowing that God's glory will come in greater force in the wake of our death than it would had we sought to preserve our life. This is what it means to have higher regard for God's glory than your own life.

Jesus knew that surrendering to the work and will of the Father was the most pleasing and glorifying gift to His Father. Jesus surrendered even to the point of His own death by crucifixion. God's glory is not easy but it is worth more than anything we could possibly lose as a consequence of living for His glory; thus, deeming our loss a gain. In my senior year of high school, our cross-country team qualified for state. During this time my body was plagued with injuries. Among other things, I had shin splints and a stress fracture in my lower left shinbone that made running extremely painful. However, our team had a shot at winning state. I ran hard even though my body screamed. As I passed a runner from our rival team near the finish line, he intentionally spit on me. I didn't care. What mattered was finishing the race. The pain in my legs, the green loogie slithering down the back of my right leg, somehow made our state championship even sweeter. Jesus said that He would always be with us but that we would also be persecuted. He told his disciples that if 'they' hated Him, 'they' would surely hate them too. *Does anyone hate you because of your faithfulness to Jesus?* It's a troubling question because for most of us our greatest need is to be liked. God is not calling us to an easy life. When you begin to pray for God to be glorified you can be assured that indeed He will be glorified and you can be assured that it will hurt. Paul said that he wanted to share in the *sufferings* of Christ so that he could share in the *resurrection* of Christ. God's glory seemed to matter most to Paul. Whatever was to his benefit, he considered a loss. More so, he considered all things to be a loss compared to the greatness of God for whose sake he had lost all things. These things that he lost he now considered to be poop (literally). If you lost some poop, would you try to find it? 'Excuse me, has anyone seen my poop? I lost it a couple of days ago.' Paul flat-out was not interested in protecting or maintaining anything that wasn't directly related to God's glory (see Phil 3:7–14).

Does praying for God's glory to be displayed in your life scare you? It should. Write your thoughts below. And what do you think the difference is between praying for God's glory vs. praying for a personal shopping list?

_____

_____

_____

What practical and tangible steps do you feel led to take this week? Write them down and be prepared to share them this week. We will help each other take them, together and in the strength that God will supply for us to do so.

_____

_____

_____

_____

CHAPTER 4

The Unseen Becoming Seen

"The Lord has drawn a line in heaven. On one side are the former things—strategies, programs, ideas, and structures that once worked but are being discarded. They may still be effective, but they are not required. The biggest danger to a new move of God is the last move that is still working! We have to move in obedience to the word of God. As we move, we progress into a place where we can hear and understand the next thing that God is communicating. If we fail to move, then our capacity to understand what God is saying and doing is diminished."[1]

OVERVIEW:

Core Scripture: Acts 8:26–40

The Kingdom of God is at Hand: God reveals Himself to us in Jesus and Jesus is neither dead nor absent. Jesus said we would be able to discern His voice from other voices. Jesus promised that He would send His Spirit to us to reveal the heart and plans of the Father. Thus, God's presence among us and in us is a revealing presence that stretches far beyond the doors of church buildings and into unsuspecting and ordinary venues like our sidewalks and checkout counters. The ancient secrets are being made known to us and through us.

Repent: God has left us a moral code (the Bible) to guide our behavior and a collection of stories (also the Bible) to inspire nostalgia in us for how great God must have been in biblical times. If we can work up enough nostalgia, then we can pass the time quicker and stay out of trouble between now and when we go to Heaven. The best we can really hope for is to live up to God's moral expectations and be consciously aware of who God was 2,000 years ago.

Believe the Good News: We can make decisions and relate to others in faith that God is alive, active, and has something in mind for every moment. We seek to live our days in attentiveness to and conversation with Jesus in order to find Him, reflect Him, and point others to Him in the midst of the otherwise ordinary and avoidable details of life.

Therefore Go: Ask God to show you what He is doing in regard to a specific person or situation. Actively watch and listen for what He is doing. Write it down and share it with your community. Also, come up with a plan to listen to God and ask someone in your community to hold you accountable to your plan and help you in the journey.

[1] Cooke, *Confrontation*, 39.

Part 1: Is God Really HERE?

"There is only one Jesus, and there is only one history. The question is whether the faith that finds its focus in Jesus is the faith with which we seek to understand the whole of history, or whether we limit this faith to a private world of religion and hand over the public history of the world to other principles of explanation."[2]

Read Acts 8:26–40
What is God showing you in this story?
Write down any thoughts, questions, or promptings.

_____

_____

_____

_____

What was the source of the knowledge that put Philip into motion?

_____

Could any amount of Bible reading have set him into motion on the dessert road? Did Philip's Bible reading *prepare* him to help the Ethiopian understand the writing of the prophet Isaiah?

_____

_____

One day my three-year-old daughter was sitting on my lap and we were chatting. She casually picked up a cloth coaster from the table next to us and gently began wiping my forehead while in a soft and tender voice she said, 'oh, there's a little blood.' She then looked at the left side of my chest and said, 'oh, there's a little blood here' while she gently wiped the cloth coaster over my heart. Instantly I thought to myself, 'my daughter is covering me with the blood of Jesus and she doesn't even know it.' Simultaneously as I thought this thought, Bailey looked at the coaster and physically jolted in surprise, her eyes widened, she cocked her head, furrowed her eyebrows and held it up for me to see exclaiming, 'It's Jesus' blood!'

There is simply no human or scientific explanation to this. God showed up, spoke to my three-year-old girl, and declared Himself through her.

Sometimes I feel foolish when I 'listen' for God's voice. I've never actually audibly heard God speak like Moses and many others did. There are countless stories in the Old

[2] Newbigin, *Foolishness*, 61.

72

Testament about God interacting with people. The text will say something like, 'and then God told Noah,' or 'Then the Lord reached out His hand and touched my mouth and said to me . . . .' Once I visited a prayer tent that was in town for a few days. I walked into the tabernacle-like tent, dropped to my knees, and asked God to share His thoughts with me. I 'felt' like He was telling me to prepare another place for someone to join me in prayer. I awkwardly obeyed and couldn't help feeling silly. I got up from my kneeling pad and brought over another and placed it next to me. I prayed for another 20 minutes or so and felt like the conversation was over. But no reinforcements had showed up. My kneeling pad sat there with no one on it. I began to feel silly. I asked God what the meaning of it could be. Again, I 'felt' like He was telling me that there was someone praying with me. He told me that He had sent me a guardian angel and that my angel met me there in my time of prayer and was praying with me. I don't tell many people this story because they give me a sideways look and say, 'yeah . . . so, did you see the game last night?' Maybe you're skeptical as you read this and wonder if it was all in my head. I might think I was schizophrenic or foolish too had it not been for my friend Jeanette who I visited the next day. I walked into her office and her eyes got really big and she said, 'You brought an angel in here with you!'.

We may believe God is real but we never expect Him to show up here and now. Why?

_____

_____

_____

We talk about God as if He is living in another world but is hindered from living in *our* world. We talk about God like we talk about loved ones that have died. When someone dies, we miss their presence so we do what we can to comfort ourselves by recalling the times when they *were* present. We create shrines or hang on to objects that remind us of the person in some way. We picture our deceased loved-one as we think they are in their after-life of choice and maybe we seek out spiritual mediums to bridge the chasm between this world and the world where they now dwell. This is what Christianity has turned into in America. We wrongly believe that we must somehow reach as high as we can so that we can touch this God who lives beyond the clouds. One of the most widely circulated pop slogans in Christian America confirms this wrong belief: "What would Jesus do?" The statement implies that Jesus is not here. He left us 2,000 years ago and we are to do our best to do what He would do *if* He were here. This is the type of language that turns our faith from relationship to religion. Followers of other religions can rightly say, 'What would the Buddha do if he were here?' or 'What would Mohammed do in a situation like this?' Instead of 'WWJD' we must ask, *"What in fact is Jesus actually doing in this moment and in this place and how am I to orient my life to His actions?"* We read the Bible as if it is a collection of memories vs. the revelation of a living God who is still alive and doing things here and now. We wish that we could have been a character in the Bible because they got to interact with God directly. We comfort ourselves by recalling the Gideon's and Moses' or the disciples and we say, 'Wouldn't it have been great to have been them!?'

On the eve of his crucifixion Jesus said to his disciples whom He had spent three solid years of His life with, 'It is good that I am leaving you so that I can send the Holy Spirit to be with you at all times and in all places' (John 16:7). Apparently being given the Holy Spirit (invisible) is better than job shadowing Jesus (visible). Write down below why this truth is difficult for you to accept.

_____

_____

_____

Sometimes I read stories in the Bible and I think, 'okay, if I could have seen that (referring to some dramatic event like witnessing a miracle that clearly defies the laws of nature), I would never doubt the existence of God'. Sound familiar? Yet over and over we see grumbling, doubting, and faith-wavering pilgrims. Can you imagine crossing Lake Michigan on dry land with two walls of water stacked up like bricks on either side of you and six weeks later grumbling to God that He forgot about you? Thousands of Israelites did. God is the only hero in the Bible. Everyone else is a sinful and faith-wavering mess.

Have you ever seen God manifest Himself and your mind immediately began playing games? 'That was just a coincidence,' you might have said to yourself. Ever since Christ walked on earth, man has been trying to 'explain' the miraculous. Dead people that were resurrected weren't really dead—they were just sleeping. People cured of disease were never sick; they made the story up in order to have something to talk about. Jesus walked on water because there was three inches of ice on the water and anyone can do that.

Everyone lives by faith. The reason that I do not jump from tall buildings is because I have faith in the law of gravity and my inability to defy it. If I believed that gravity only applied to me on Monday's I might try floating off a tall building on Tuesday. The degree to which westerners have accepted pluralism is astounding to me. We are taught that 'pluralism' is how we tolerate and respect one another's opposing beliefs. In this system of thought we can all be right and not have to worry about offending one another with our arrogant superstitions. We say goofy things like 'what is true for you is not necessarily true for me.' Ascribing to an absolute (something that is true at all times, in all places, and for all people) is downright arrogant since all of us are on the same playing field when it comes to discerning what is truth and what isn't. Therefore, if I claim for something to be true for me and you, you have the right to scold me because the only person who has the authority to define truth for you is you.

It seems quite natural for Americans to think this way without questioning it. It is helpful to see that pluralistic thinking is historically pretty young. In the 1600s a philosopher named René Descartes radically changed the face of Western culture. Descartes is known for his words, 'cogito ergo sum'—I think, therefore I am. Prior to Descartes, westerners sought understanding through faith. Descartes introduced the concept of seeking faith through understanding. Descartes convinced his colleagues that our senses are unreliable and therefore we can't be sure of what we know and don't know. Just because I see something with my eyes doesn't mean that the thing, which I see, exists the way I see it. All I can know is that I exist because my mind is actively receiving stimuli that could be real and true or delusions of my own senses. What matters is that I am thinking. Reality is essentially unknowable. In the 1700s, the philosopher Immanuel Kant reinforced the work of Descartes by declaring that we can only know what *appears* to our senses and since we all perceive things differently, reality is unknowable and unreachable. This is why it is more virtuous in our culture to doubt something then it is to believe something. The one who doubts, questions, and scrutinizes is intellectual because they understand that there is no single quest for an absolute truth because even if there was an absolute truth, none of us could ever know it. The one who can claim to know something is arrogant or foolish. God wants to give us guidance for living that comes from concrete realities; namely His character and His activity in our midst. As long as we buy into the philosophy of our culture, we are settling for a safe, domesticated religion.

There is an enormous double standard in pluralism. Imagine sitting in a classroom. A professor is lecturing on the properties of water. She declares that water is comprised of molecules with three atoms; two hydrogen and one oxygen. Suddenly a student raises their hand and they say, 'I think water is made of iron and calcium'. The professor gets really excited, 'that's great! I never would have thought of that! How about the rest of you, what do you guys think about water?' Another student pipes up, 'I think water is made of uranium and sodium.' 'Wow!', says the professor, 'that's really cool—I never thought of that possibility either!'

This would never happen in a chemistry class. Why? We neatly separate facts from values. The molecular content of water means nothing to me yet water has tremendous value. It quenches my thirst and sustains my life—this is the value of water. If scientists discovered that water has three hydrogen atoms instead of two, I don't think we would stop drinking water. The facts of water don't really matter. Millions of people drink water everyday and have no clue what it is made of but they understand the value of water. We keep our facts in one column and our values in the other column.

Facts of Water
- Two Hydrogen atoms
- One Oxygen atom
- Freezes at 0 degrees C.
- Boils at 100 degrees C.

Values of Water
- Quenches my thirst
- Gives life to the plants and animals that we eat.
- Keeps me alive

We don't tolerate pluralism in the first column and so scientists work hard to get at exactly what the facts are. In the values column, we are free to call the shots because in Western thought, values do not have a correlative relationship with facts or events. Values are free–floating and are subject to be determined by each individual. People become very uncomfortable when they see facts collide or coincide with values. For example, Jesus claiming to be God (value or belief) does not threaten me until He raises Lazarus from the dead (fact). This statement makes me uncomfortable if *I* want authority to determine what truth is and invent my own values. I must find a way to sever the value from the fact or else I will be confronted with a truth that I am not willing to accept and embrace. When God does something (fact) it is always to demonstrate His character (value). We don't have the luxury of separating God's facts from His values like we can in chemistry class.

Facts of God
➢ Raised Lazarus from the dead . . .
➢ Jesus died and rose from the dead . . .
➢ Jesus promised us the Holy Spirit . . .
➢ Jesus died . . .

Values of God
➢ Thus God has the power to give life
➢ Thus God has authority over all things
➢ So that we will do greater works than He did.
➢ Because it was the only way to redeem creation.

Do you see how these two columns cannot be dissected from each other? To accept column one is to accept column two.

Due to our fear of appearing foolish, we have weakened the power of the Gospel by believing that it has no relevance to the factual world of the here and now. The gospel is just a system of values that we are to try and live up to (be nice to people, go to church, help the poor, don't cheat on your spouse). This is religion. Religion is very safe. As a religious person I am simply saying, 'this is the manner in which I am choosing and aspiring to live'. Everyone chooses to live one way over another so in that sense we are all religious. As a religious person, I am saying, 'the way I live my life is for me and not necessarily for anyone else—it is a personal decision and I'm not going to impose my beliefs on someone that believes something different.' To claim that my belief is also true for you is arrogant and judgmental.

Our accepted ethos of separating values from facts has had detrimental effects on the way we live our lives. We have bought into this strange notion that God will always remain invisible and uninvolved (practical atheism) because the values of God (love, joy, peace, patience, etc) never cross over into His factual existence here and now. The things that makes Christianity different from all other religions is our belief that God makes Himself visible and directly intervenes in the affairs of men everyday. Buddhists are just trying to implement the teachings of the Buddha. Muslims are doing their best to live their lives in a way that would make Allah proud. Many Christians are doing the same thing; trying to live their lives as closely as they are able to a set of teachings or doctrines. This is dead and empty religion. The Bible illustrates through its own history that God continually shows up and intervenes and involves His people in supernatural undertakings. If you take the facts of God out of the picture there is nothing!

Write down your fears and hopes regarding your Christian values (love God; love your neighbor) intersecting with the facts of God (God showing up, intervening, and involving you in supernatural undertakings)?

_____

_____

_____

_____

Part 2: Rethinking What is Reasonable

Read Acts 8:26–40
What is God showing you in this story?
Write down any thoughts, questions, or promptings.

_____

_____

_____

_____

What would your response be if a friend excitedly told you this had just happened to them?

_____

_____

Does this encounter seem reasonable or unreasonable to you? Deep down, do you suspect that it might be made up or embellished a bit?

_____

CNN reported a story about a 12-year-old girl in Ethiopia who was kidnapped by several men. She was held and repeatedly beaten for seven days. On the seventh day, three lions emerged from the bush and chased away her attackers and stood guard over her for several hours. The sergeant who found her reported that the lions "stood guard until we found her and then they just left her like a gift and went back into the forest." A wildlife expert believed that the lions probably mistook her for a lion cub or perhaps were preparing to eat her and the police interrupted them. (You can access the whole story at http://outside.away.com/outside/news20050622_2.html.)

How do you explain this story?

_____

_____

The Matrix is one of my favorite movies. It illustrates our need for freedom in a culture that enslaves us by its false promises. We go to great lengths just to 'fit in' and acquire everything necessary to feel like we are human beings who belong to something bigger than us. Some who are plugged into the Matrix are happy while others remain discontent. Feelings though, are irrelevant since both happiness and sadness are derived from an artificial existence created by a computer program. In reality, millions of people are sleeping in little pods hooked up to feeding tubes being kept alive by machines so that their body heat will keep the batteries charged that power these machines. Each person's mind is hooked up to a cosmic video game that tricks them into thinking they are living 'normal' lives. But everything is fabricated. The woman who was promoted at work is in the same condition as the guy who got canned; one feels happy and the other sad but they are both poor saps sleeping in a human-sized eggshell. Their lives are not real. Neo, Morphius, Trinity, and others are on a mission to free people from the Matrix. It is delicate work though. You can't just barge into someone's life and inform them that everything they thought was real is in fact nothing. If someone told you that everything you sense around you is an illusion created by a super computer, would you really believe them?

The relationship between the physical and spiritual worlds is similar to the worlds described above. Spiritual realities are the foundations on which physical realities are built. If Jesus did not exist then neither would you or anything you see yet most people do not live like Jesus is who He claims to be. Most people are concerned with what is clearly visible and is immediately in front of them. God calls us to be concerned with what is invisible and hidden.

The empirical scientific method has undermined our ability to see an invisible God by faith. The scientific method has taught us to put our faith only in what we can directly observe with our physical senses and test in a controlled environment.

For some reason, we expect mediocrity. I'll never forget being told that 'a girl liked me' in junior high. 'This couldn't be' I thought. Why would a girl like me? When she called me (I never actually met her—she saw my picture and thought I was 'cute') I still didn't believe that she liked me. I was convinced that it was a practical joke and that there were a dozen people listening on speakerphone waiting for me to take the bait. My heart and mind was not prepared to receive good news—it wasn't reasonable.

In high school I met this guy in a Teriyaki joint. He said that he was 'on a mission to thwart the aliens from taking over planet earth' and that if he was successful that he would rule the universe together with La Toya Jackson. I didn't believe him but when you looked in his eyes there was no questioning his sincerity. *He* certainly believed it. He called himself 'Numero Uno.' Numero Uno had a completely different construct of reason than I did. Thwarting aliens and ruling the universe wasn't on my agenda. What I would call 'common sense' would be much different than what 'Numero Uno' would call common sense. We say that something is 'reasonable' or 'makes sense' because of the tradition that we have grown up in. What makes sense to most Americans would be absurd in most other cultures. Americans value skinny. Other cultures value fat. It makes sense in America to go on a diet. This would not make sense or be reasonable in a culture that valued fat more than it did skinny. Americans value fashion so it makes sense to Americans to spend $100 on a pair of jeans or to have two-dozen pairs of shoes to choose from. This behavior would not be reasonable to a family in Africa that has no food and no shoes.

DOXA

When you think of the American church, what is normal, reasonable, or expected?

_____

_____

_____

_____

Drawing from the stories we've covered in Acts so far, what is normal, reasonable, or expected?

_____

_____

_____

_____

Do the differences in your answers in the two questions above disturb you? What is God telling us?

_____

_____

_____

_____

We speak about our existence and experiences as if we are the center of things. When we witness an event, we speak about it, not as an event happening independent from us, but as something that we are to question, analyze, and scrutinize. We become the judges of what *really* happened based on what we believe to be 'reasonable'. We refuse to accept the event or reality as it comes to us.

We take the opposite approach in our movie theatres. We remove our filters that tell us what is believable and what is unbelievable; we allow the story to unfold in complete freedom. We abandon ourselves and surrender to the story. This allows us to be caught up in the mystery, romance, suspense, or tragedy in the story. We do not go to movies to question them. We go to movies to be gripped by passion. We long to be actors and actresses in the movies we watch. We are unable to be actors and actresses in God's drama because we have given ourselves unmerited authority to accept, reject, or revise the things of God. There is a subtle yet profound difference between saying, "I have discovered" and "God has spoken". Our culture tolerates the first and rejects the second. Our culture respects delusional and paranoid personalities because they are sincere in their personal

80

beliefs. We are free to 'discover' pretty much anything as long as we remain mindful that it is our own personal discovery and does not apply to anyone else. If I say, 'God has spoken,' I am saying, 'it is a fact independent of what anyone believes—God actually spoke and it had nothing to do with me or anyone else.' If I say, 'I have discovered God,' people will applaud me for pursuing 'my path to enlightenment.'

I saw the movie *Quick Silver* when I was in junior high. It's a story about some Average Joe's who deliver documents and blueprints on bicycles between office buildings in a large metropolitan area. Something about the story gripped me and after seeing the movie I became obsessed with bike riding. For some reason, I wanted to be just like them. We never really grow out of this—it is how we are wired. Our hearts are inexplicably drawn to great stories. We see this in the endless product lines that follow in the wake of epic movies like *Star Wars* or *Lord of the Rings*. Deep down, we just want to be involved in a really cool story. It's not enough to just watch it; we must be part of the action. The story of God is the greatest story ever told and it's the greatest story that is *still happening*. Our job is not to critically analyze it or reduce it to neat little sets of teachings (Seven Principles To A Great Prayer Life, The Three Steps To Achieving Intimacy With God, The Ten Keys To A Perfect Marriage, etc.) Our job is to participate in the story as Jesus is writing it. The most difficult thing about participating in God's story is that He is the Author and we are not.

To participate in God's story means we must surrender our control. To participate in God's story means that our definitions of reasonable and believable come from Him and not us.

If I determined what was reasonable based on my culture and my feelings I might come up with things like:

- *It is reasonable that I be happy most of the time.*
- *It is reasonable that if someone wrongs me I can choose to not forgive him or her.*
- *It is reasonable that if a situation is uncomfortable, I can walk away.*
- *It is reasonable to protect myself even if it means hurting others in the process.*
- *It is reasonable to live in fear.*
- *It is reasonable to buy what I want with the money that I rightfully earn.*
- *It is reasonable to avoid conflict.*

How do our stories in Acts thus far challenge these assumptions?

DOXA

Can you identify any obstacles that keep you from fully stepping into God's story? (beliefs, fears, false hopes)

_____

_____

_____

_____

Part 3: Discovering a God of Supernatural Facts

It's ironic how many people are looking for God yet fail to recognize Him as an independently thinking, feeling, and acting person. To most, the word 'god' represents their ideal life experience. I am both grieved and angered when I hear people who know nothing of the God revealed in the Old Testament, Jesus, and the Church after Him, saying things like, 'God speaks to me in the wind.' I ask them what He tells them in the wind. 'He wants me to be happy,' they say. We listen to our own voice and wishes and call it God's voice and God's wishes. This is our (the Church) fault. Jesus and the Apostles warn us to resist Satan, our enemy, who is hard at work seeking to deceive us for the purpose of destroying us. We are like the frog in the pot of water that is heating up slowly and is unaware that he is about to be boiled. I was driving on a highway when a semi came after my vehicle (literally and intentionally). We had done nothing to provoke the driver. It was as if he just wanted us dead for no visible scientific reason. I believe this man was under Satan's control. I have no scientific evidence of this and because of that, maybe you think this explanation is unreasonable. My explanation may be wrong but we should not think it to be unreasonable. It this explanation is unreasonable than so are most of the events recorded in the Bible. I met a friend in a coffee shop and part way into our meeting a woman sat right next to our table and began reading curses from a book on witchcraft. We met at the same place a few weeks later and the same woman was sitting in her car outside watching us. Most Americans say they believe in God but very few reflect Him with their lives. Jesus said that we would be known by our fruit (the work of the Father happening through us)—not by our words or doctrinal statements. I've had countless conversations with people who are seeking God and truth (values yet to be determined) but they don't want to talk about Jesus or the Bible (facts already established). They don't want to limit god to a single person or source of information. For most people 'god' is a word they use to sum up their worldview. 'God' wants me to be happy. 'God' just wants everyone to get along. 'God' wants to promote the agenda of America in the world. 'God' is on our side. People feel close to god when they're having extramarital sex. People feel close to god when they're stoned. People feel close to god when they're in the woods. People feel close to god when our country wins a war.

Can you think of assumptions that you thought originated from facts surrounding the person and works of God but through a deeper examination can see that these assumptions are not grounded in a concrete revelation of God? *[For example, I used to think that God would not stand up for or advocate for a criminal and would favor those in powerful positions until I took a deeper look at how God has actually treated criminals and those in powerful positions. Jesus said part of his mission was to release criminals from prison. He often had harsh words for those in powerful positions. He chose a tax collector (notoriously known for ripping people off) to be one of his disciples. He defended a murderer and would not allow him to receive the death penalty (Cain). He offered paradise to a convicted felon during His own execution. He turned one who systematically murdered Christians into one of the most influential apostles in the New Testament (Paul). Throughout the Old and New Testaments, God repeatedly invests Himself and reveals Himself through the nobodies of societies.]*

_____

_____

_____

_____

I am not downplaying the importance of *experiencing* God. God extends Himself to us because He wants to make Himself known to us through daily experiencing His character and activity. I'm sounding an alarm on the dangerous language that assumes God is knowable without encountering Him as an *independently thinking, feeling, and acting Person* who is directly revealed to us in Jesus Christ. We have all these ideas about God but we've never asked Him about them.

If we want to know God, we must take a look at how God has revealed Himself to the world in Jesus Christ. Every assumption and every idea that we have about who God is, what He thinks and feels, and what we believe He is doing today in our midst can and must be tested against the word, character, and promises of Jesus.

Here are some facts that Scripture teaches us about the relationship between the earthly ministry of Jesus and what we still have to learn on an on-going daily basis.[3]

1. God was completely and fully revealed in Jesus Christ. "He who has seen me has seen the Father" (John 14:9).
2. There is however, much more to learn. Jesus gives us the Spirit of His Father who will be our teacher to help us interpret and discern the revelation of the Father. (John 14:16) The promise of this Counselor is for the Church only, for the world cannot receive the Holy Spirit (John 14:17).
3. The gift of the Holy Spirit is not intended to be a private possession but is given to us in order that Christ may declare who He is to the world through us (John 15:27).
4. When Jesus declares Himself to the world through the Church it will become evident that Jesus contradicts the world's most fundamental beliefs (John 16:8–11). The work of the Holy Spirit takes place in the Church as the Church contradicts the fundamental beliefs of the world (taking up our cross).
5. In the Church, the Spirit's work will be "to declare the things that are to come," to interpret coming events, and to enable the Church to be the community that brings significance to history (John 16:13).
6. In so doing, the Spirit brings glory to Jesus. As the Spirit guides and teaches the Church, it will be made visible to the world that the crucified Savior is the Lord of all things (John 16:14).

---

[3] I give credit to Newbigin for expounding these points in, *The Gospel*, 78.

7. The scope of the Spirit's work is as wide as the universe for "all that belongs to the Father" (the universe and everything in it) has been given to Jesus (John 16:15).

> "What is affirmed here is that a particular community in history, that community which bears the name of Jesus, will be given, through the active work of the Spirit of God, a true understanding of history—the ongoing history that continues through the centuries after Jesus, and understanding which is based on the particular events of whose memory they are the custodians. *But this privileged position is not for their sake but for the sake of the world into which they are sent as witnesses to Jesus in whom God's purpose for his entire creation has been disclosed. What I am affirming, in other words, is that, just as the experience of Israel is to be interpreted not merely as a chapter in the history of religions but as the self-revealing action of God, so the history of the Church is to be interpreted not merely as one among the varieties of religious experience but as the fruit of the promised work of the Spirit of God.*"[4]

Study the seven points above. In what ways do these challenge or confront how you currently think and live?

_____

_____

_____

_____

We can know what Jesus did 2,000 years ago. Can we know what He is doing today? If so, how? If not, why not?

_____

_____

_____

_____

[4] Ibid., 78–79.

Is reading about the life of Jesus the same as experiencing Him? What is the difference?

_____

_____

_____

Our culture teaches us that we can be pluralists in respect to our beliefs but not in respect to what the facts are. Belief is a matter of personal choice (religion). Facts are public knowledge (science). Science is what all people know; religion is what some people believe. Lesslie Newbigin sums up this sentiment well: "What matters is not the factual content of faith claims but the sincerity with which they are held. They are matters not of public knowledge but of personal faith. Knowing is one thing, and the schools are there to see that everyone knows what we all need to know about the real facts. Believing is something else, that is, it is a personal matter for each individual. Each of us should have a personal faith of our own."[5]

Our culture has created two categories of information. There is information that we believe and there is information that we know. The traditions of Western culture are rooted in a commitment to understand the relationship between happenings and the causes of those happenings. "The way to 'explain' things is to analyze them into their smallest parts and show how everything that happens is ultimately governed by the laws of physics. If a thing or a happening can be understood as the mathematically calculable interaction of its parts, then it is 'explained.' Things are not to be explained in terms of purpose, because purpose is a function of the beliefs and values of the person whose purpose it is. Things are to be explained in terms of their causes, of what makes things happen. All happenings have causes, and all causes are adequate to the effects they produce. The ultimate goal is to understand everything in terms of the physics and chemistry of its constituent parts. Human life is ultimately to be understood as the product of an endless series of random happenings in the physical world. Chance and causality are the sufficient 'explanation' of all that is and all that happens. The main intellectual drive of our culture is in this direction—to understand everything in terms of the fundamental laws of physics."[6]

How would the intellectualism described above undermine our understanding of faith and relating to God?

_____

_____

_____

[5] Ibid., 26.
[6] Ibid., 36–37.

Read Acts 8:26–40. What does God show you in this story? What stands out to you? What questions does it raise for you?

_____

_____

_____

_____

_____

Based on the above statement by Lesslie Newbigin, why is it difficult for us to accept accounts like this in Acts as factual events?

_____

_____

Is it more comfortable to say, "I believe God is real" vs. "I know God is real"? Do you think there is a difference between knowing something and believing something?

_____

_____

_____

"It is the concept of a cosmos without purpose which provides the validation for the division of our world into two—a world of facts without value and a world of values which have no basis in facts."[7]

---

[7] Ibid., 38.

Part 4: Aligning Our Values with the Facts

Read Acts 8:26:40. What does God show you in this story?
What stands out to you?
What questions does it raise for you?

_____

_____

_____

_____

_____

Review the seven facts in yesterday's study pertaining to the life of Jesus 2,000 years ago and the life of Jesus today. Write down any questions or thoughts you have regarding this.

_____

_____

_____

_____

I was driving to work one morning when I clearly heard God tell me there would be a train at the railroad crossing ahead of me, which was not yet in view. As the tracks came into view, sure enough there was a train barreling along. There are rarely trains on these tracks. I've only seen a train on these tracks twice in one year. At first I thought it was silly. 'I must have made it up,' I said to myself. I chuckled as I sat there watching the train race by. I arrived at work and there in the doorway stood my coworker whom I worked closely with each day. Instantly when I looked at him, God told me an intimate piece of information about his life. I prayed about this information for two months and then one day at work as we were having a conversation, he told me the same piece of confidential information that God told me two months earlier. I told him that God had revealed it to me two months prior and that I had been praying for him. He cried when I told him this. I know that God told me about the train to get my attention. It was like He was saying, 'I'm going to tell you something obvious and silly so that you'll be listening because I have something important to say later on that won't be as obvious and I needed to make sure that you would be listening closely.'

God is waiting for us to put our faith in facts that we cannot prove.

'We live by faith, not by sight.' Jesus did miracles, not *so that* people could have faith in Him, but to honor those who *already demonstrated* faith by their active response to His invisible workings. How many times have we told God, 'if you do this, then I'll believe'? Jesus did the fewest miracles in His hometown 'because of their lack of faith' (Matt 13:58). Maybe the American church is the equivalent of Jesus' hometown—we have little faith so God is withholding His hand.

Jesus repeatedly granted the requests of individuals who demonstrated faith in Him. "Dear woman," Jesus said to her, "your faith is great. Your request is granted." And her daughter was instantly healed" (Matt 15:28). "Master," Simon replied, "we worked hard all last night and didn't catch a thing. But if *you say so*, I'll let the nets down again." And this time their nets were so full of fish they began to tear!" (Luke 5:5–6). "In one of the villages, Jesus met a man with an advanced case of leprosy. When the man saw Jesus, he *bowed with his face to the ground*, begging to be healed. "Lord," he said, "if you are willing, you can heal me and make me clean."

"Jesus reached out and touched Him. "I am willing," he said. "Be healed!" And instantly the leprosy disappeared" (Luke 5:12–13). "*Seeing* their faith, Jesus said to the man, "Young man, your sins are forgiven"" (Luke 5:20). "[Jesus] looked around at them one by one and then said to the man, "Hold out your hand." So the man *held out his hand*, and it was restored!" (Luke 6:10). "I am not even worthy to come and meet you. Just say the word from where you are, and my servant will be healed. I know this because I am *under the authority of my superior officers*, and I have authority over my soldiers. I only need to say, 'Go,' and they go, or 'Come,' and they come. And if I say to my slaves, 'Do this,' they do it." When Jesus heard this, he was amazed. Turning to the crowd that was following Him, he said, "I tell you, I haven't *seen* faith like this in all Israel!" And when the officer's friends returned to his house, they found the slave completely healed" (Luke 7:7,9–10). "And Jesus said to the woman, "Your faith has saved you; go in peace"" (Luke 7:50). "The disciples went and woke him up, shouting, "Master, Master, we're going to drown!" When Jesus woke up, he rebuked the wind and the raging waves. Suddenly the storm stopped and all was calm. Then he asked them, "Where is your faith?" The disciples were terrified and amazed. "Who is this man?" they asked each other. "When he gives a command, even the wind and waves obey him!"" (Luke 8:24–25). "Daughter," he said to her, "your faith has made you well. Go in peace"" (Luke 8:48).

How can we tell when we are or are not demonstrating faith in God?

———————————————————————————

———————————————————————————

———————————————————————————

When I look at the stories above, I see Jesus looking for people who are willing to take Him at His word. He gave them simple instructions that were easy to perform. 'Stretch out your hand . . . let down the nets on the other side of the boat.' Jesus' words are fact-forming. He speaks a word that alters reality due to His word. Nets are full of fish because Jesus commanded them to swarm on one side of a fishing boat. A withered hand is restored as it is obediently stretched out. We are always looking for proof as a prerequisite for action. Jesus is always looking for us to act without proof. God demonstrates His character and power in the middle of our acting; not prior. Religion teaches us to do certain things in order that we might gain certain things. Religion is a man–made attempt to arrange for happiness and feel right and holy while we go about it. Religion is obsession with cause and effect. '*If* I go to church every week *then* I will be blessed and happy.' If we are living religiously (adhering to a set of 'if-then's'), then we are living as if God is neither speaking nor acting here and now.

We most often apply religion to the areas of our life that are paralyzed from fear or pain. If my deepest fear is rejection then I will make sure I am on my best behavior so that I can stay in God's favor. If my deepest fear is abandonment then I will make sure I am doing important things for God. Religion, religion, religion—it always comes back to us and our efforts to control and make life work apart from the life-giving and life-guiding Word of Jesus.

More facts . . .
- Faith without works is dead (Jas 2:14–26). Simply professing, 'I believe in God,' does not mean we are living in faith. "You say you have faith, for you believe that there is one God. Good for you! Even the demons believe this, and they tremble in terror" (v. 19).
- The work that we have been commissioned to do belongs to the Father and is made known to us by the Spirit. We cannot know what God is asking us to do apart from knowing His heart and mind and listening to Him! (John 16:13–15).
- Faith is taking God at His Word. When we are listening, we are postured to live faithfully. If we hear God's voice, we must then choose to either obey His voice in faith or rebel (John 10:2–4).
- When we are not listening, we are not even *postured* to live faithfully. Faithful obedience is not a possibility until we listen.

In what ways do you need to re-arrange your life so that you can hear the words of Jesus that He is already speaking to you?

_____

_____

_____

_____

It's frightening to make the leap from religion to relationship (actually listening to God). Our desire to control our circumstances and manipulate our own happiness will immediately be attacked. God told Abraham to kill his one and only son. At times, our instinct will be to run away when we hear God's voice. Write down some of your fears and apprehensions about listening to God.

_____

_____

_____

Apart from God, the only thing we are capable of doing is destroying our lives. Middle and upper class Americans do it slowly and often unknowingly because we are able to buy numbing agents in the process. We know we are dying but at least we don't have to *feel* like we are dying. Our numbing agents increase our self-centeredness causing us to ignore those in our midst. Others destroy their lives more quickly through a life of crime and violence. The suburban churchgoer is a respectable image in our culture. Adhering to a set of religious principles and values seems to keep our nation intact. We have conveniently convinced ourselves that God wants us to be happy *on our terms*. Lifestyles of consumerism, gluttony, escapism, comfort, leisure, and recreation are now justified as 'what God wants for me.' What will it take for us to see that there is no hope in this sort of dead-end religion?

> Religion can only accomplish what *it* can accomplish. Listening to God will accomplish what only *God* can accomplish.

Religion cannot bring us closer to God. Religion cannot heal our hearts or our bodies. Religion is deception. Religion is a counterfeit. Religion is a lie, a hoax, a scam from Satan to make us think we are redeemed from a deathly way of life when we are not. Get out while you can.

Can you identify priorities (major chunks of time, energy, or thought) that are devoted to fulfilling religious duties that stave off guilt or feelings of insignificance?

_____

_____

Do you want out?

_____

How, with the help of your community, can you move from a life of religion to a life of listening?

_____

_____

CHAPTER 5

Becoming Risky

"The more confidence we have in our own strength and abilities, the less we are likely to have in Christ. Our human weakness is no hindrance to God. In fact, as long as we do not use it as an excuse for sin, it is good to be weak. But this acceptance of weakness is more than acknowledging our limitations. It means experiencing a power much greater than our own and surrendering to it."[1]

OVERVIEW:

Core Scripture: Acts 16:16–40.

The Kingdom of God is at Hand: God is alive. He is both good and able to deliver His goodness to us. We are not on our own. God's greatest desire is to glorify Himself. He is committed to this mission and has chosen to use us, His Church, for this mission. We have nothing that weighs more than God's glory yet we cling to these things as if they were of ultimate importance. And so we choose to live safe lives. God is inviting us to discover the grandeur of His glory by calling us into a risky vocation of kingdom living.

Repent: Missionaries in Africa are the real Jesus Freaks. Only missionaries in Africa encounter danger, hardship, and loss. We are not like them—our lives are relatively calm and predictable because we live in America. We'll give 25 bucks a month to the mission in China so we can be part of the action though, since that's where the real action actually is.

Believe the Good News: My relationships and circumstances can be surrendered to what God wants. My decision-making no longer needs to be filtered through desired outcomes of comfort, safety, ease, and pleasure but through the desires of God. God will invite me to risk what is important to me so that He can demonstrate His goodness and faithfulness to me. Since God supplies all that I need to do His will I am able to let go of my need for relational safety and material comfort.

Therefore Go: Ask God to show you something that He is asking you to do in faith. It could be as simple as asking someone for forgiveness or introducing yourself to your neighbors. Or maybe God wants to uncover a Pandora's box. Maybe He's sending you to Africa but more than likely He's sending you to befriend an enemy or resolve a conflict. Act on God's leading and write down why it was fearful and write down what you think God will do with your faithful obedience. Share this journey with your community.

---

[1] Arnold, *Seeking Peace*, 51–52.

Part 1: Shift Out of Neutral

"The most spiritual activity you will engage in today is making choices. All other activities that we describe as spiritual—worship, prayer, meditation—are there to connect us to God and prepare us to live."[2]

Read Acts 16:16–40.
What is God showing you in this story?
Write down any thoughts, questions, or promptings.

_____

_____

_____

_____

Write down all the choices that Paul and Silas made throughout this drama. What do their *choices* tell us about what they believed?

_____

_____

_____

_____

_____

What do your *choices* (what you do with you money and time) tell you about what you believe?

_____

_____

_____

I had a friend in high school who was willing to do pretty much anything. Hanging out with Sean was like having your own personal stunt man and comedian all in one. 'Hey Sean, see how fast your car will go.' He'd floor it until the speedometer was buried to the right of '130.' 'Sean, go tell that girl that you think she's cute.' He would return to our huddle with her phone number. Sean was marvelous at rallying others to his various causes. Egging houses at two in the morning, breaking into schools by scaling the flag-

[2] McManus, *Seizing*, 19.

pole, jumping from rooftops in the dark onto unknown terrain, asking beautiful women for their phone numbers, prank phone calls, firefighter training, stealing luggage at the airport, robbing pawn shops, stealing credit cards and spending thousands of dollars with them. Sean could easily get out of control. Sean didn't seem to have all the filters we had. 'What if the cops come . . . what if we get caught . . . what if we look stupid . . . what if we fall . . . what if they try and kill us?' Sean didn't have a 'what if' checklist that he went through before embarking on risky behavior. He just did it. I've always wished I could embrace a moment like Sean does. Today Sean continues to engage in risky behavior. At his wedding near the end of the ceremony, he boldly and joyfully spoke of God's love for all people. He asked for a show of hands from people who needed healing and restoration in their lives. He prayed for these people for about 10 minutes. Sean used to take risks for himself. Today he takes risks to advance God's kingdom.

They say experience is the best teacher. I climbed a tree once. When I was about 20 feet in the air, the branch that I was clinging to for balance snapped. I plummeted 20 feet into blackberry bushes. They broke my fall but I lost a pint of blood wading my way out of them. This experience kept me from testing my luck on a rope-swing. I thought I would be safe if I just watched my friend. I stood on the side of the embankment watching. David wanted off the rope-swing so I reached out my hand to help him. He ended up pulling me off the embankment. I landed flat on my back about 15 feet below. I tried a trampoline once. Somehow I wound up upside down in a clothesline about 10 feet from the edge of the trampoline. There was also the time I rode my bike with my eyes closed. A concrete wall is a lesson that is hard to forget. I once told a girl that I liked her. She said, 'So?' and just stared at me with a blank stare and walked away.

Risk is about jeopardizing something you already have in order to acquire a something you don't have. A low risk situation is one where we will most likely not lose what we are jeopardizing. A high-risk situation is one where we will most likely lose the thing we are jeopardizing. Decision-making primarily happens through this sort of grid. We have learned to perform cost-benefit analyses in our heads in mere nanoseconds before we make a decision involving risk; especially when it comes to risking our personal identity.

The first thing we risked when we were children was our dignity. We went off to school assuming that all the children would be friendly. We naively trusted that we could be known and loved at the same time; only to have our dignity crushed by the mean kids. We weren't even aware of the risk because we weren't aware of the investment. Simply by being friendly and making ourselves known we were creating an invitation to be hated or excluded. Prior to this experience we felt valuable; afterward we felt diminished and unwanted. From now on, we would be careful investors. A pretty face gets a much better return than an ugly face. Therefore being ugly is risky; being pretty is safe. I must always be pretty and never ugly. Experience teaches us that the safest bet is for us to stay in control of our relationships and circumstances at all times. Once we wander outside of these borders of security and control, we are jeopardizing something that is valuable to us (dignity, identity, happiness, or physical safety). The first time I drove on the freeway at age 15, my grandpa was in the backseat directly behind me. He was leaning forward and coaching my every move. His mouth was about a half inch from my right ear— 'Now the road bends up here to the right a little . . . there's a wet spot up ahead there . . . there's a semi up ahead in the other lane.' It was like he was helping a blind person drive. Fundamentally, my grandpa did not trust me and so he needed to intervene and take matters into his own hands. He believed that his guiding words would make up for what he believed was lacking in me. He was minimizing perceived risk based on his belief that I was incompetent to operate a vehicle at 60 mph. Further, he believed that his coaching would make up for my lack of competence.

Fundamentally, we believe that to trust God with our lives is so risky that at times we just can't bear to do it. We are comfortable and safely functioning in the controlled environment we have created with our cultural identities and entertainment gadgets. It just seems too good to leave. So we become Christians who neither listen to God nor intend to follow Him. We just want the security of not going to hell when we die. We cling to our things as if they were ours. We cling to our lives as if they belonged to us. We believe that our own efforts to bring ourselves the life we crave will make up for what we believe is lacking in God's ability to *relationally and experientially* fulfill our needs and guide us in His will. In what way does this paragraph describe you?

_____

_____

_____

_____

If you asked people on the street what behaviors defined the life of a Christian, what do you think the most common answer would be?

_____

_____

_____

_____

"It is rarely counted as evil when we live in neutral."[3] Paul and Silas were not living in neutral. What motivated their bold and risky living?

_____

_____

[3] Ibid., 44.

Reflect on your view of God and your relationship with Him. What is the risk for you in following Jesus?

_____

_____

_____

_____

What is the risk for you in *not* following Jesus?

_____

_____

_____

_____

Has it ever occurred to you that there is risk in *not* following Jesus? We live in a posture of defense. We are wrapped up in defending our rights, protecting our wounds, and tending to our own felt needs that *it seldom occurs to us that selfish living could be more risky than Christ-centered living.* Morbid preoccupation with our own needs blinds us to the world around us. We believe that the most important thing at any given moment is our most pressing need at that time. In the time it takes me to decide which flavor of syrup I want in my latte, 4 children die because they lack water, food, or medicine. [4] Jesus cares more about children who lack their most basic needs than he does the enjoyment factor of my coffee. I am not saying that enjoying coffee is evil. I'm saying we are far too wrapped up in our coffee, our clothes, our cars, our entertainment venues, and our technological devices. How many conflicts in our friendships occur because we cannot set aside our selfish preoccupations long enough to genuinely listen without becoming defensive or self-conscious?

We have become slaves to ourselves. This makes us both the slave and the master. In this state, our vocation (what we are actually doing with our life on a day-to-day basis) is that of a slave—meaningless toil in which we never reap the rewards for the labor. We have been deceived into believing that our vocation is that of the master—we call the shots, we are in control, we command our world and manipulate it to match our desires. On the contrary, we are the masters only in the sense that we have commanded ourselves to live a life of meaningless toil in which we will never reap any benefit or reward from our toil. What a scam! Jesus died to redeem us from this life of slavery.

---

[4] Assuming a 12 second decision time.

If the most important gig in the universe is God's agenda than the riskiest thing you can do today is fail to listen to God and obediently respond to what He is telling you!

Jesus told us that 'the work God requires from us is to believe'. Jesus wants to take you from believing that *your* gig is central to believing that *His* gig is central. God wants to show you that the safest place to be is in the center of His will. Everything else is a foolish and worthless investment.

What fears, doubts, or apprehensions do you have about surrendering your gig and joining God's gig? Are you afraid because you already know how God is asking you to change or because you don't yet know how God is asking you to adjust your life to His?

_____

_____

_____

_____

Take a few minutes to chat with God. Confess, repent, and ask Him to change your heart and align it with His agenda.

Part 2: Risky Listening

Read Acts 16:16–40.
What is God showing you in this story?
Write down any thoughts, questions, or promptings.

_____

_____

_____

_____

There were logical things that Paul and Silas could have done in response to their circumstances yet most of their actions ran contrary to human nature. To me it seems the girl possessed by a spirit wasn't a hindrance; after all, she *was* speaking the truth. If I'm beat up and locked in jail on account of my God; worship and praise would not be my first inclination—I think I'd feel let down or abandoned. If I'm chained up in a locked jail cell and suddenly my chains fall off, the door opens and the guard is fast asleep; I think I'd be outta' there in a flash. Paul and Silas remained and further they kept the guard from committing suicide. Paul and Silas were deeply aware of things that were taking place due to the Spirit's presence in their hearts and activity in their midst. What do their actions indicate they were aware of?

_____

_____

_____

A leader in the kingdom of God is someone who is close enough to God to hear His voice and as a result, alters his or her life to the loving and guiding words from the Father. The result of this is that their life appears strange to those who are not hearing the voice of God. If someone is only doing what seems natural and good to everyone else, they are not leading; they are joining an already existing movement commonly known as pop culture. A kingdom leader breaks new ground because God is daily doing a new thing. A kingdom leader boldly says, 'We *will* walk through the forbidden forest.' A kingdom leader is willing to break the rules of their culture in order to expose its foolish, controlling, and destructive nature. Paul said that the wisdom of God *appears* foolish and the wisdom of man *is* foolish (1 Cor 1:20–25). This is hard for us to embrace in a culture where appearance is everything and substance is of little value.

We long to appear wise and strong. "Instead, God chose things the world considers foolish in order to shame those who think they are wise. And he chose things that are powerless to shame those who are powerful. God chose things despised by the world, things counted as nothing at all, and used them to bring to nothing what the world considers important. As a result, no one can ever boast in the presence of God" (1 Cor 1:27–29). 'A chain is only as strong as its weakest link'. We fear being the weakest link in our workplaces, our friendships, and in our churches. We fear being 'a burden' on those around us. God tells us that the weakest links are actually the most valuable and necessary (1 Cor 12:22). Maybe it is comforting for you to hear this because you know that underneath all your puffed up wisdom and strength is a lonely, scared, and weak soul. However, we must progress from simply being consoled by this truth while still wishing we were not weak and move towards embracing this truth so that its power might be displayed. God uses us, not in spite of our weakness but *because* of our weakness. We must go public with our weakness because it is the most valuable commodity in the hands of God. Our strength and wisdom is of no use to God—in fact it is actually a hindrance because we rely on it as a substitute for God's strength and wisdom.

Religious people are respected in America. Our nation's leaders hold prayer breakfasts; our anthems and pledges acknowledge a religious fabric in our society. Religious people are busy doing work for God. Godly people are allowing God to work for them, through them, and in them on behalf of themselves and the world. All religious work apart from Jesus is irrelevant. Jesus said that apart from Him, we could do nothing (See John 15). Yet somehow we are very busy and all the while believing that our busyness is a pleasing offering to God. "It is much easier to do something than to trust in God; we mistake panic for inspiration. That is why there are so few fellow workers with God and so many workers for Him. *We would far rather work for God than believe in Him.*"[5]

John 15 gives us further clues as to what we can anticipate when we join our lives to the Master's life through a posture of listening.

- "I no longer call you slaves, because a master doesn't confide in his slaves. Now you are my friends, since I have told you everything the Father told me" (v. 15).
  - We can know what our Master is doing (by listening).
  - Jesus wants to make known to us (by listening) everything that He has heard from the Father.
- "You didn't choose me. I chose you. I appointed you to go and produce lasting fruit, so that the Father will give you whatever you ask for, using my name" (v. 16).
  - Jesus comes to us and personally addresses us. Have you heard Him address you?
  - We can go to the Father and personally address Him. Are we talking to the Father?
  - We can ask God for anything that falls within the boundary of the name of Christ. We can know the things of Christ because He reveals those things to us. Are we listening to know the things of Christ?

---

[5] Chambers, *My Utmost*, June 1st.

- "If the world hates you, remember that it hated me first. The world would love you as one of its own if you belonged to it, but you are no longer part of the world. I chose you to come out of the world, so it hates you. Do you remember what I told you? 'A slave is not greater than the master.' Since they persecuted me, naturally they will persecute you. And if they had listened to me, they would listen to you" (vv. 18–20).
  - When we have heard Jesus call us, appoint us, and are bearing eternal fruit, the world will hate us. Being hated is not our goal but it is a *guaranteed* by-product of being faithful to Jesus.

What do you see as the primary differences between a religious life and a life joined to Jesus as described in these verses from John 15?

_____

_____

_____

_____

Prior to and apart from listening to God, we are simply living religious lives that quickly earn the respect of men and society but not God. "U.S. News & World Report" featured a special report in 2003 that attempted to define the uniqueness of America. Here is a bit of what they found. Fifty-nine per cent of Americans said that religion plays an important role in their lives; yet in 2005 we accumulated $985 billion of credit card debt; we produce 1, 637 pounds of garbage per year per person[6]; over 18% of our households own three or more cars; we work more than those in any other nation; and we have more lawyers per thousand than any other nation.[7]

The same report continued to highlight values that are quintessential in the American psyche. Among them was a strong sense of rugged, self-made individualism; homogeneity (we make efforts to live with those that are like us); religious experience for the individual along with suspicion for established sects; consumerism as a status symbol; individual economic advancement by any means; and moral superiority.[8]

Individualism, amassing wealth in unseen proportions, consuming products to ensure our comfort and secure our status in society, freedom to determine the course of one's prosperity, *and* peace with God—welcome to the American Dream. One in four children in America will utter a brand name as their first word.[9] America continues to

---

[6] "The dollar value of the food North Americans throw in the garbage each year equals about one-fifth of the total annual income of Africa's 120 million Christians." Sider, *Rich Christians*, 110.

[7] Brian Duffy. "Defining America" US News and World Report, (June 28–July 5, 2004): 36–57.

[8] Ibid.

[9] *Adbusters*.

be a nation where the poor get poorer and the rich get richer. The gap between the rich and poor is currently wider than it has been since WWII.[10] As a nation, we have enjoyed an ever-increasing GNP; however, the number of children born poor and disadvantaged is growing and currently up to 40% of children in America will experience poverty.[11] In 2002, Americans lost nearly $17 billion at our casinos and online gambling venues.[12] Clearly religious living in America is not the equivalent to listening to God and knowing His heart, mind, and plans.

Rees Howells was a man who exemplified life in the Spirit. Check out the following excerpt from his biography.

> "One night, when Rees Howells and his friends were walking, they passed a group of women who never came to the local meetings of the church. It was evident by their voices that they had been drinking. One of the party exclaimed, 'Where is the power to change these people?' It was a challenge, and Rees Howells took it. There and then the Spirit gave it to him that he was to pick out the ringleader of those women, who was a notorious character and a confirmed drunkard, and pray her into the Kingdom by Christmas Day!

> "This was something new! He had seen many drunkards converted, but the Lord had worked through his personal contacts with them; in this case, however, he had no connection with the woman and the Lord told him that he was to use no personal influence, but to reach her by way of the Throne. It would be a real test of strength. Could the Holy Spirit through him use the power of the atonement to break the devil's dominion in her life and fulfill the Savior's word in Matthew 12:29, about binding the strong man and stealing his goods? He was told that if he could get this one visible proof of the devil's defeat, the Holy Ghost could apply the victory through him on a large scale.

> To do this, the Spirit gave him John 15:7: 'If you remain in me and my words remain in you, ask whatever you wish and it will be given to you.' It would all depend on his abiding. As this 'abiding' was to take such a central place in his future life of intercession, it is important to see what the Holy Spirit taught Mr. Howells about it. This key text, John 15:7, makes it plain that the promise is unlimited, but its fulfillment depends on the abiding . . . The scriptural key to abiding is in 1 John 2:6, 'Whoever claims to live in him must walk as Jesus did'. In other words, it meant being willing for the Holy Spirit to live through him the life the Savior would have lived if He had been in his place . . . Any command the Spirit gave him, he must fulfill because the way of abiding is the keeping of His commandments (John 15:10) . . . As Mr. Howells would continue in this place of abiding day by day he would be increasingly conscious that the Spirit was engaging the

[10] Sine, *Mustard Seed*, 116.

[11] Ibid.

[12] Kevin McCoy. "Online Gamble Pays Off for Internet Sports Books," *USA Today* (March 29, 2002), http://www.usatoday.com/money/covers/2002-03-29-online-bets.htm (accessed June 6, 2006).

enemy in battle and overcoming him, until finally he would become fully assured of the victory. The Spirit would then tell him that the intercession was finished, the position gained, and he would await the visible deliverance in praise and faith . . . A great number of people became onlookers as they had heard of the prayer. It was now a case of praising before the victory, and in the remaining weeks before Christmas the Holy Spirit did not allow him to pray for her."[13]

Contrast this story with typical religion. What is the biggest difference between the two?

_____

_____

_____

_____

When I was in college I had a long distance relationship that led to an engagement. Two months before the wedding God began giving me indicators that I was not to marry this girl. I didn't want to listen—who wants to hear something like that? In his grace, He began to speak louder as I worked harder to shut my ears. Two weeks before the wedding He told me in a dream not to marry her. I had the same dream three times in one night. Finally I acted on what God was telling me. Justifying our actions with 'God told me,' or God said' is a tough sell. It is often dismissed as downright arrogance or a pious scapegoat to not take ownership for decisions or mistakes. It can certainly become this. Jihad, Jim Jones, American Imperialism, and David Koresh are fine example of self-centered arrogance acted out in the name of a deity.

Conservative and fundamentalist theologies[14] evolve from fear and paranoia of knowledge that is acquired outside of the scientific method. These theologies rely on scientifically extracting rules and principles from the Bible. These theologies spring from a desire to scientifically know right and wrong. Ultra-conservative communities then enforce their rules legalistically and abusively. The religious leaders in Jesus' day kept over 400 rules on a daily basis. They forbade people with false teeth to eat on the Sabbath (which God intended to be a day of rest and celebration) since technically they were 'lifting a foreign object' (their teeth) which technically was work which was forbidden on the Sabbath. Crazy, huh? When Jesus' disciples were rebuked for casually picking wheat (technically considered work) as they walked along a road on the Sabbath; Jesus announced to their rebukers that there was now something greater than the law (Matt 12:7). The greater thing that Jesus was referring to was Himself and the possibility of a living relationship with Him guided not by rules but by His Spirit (an actual Person). Jesus is not interested in rule keeping. Jesus was obsessed with the *story* the Father was writing because it's in the

[13] Grubb, *Intercessor*, 63–65.
[14] Generally speaking.

story that God's character and glory is revealed. Our obsession is not to be with rules but the story the Father is still writing this day.

The word 'gospel' means good news. The gospel is a story—the story of God redeeming us from sin, death, the devil, and our selves. It is the story of God freeing us to participate in His character and nature today, tomorrow, and the next day and every day until we are reunited with Him for all eternity. God's character is revealed in the Bible by what He *did*. If we don't know what a person has done than we have no criteria by which to discern their character, values, and vision. We can *intellectually* know God's character by being familiar with how God acted on behalf of people. This, however, is just the beginning. In the '80's there was a popular TV show called, 'The Dating Game' that illustrates the progression from *knowledge of* to *experience with*. A woman blindly interviews three bachelors. She asks questions to get a picture of their personalities and values. Most of the questions are related to hypothetical situations or inquiries into the past. 'If you had one million dollars, how would you spend it? If you were an animal, what kind of animal would you be and why? What was your most embarrassing moment? What did you do last weekend?' The contestant then selects one of the three bachelors with whom to go on a date. Their selection is based on which bachelor they believe would provide the best *experience* based on the *knowledge* they had to work with. The Bible gives us knowledge about God; what He has said and done in ages past. When Christians only explore God in their bibles or through listening to weekly sermons, they are playing the Dating Game without ever going on the date. We read stories in the bible and conclude that God did a good thing when He sent Jesus to die for us or when He promised to send His Spirit to teach us, guide us, and live in us. Yet we continue to live in slavery to our culture, to addictions of all sorts, and to self-focused living. God wants to *date* you. You've read His profile, now what? That's great that you can read about Him. That's great that your friends experience His power in their lives. God wants more for you though. He wants us to discover that He is still doing good things. The Bible gives us information about God. It is true and inspired but it is not a substitute for a *relationship* with God. He speaks, we respond, He responds, we speak, He listens, He acts, our lives change, etc. etc. The Scriptures give us a platform and concrete definition to words like godly, patient, loving, kind, truthful, humble, Christ-like, and self-controlled. Yet God is doing something special and unique to lead you into these realities *today*.

Write down the new possibilities God is showing you for what it means to be in relationship with Him.

_____

_____

_____

_____

Part 3: Knowing What Is at Risk

"God can, when he pleases, change all other obstacles into aids for spiritual progress. For to him, everything is the same, equally useful or useless. Without him everything is nothing, and with him nothing is everything. We may meditate, indulge in contemplation, pray aloud, practice interior silence, live an active life or one withdrawn from the world, and though they may all be valuable, there is nothing better for us than to do what God wants at any particular moment. We must regard everything else with complete indifference and as something worth nothing at all. As we see only God in everything, we must take or leave all things according to his will, so that we neither live, nor develop, nor hope except as he ordains, and never try to use things which have neither power nor worth except through him . . . All is nothing unless [God's] will gives it meaning."[15]

Do you believe that what God wants at any given moment is the best and most significant thing at that time?

_____

What beliefs or forces in your life prevent you from embracing the sort of life described in the above paragraph?

_____

_____

_____

Read Acts 16:16–40.
What is God showing you in this story?
Write down any thoughts, questions, or promptings.

_____

_____

_____

_____

What were Paul and Silas risking through their bold actions in this story?

_____

_____

[15] Caussade, *Abandonment*, 30.

In some cases Paul and Silas lost what they risked. They risked their physical safety and they lost it. They risked their comfort and they lost it. They risked their reputations and they lost them. They risked their dignity before a crowd of people and lost it. Paul and Silas seemed indifferent to these losses though. There were other things at stake that their eyes were set on. Paul and Silas were tuned into what God was doing. God's activity was the *ONE* thing that could not be compromised. Dignity before a crowd and a public flogging seemed a small price to pay to see God come through in all His glory.

Choosing to *not* live our lives listening to and responding to God is riskier than anything else because we are squandering opportunities to bear eternal fruit (God is doing something and is willing to use us to do it but we fail to see Him and the opportunity passes us by). Circumstances that are engineered by God to yield eternal rewards do not have a shelf life beyond that particular moment. If we do not see the opportunity, it will go away. We are told that when Jesus returns, He will wipe the tears from our eyes (Rev 21:4). Why would we be mourning in the first place? I've always pictured a joyful reunion with God from the get-go. Some interpret this Scripture to mean that God is going to give us a brief picture of the almost countless opportunities that we have thrown away, disregarded, ignored, pushed away, or retreated from in fear. We will mourn because we will see that our choices rooted in selfish living actually impact eternity. Ouch . . .

Selfish living *feels* less risky than godly living because selfish living caters to our felt-needs for happiness, security, and comfort. Life in the Spirit *feels* risky because obeying God demands that we put things that are important to us (like our felt-needs for happiness, security, and comfort) on the alter. We must be prepared to lose them. Faith in the invisible and allowing God to have authority over our circumstances and relationships feels self-destructive and foolish. Yet God promises to care for us in spite of this. 'Seek my Father's kingdom, I got your back' (My interpretation of Matthew 6:33). There is no safer place to be than in the center of God's will. No person or plan can bring greater significance and fulfillment to our souls than a living relationship with God. And no one can offer greater comfort than the gentle and compassionate hand of God.

It all comes down to *perceived* risk vs. *actual* risk. I had a friend in college who would get severe hallucinations when he smoked pot. One night, as he was sitting in his desk chair in his dorm room on the 8th floor, he began hallucinating that the only floor space in his room was a small section directly underneath him. We liked to mess with Jason when he was stoned. We tried to coax him away from his chair and onto the portion of floor space, which in his mind, would result in plummeting 8 stories. The fear in his eyes was unmistakable. Next we would physically drag him from his chair. Jason was a big guy. One time, one of us got a nosebleed because he would fight so hard against us. In Jason's mind, the perceived risk of falling felt and looked real; nothing would convince him otherwise. Jason slept in his chair that night and he insisted that we double and triple check that there was adequate distance between his chair and 'the edge' before we left his room for the night.

A falsely perceived risk has tragic consequences.
- *Fear and/or insecurity* creates a perceived risk which leads to an:
- *Altered Picture* of the character and reliability of God which becomes an:
- *Obstacle* to trusting God to meet our emotional needs with *His* resources. Our only alternative to get our needs met is to have a:
- *Lifestyle of Control* centered on getting our immediate felt needs met with our own resources.

What areas of your life do you see the above progression of logic?

_____

_____

_____

_____

Meditate on the following words and think about what is truly at stake in life.

"The opposite of eternal life is not annihilation. It is hell. Jesus spoke of it more than anybody, and he made plain that rejecting the eternal life he offered would result not in obliteration, but in the misery of God's wrath: "Whoever believes in the Son has eternal life; whoever does not obey the Son shall not see life, but the wrath of God remains on him" (John 3:36). And it remains forever. Jesus said, "These will go away into eternal punishment, but the righteous into eternal life" (Matt 25:46). This is an unspeakable reality that shows the infinite evil of treating God with indifference or contempt. So Jesus warns, "If your eye causes you to sin, tear it out. It is better for you to enter the kingdom of God with one eye than with two eyes to be thrown into hell, 'where their worm does not die and the fire is not quenched'" (Mark 9:47–48). So eternal life is not merely the extension of this life with its mix of pain and pleasure. As hell is the worst outcome of this life, so "eternal life" is the best. It is supreme and ever-increasing happiness where all sin and all sadness will be gone. All that is evil and harmful in this fallen creation will be removed. All that is good—all that will bring true and lasting happiness—will be preserved and purified and intensified."[16]

Pop culture in America has trained us to allow our feelings to be the most powerful motivators and most truthful or reliable indicators of reality. If I feel afraid, there is a real danger. If it feels good to buy things than it must be good. If I hate myself then I am a bad person. Our emotional state seems to be the most reliable witness. A thousand people can tell a woman suffering from anorexia that she is beautiful but more than likely she will give more validation to her own emotional self-hatred.

It is important that we begin to discern what is actually a risk and what is a perceived risk. Entering into a situation that addresses a perceived risk is frightening because the

---

[16] Piper, *The Passion*, 56–57.

risk was planted there by a painful experience in the past. Being in the presence of a bee is a perceived risk for me because when I was a child I was attacked by bees while on roller skates. When I see a bee I automatically assume the bee's deepest longing is to inflict pain on me.

Ignoring my neighbors doesn't feel risky but it is very risky. I know people that don't know Jesus. Engaging my neighbors in relationship feels risky because they look at me weird when I try and make conversation. They give me this look that says, 'Why are you standing here talking to me like this?'.

> *By pursuing relationship with my neighbor, I could potentially discover that there is one more person in the world that thinks I'm an idiot. That knowledge injures me so I avoid my neighbor.*

If I could understand that God's declaration of love and rejoicing over me is authoritative and cannot be altered by man's opinion of me, I would see no risk in making conversation with my neighbor for Jesus' sake. Likewise, if I could feel what God feels for my neighbor, I would be willing to do everything I could to communicate His love to them. If I could realize that Jesus suffered and died on a cross simply so that my neighbor could know the benefits of His grace and peace I would be willing to 'risk' my fragile ego being bruised. I would see that the only risk in this situation is in *not* seeking and obeying God's plan to redeem my neighbor.

For you, why does it *feel* risky to entrust your emotional well being to God?

_____

_____

_____

_____

What are some attitudes or behaviors in your life that you now see as being eternally risky?

_____

_____

_____

_____

Part 4: Risky Living—The Way of the Cross

"If Jesus ever gave us a command He could not enable us to fulfill, He would be a liar; and if we make our inability a barrier to obedience, it means we are telling God there is something He has not taken into account. Every element of self-reliance must be slain by the power of God. Complete weakness and dependence will always be the occasion for the Spirit of God to manifest His power." [17]

Read Acts 16:16–40.
What is God showing you in this story?
Write down any thoughts, questions, or promptings.

_____

_____

_____

_____

Recall some familiar commands that Jesus gives those who would follow Him. Write them below and ask God how He wants to enable you to fulfill those commands.

_____

_____

_____

_____

_____

Religion requires no listening. Religion involves knowing and keeping rules. Sometimes Christians base everything on the Ten Commandments or The Great Commandment and Great Commission. These are good things spoken by God Himself. Jesus affirmed the law. He was not a rebel to God's law but He was and is a rebel to *our* religion. When we distort God's law to be little more than absolute rules of conduct; we are setting ourselves up to live moral lives independent of God. Our actions may be 'Christian' but there is no power in them because it is just us doing our best to follow God's commands. God's aim is to display His character and strength in our lives via supernatural means (giving us His living Spirit). We are trying to copycat God. He wants to spiritually dwell within our physical bodies. We are a vessel. He is the Treasure inside.

---

[17] Chambers, *My Utmost*, May 5th.

Glenn Stassen and David Gushee identify four levels of moral norms in their book, *Kingdom Ethics*.

1. The particular / immediate judgment level: A moral declaration about a particular case without a reason given for the judgment. This alone leads to situationism or *moral subjectivism*—I can't impose my ethics on others because every person and situation is different than mine (moral decisions are personal, private, and emotive).

2. The rules level: A rule applies not just to one particular case; but to all similar cases. A rule tells us directly what to do or not do. This alone leads to *legalism*. We read the Bible looking for rules and we see God as the rule-giver and rule-enforcer. Legalists fall into sin when they encounter situations for which there is no applicable rule—they are without guiding principles by which to formulate rules.

3. The principles level: Principles either support or criticize a rule. Principles are more general than rules and do not tell us concretely what to do. 'Love your enemies' supports the rule—'go a second mile with your enemy'. Understanding the principles that underlie the rules prevents us from becoming legalists. This alone leads to *principlism*. Even at this level, principles can conflict. Without a grand narrative—a story, it would be impossible to discern which opposing principle was morally superior (which are grounded in God's will, action, and character). Principlism also ignores concrete rules and can entice us into broad principles of uninvolvement (Matt 5:24).

4. The narrative level: Our lives are grounded in the story of what God has done and continues to do on this day. This story gives us our most basic convictions about the *character, activity, and will of God, as well as our nature and response as participants in that will.* It is this story that leads us to act, feel, and think the way we do.[18]

Which of these four levels comes closest to describing what you see being lived out in Christian America?

_____

_____

Level one feels safe. We like level one because we have a sense of control knowing exactly what is required of us. I am my own boss. I know what's right for me and no one can tell me differently. All we need to do is know and keep the rules. Level four feels risky. It feels ambiguous, scary, mystical, and invisible. How can I know for sure what God is up to today? How do I know when He is speaking? How can I be sure that what I am seeing is the work of God and not just my imagination or wishful thinking? We live by faith, not by sight.

Jesus calls us to deny ourselves, to take up our cross (road of suffering and voluntary weakness) and follow Him. On the surface, this seems self-deprecating. If God is not

---

[18] Stassen and Gushee, *Kingdom Ethics*, 100–106.

sovereign than yes, the way of the way of the Cross is a self-deprecating journey. But only God is able to fulfill the destiny we long for. He's inviting us to learn what it means to trust that *the way of the Cross is the only possibility that affirms our value as image-bearers of God.*

Reflect on why this seems so absurd and contradictory.

_____

_____

_____

Anything less than the way of the Cross is vocational prostitution. Nobody *wants* to be a prostitute. A prostitute is not desired for their personhood. A prostitute is valued only to the degree that he or she can deliver a service at the expense of denying what is fundamentally real within them. We have become prostitutes when we deny what is most fundamentally real about ourselves (bearing the image of God by way of the Cross) and adopt lesser forms of life. A Lamborghini bears the image of speed. An invitation to a Lamborghini is thus, 'you must give up cruising speeds below 150mph. You must always aspire to be in 6th gear. Resist braking; embrace acceleration.' It's tragic to see this sort of car sit in a garage or only be driven slowly by a wealthy 78-year-old man who is legally blind. It's a tragedy when human beings live below their full capacity to bear the image of God. Anything else that we might choose is prostitution. We cheapen our worth when we chase after our false gods. Things are lost in eternity when we live below capacity.

To deny your self does not mean to hate yourself or have no regard for yourself. It means to trust that your life is valuable and because of its value, it is to be placed only in the hands of the One who created it and can best care for it. When Jesus says to us, 'deny yourself, take up your cross, and follow me'—He is giving us an invitation to follow the same road the Father gave Him—the way of the Cross which entails suffering, shame, and weakness. Jesus trusted the Father, that when faithful to *this* road, the result would be glory to the Father. Apparently enduring crucifixion had a worthwhile payoff. The Father raised Jesus in power and might after his shameful, humiliating, and painful death. God wants to display His power and might in your life but it will happen by way of the Cross. This seems contradictory to us. It feels cruel to be led into allowable suffering. However, through our suffering, God promises us His glory. Let us carefully consider that "what we suffer now is nothing compared to the glory he will reveal to us later" (Rom 8:18). We can live in confidence because we know that in all things God works for the good of those who love him, who have been called according to his purpose and predestined to be conformed to the likeness of Jesus (Rom 8:28–29). We can live in assurance that Jesus, who now sits at the right hand of God, is praying for us and neither trouble nor hardship nor danger nor sword can separate us from his love. "Despite all these things, overwhelming victory is ours through Christ, who loved us. And [may we be] convinced that nothing can ever separate us from God's love. Neither death nor life, neither angels nor demons, neither our fears for today nor our worries about tomorrow—not even the powers of hell can separate us from God's love. No power in the sky above or in the earth below—indeed, nothing in all creation will ever be able to separate us from the love of God that is revealed in Christ Jesus our Lord" (Rom 8:37–39).

Our Father's glory is the highest prize. We are most hateful of ourselves when we insist on self-reliance, self-gratification, and self-actualization. In essence we are stating that our momentary pleasures and comforts are of greater worth than our Father's glory. Ouch. In this state we are refusing to enter the arms of God who is ready to care for our needs and equip us to participate in His work.

Agree or disagree—my state of being (emotional, physical, spiritual, mental) effects God's work.

_____

Cause and Effect:
It's uncomfortable to think that our decisions have the capacity to influence God's decision-making process. Read the following Scriptures and write down the human condition or action and the resulting action or decision from God.

- 2 Samuel 22:26–28

  - Man's action:

  _____

  - God's re-action:

  _____

- 2 Chronicles 24:20

  - Man's action:

  _____

  - God's re-action:

  _____

- Matthew 13:54–58

  - Man's action:

  _____

- God's re-action:

_____

- 1 Peter 3:12

  - Man's action:

_____

  - God's re-action:

_____

- James 4:1–10

  - Man's action:

_____

  - God's re-action:

_____

Based on these factual accounts of God relating with His people, does the conduct of your life have an effect on the degree to which God works through you? Is that not just a little disturbing?

_____

_____

_____

"The more confidence we have in our own strength and abilities, the less we are likely to have in Christ. Our human weakness is no hindrance to God. In fact, as long as we do not use it as an excuse for sin, it is good to be weak. But this acceptance of weakness is more than acknowledging our limitations. It means experiencing a power much greater than our own and surrendering to it. Eberhard Arnold, a founder of the Bruderhofs, said, 'This is the root of grace: the dismantling of our power. Whenever even a little power rises up in us, the Spirit and the authority of God will retreat to the corresponding degree. In my estimation this is the single most important insight with regard to the kingdom of God.'"[19]

[19] Arnold, *Seeking Peace,* 51–52.

What makes you feel powerful and in control?

_____

_____

_____

How does it make you feel that God wants to tear down the things that make you feel powerful and in control?

_____

_____

_____

Paul and Silas could have chosen the road of power. If they were seeking power or control, how might they have acted differently? (Especially in vv. 19, 25, 28, and 38).

_____

_____

God is inviting us on a journey that feels like death. He demands things of us that cause us pain and turmoil. Yet Jesus was clear, "Come to me, all of you who are weary and carry heavy burdens, and I will give you rest. Take my yoke upon you. Let me teach you, because I am humble and gentle at heart, and you will find rest for your souls" (Matt 11:28–29). Paul and Silas sat in a jail cell not knowing their *earthly* fate. Apparently Paul was unconcerned about his earthly fate. As he told the Philippians, "For me, to live is Christ and to die is gain." In Paul's view, all things were eligible to be used by God for His glory. Paul and Silas were beaten badly and publicly humiliated yet they sang their lungs out to God. They did not feel sorry for themselves. They were not discouraged. They engaged in risky behavior that appeared foolish and destructive. Instead of becoming weakened though, it appears that in their hardship they became strengthened and encouraged.

> "To be grateful for the good things that happen in our lives is easy, but to be grateful for all or our lives—the good as well as the bad, the moments of joy as well as the moments of sorrow, the successes as well as the failures, the rewards as well as the rejections—that requires hard spiritual work. Still, we are only grateful people when we can say thank you to all that has brought us to the present moment. As long as we keep dividing our lives between events and people we would like to remember and those we would rather forget, we cannot claim the fullness of our beings as a gift of God to be grateful for. Let's not be afraid to look at everything that has brought us to where we are now and trust that we will soon see in it the guiding hand of a loving God." Henri Nouwen

Recall some events and circumstances in the last month that have left you bitter and ungrateful. Assume that God really is capable of using evil for good and is not shy about allowing suffering and hardships to hit us over the head. How might God be using these circumstances to glorify Himself in and through you?

_____

_____

_____

I want to clearly state that God does not need us. If none of us listened to God, He would not be any less glorious or powerful. Humanity would suffer, but God would not become less. Hanging in my garage, which is also my office, are wind chimes. I intentionally hung them there so that their silence would remind me that wind chimes only make sense in the presence of wind. We are like wind chimes. God is like a strong wind that blows in the night. If we position ourselves to be in the wind, music will be made. If we hide indoors, no music will be made yet the wind will continue to blow outside. Our hiding does not detract from the wind. Wind chimes simply indicate *the presence of wind as they are moved by that wind.* From indoors we hear wind chimes and we know the wind is blowing. We draw attention to the presence of God on behalf of a groaning creation *as we allow ourselves to be moved by Him.* He does not need us. His call is His grace. The way of the Cross is His grace generously extended to you. His work that He has prepared for us is His grace.

CHAPTER 6

Becoming Awe-struck and Humble

"They called the apostles in and had them flogged. then they ordered them not to speak in the name of Jesus, and let them go. The apostles left the Sanhedrin, rejoicing because they had been counted worthy of suffering disgrace for the name. Day after day, in the temple courts and from house to house, they never stopped teaching and proclaiming the good news that Jesus is the Christ" Acts 5:40–42.

OVERVIEW:

Core Scripture: Acts 5:12–42.

The Kingdom of God is at Hand: There is simply no one greater than God. No other person or thing in the universe is worthy of our allegiance, affection, and devotion. As Christians, we have surrendered our lives to a God who is jealous; He demands exclusivity when it comes to our faithfulness and worship. God is not willing to share His throne with any other. He stands as Ruler over all authorities, all powers, all governments, and all spirits. One day, every knee will bow to Him and acknowledge His rightful reign in the universe.

Repent: Worship is when Christians sing in church on Sunday. Good worship happens when the music suits my personal taste and is executed in a professional manner. Horrible worship is boring music performed by unskilled musicians. Worship is a 'thing,' an 'event,' that we show up to. It is to be judged and scrutinized by the same standards for other things that we would consume like a concert or movie.

Believe the Good News: We can respond personally and communally to the word and work of Jesus. It is what will happen when we see what sort of King Jesus is and the sort of kingdom that flows from His authority. Replying to Jesus reminds us that we know the beginning and end of His story. It also reminds us that our great King is at work so that we might have strength and courage to seek His rule in the middle times when His victory cannot be seen with the naked and faithless eye.

Therefore Go: Spend as much time as you need to ask God to show you that He is good and how His goodness could change your heart. Write down what you experience. Also, ask someone you know who is not a Christian what they feel is most important to Christians. Share these experiences with your community.

Part 1: We Worship What Is Most Powerful: Worship as Addiction

Read Acts 5:12–42.
What is God showing you in this story?
Write down any thoughts, questions, or promptings.

_____

_____

_____

_____

What does it seem the religious leaders are trying to achieve throughout this story?

_____

_____

To whom or what are the religious leaders loyal?

_____

_____

I visited my cousin in Ohio at age 12. The year was 1987 when it was really cool to wear untied puffy white Nikes without socks. My cousin Matt had achieved this status while I was forced to sport the substitute—'Hakers'. One day Matt and I were having one of those 'I'm cooler than you because . . . ' conversations with his next-door neighbor. Matt's best ammo was his shoes—they were simply the coolest thing a 12 year old could get in 1987. "What about *his* shoes?" said the neighbor kid while pointing his finger at my 'Hakers'. "Oh, these are Hakers", I sheepishly said. He gave me this blank look that said, 'dude you are really lame standing there in your Hakers and crew socks that stretch halfway to your kneecaps. And are those horizontal green stripes on those socks?' I knew I had been found out and my face flushed. Matt then explained that I was from Seattle and that in Seattle 'Hakers' are simply the coolest (second only to Pearl Jam). He bought it and quickly dropped his charges against me. When I returned to Seattle I whined to my parents to buy me a pair of Nikes.

That which we allow to exercise control over us (addiction) is who or what we are worshiping. Western pop culture has created entire generations of devoted and faithful worshipers. We are taught to worship images and impulses. The images we worship are most clearly seen in our shopping malls; Tommy Hilfiger, American Eagle, Hollister, Gap, Abercrombie and Fitch, Independent, Old Navy, and many others.

We give our worship to the image by becoming like it. By becoming like it, we are acknowledging that it possesses power and we want to benefit from its power.

We gladly pay the price to receive the bounty that it has to offer in exchange for becoming like it. For example, if I wear an American Eagle shirt, suddenly girls will ask me for my number and offer to sleep with me. Why does a cotton tee-shirt made by Hanes cost considerably less than a cotton tee-shirt that says 'Hollister' on it? Is it a better tee-shirt? Will it last longer? Hanes is not asking you to worship what you are buying. Hollister has already earned your act of worship the second you pay for it. A worship-able image gives us access to the impulses we worship. Our corporate addiction in the U.S. is immediate gratification. The most *powerful* foreseen possibility is the most *pleasurable* possibility. Few things have the ability to derail the impulses of a hormonal teenage boy when opportunity knocks. Their allegiance is to the moment. Acquiring the right image in order to participate in the most desirable impulses is the religious ceremony of 21st Century America. Shopping malls are our halls of worship where we tithe our earnings and find hope for our meaningless existence.

> *We gladly arrange our lives around image and impulse because it appears to be the most powerful and available source of life in our midst. We arrange our lives around God reluctantly and begrudgingly because we sincerely believe He is not the most powerful and available source of life in our midst.*

Reflect on this statement and write down how it relates to you.

_____

_____

_____

_____

We have a vision problem. "How does God deal with human fear, confusion, and paralysis? God tells a story: I am none other that the God who 'brought you out of the land of Egypt, out of the house of bondage' (Deut 5:6). Knowing that story makes sense out of the following command that Israel 'shall have no other gods before me.' The Bible does not argue that idolatry detracts from human self-esteem, or that life is better when lived without idols. Indeed, idolatry is a creative response on the part of a finite creature that has not heard about the Creator. Idolatry is condemned only on the basis of a story we know about God. Israel is a people who learn this story by heart and gather regularly to retell it . . . Story is the fundamental means of talking about and listening to God, the only human means available to us that is complex and engaging enough to make comprehensible what it means to be with God."[1] We will always be addicted to something. God

---

[1] Hauerwas and Willimon, *Resident Aliens*, 54–55.

wants us to be addicted to Him. We are either slaves to sin or slaves to Christ. Idolatry is part of our God-given DNA. Seeking a god, someone or something to worship is hard-wired into us because God wants us to seek Him. The only explanation that I can see for a nation of Christians who are not worshiping God is that we have not encountered Him in the manner that He is offering. We have settled for beliefs that are abstract and have no consequential bearing on the here and now.

Drawing from our story in Acts 5, here is what it meant for Peter to be with God:

- Performed many miraculous signs and wonders.
- People sought after his shadow.
- Healed the sick and those tormented by evil spirits.
- Angered and incited jealousy in those who held positions of authority.
- Arrested for all the above.
- Released from jail by an angel.
- Disobeyed man's authority to remain true to God's authority.
- Flogged (beaten 39 times with a band of leather embedded with chucks of pottery and other sharp objects) for his loyalty to God.
- Viewed his disgraceful flogging as an honor and rejoiced.

If you were a friend or acquaintance of Peter's, would you be drawn to worship the same thing He did? Why or why not?

_____

_____

_____

_____

A few hundred times in the Bible, God refers to Himself or is named by someone else as 'the God of _____'. For example, Shadrach, Meshach, and Abednego refused to worship King Nebuchadnezzar's golden image and were thrown into a fiery furnace. God delivered them from the flames. They walked around in the fire while accompanied by an angel. They came out from the fire without even the smell of fire on their clothes or a hair on their head singed. After this miraculous event, when people spoke of God they called Him 'the God of Shadrach, Meshach, and Abednego'. God, who was previously unknown to the Babylonians, was manifested through the worship of Shadrach, Meshach, and Abednego. In Babylon, God was called '*The God of Shadrach, Meshach, and Abednego*'. God became known because of a concrete story performed through the worship of Shadrach, Meshach, and Abednego. When people thought of *them*, they thought of *their God*. When Babylonians thought of their God, it was in the context of how God delivered Shadrach, Meshach, and Abednego.

Okay, here's a tough one. Who or what do you think those around you would conclude you worship? What stories would your acquaintances attach to the 'God of [*your name*]?'

_____

_____

_____

Take a couple of minutes to petition God to show Himself to your heart that you may be drawn to worship Him.

We worship that which we believe possesses the ability to deliver us from what feels most threatening to us and provide for us what we most desire. God was the most powerful and compelling force in Peter's life, not because he read it somewhere, but because he experienced it to actually be the case. The story of God's activity in his midst compelled Peter to arrange his life to God's liking (worship). It's helpful to recall that it wasn't always this way. We have numerous examples of Peter's shortsightedness and rebellion during his three years with Jesus; 'Peter, put your sword away . . . before the rooster crows you will deny me three times . . . get behind me Satan . . .'. Peter went from manifesting the will of Satan to possessing a shadow that would cure people of their illnesses. Most of us are unwilling to worship something that we cannot control. It's the end result we worship (acquiring the right image to be able to act on our impulses). We are all searching for something that will always deliver, never disappoint, and satisfy us completely. For many Christians, God is not deemed capable of this. We have a vision problem. Instead we have chosen to pursue material gain, comfort, and safe relationships but remain 'Christian' in the process. I see little safety and comfort when I look at Peter and others who have gone before us. The Christian compartment of our lives primarily revolves around selecting a church service once per week that most closely syncs up with our personal tastes and preferences in things like 'warm and friendly people, relevant sermons, and good music'. God is, at best, the religious or moral compartment of our lives. At worst, He is simply a mascot in our lives that we have come to believe cheers us on in all of our plans, projects, and dreams.

The mascot is traditionally brought out when we're depressed for the purpose of helping us believe that maybe the tides will turn in our favor. A mascot has no effect on the outcome of the game. A mascot has no power. A mascot has the ability to do nothing but create false hope by stirring up positive emotions about a bad situation (i.e. the home team is down by 168 touchdowns but the blue chicken is still dancing on the sidelines like there's something worth believing in).

On the other hand, a coach makes or breaks the outcome of a game. The coach calls the shots and orders the steps of the players. To work under a coach requires trust and submission. A coach has power because they have the ability to affect an outcome. A coach is submitted to or 'worshiped' when they demonstrate that they have the ability to win games. We will worship God when we see that He has the ability to take evil and make it good. We will worship God when we see that He is willing and able to do things far beyond our abilities and imaginations. We will worship God when we see that He graciously wants to perform His work in and through us.

In what ways do you view God as a mascot and in what ways do you view Him as your coach?

_____

_____

_____

At the end of the day, Peter and the other apostles worshiped God for what He did. There is no distinction or separation between God's word, works, and personhood. God expresses His infinite capabilities, eternal sovereignty, and unending love in the things He does for us on our behalf.

> *If we have not seen that God has done, is doing, and will continue to do something worthwhile on our behalf than we must ask ourselves why we think we are worshiping Him.*

Further, we must examine why we think we are *not* worshiping the things that we continue to allow to bail us out of our emotional turmoil and to be the focal point of our desires. Just because we sing songs about God doesn't mean we are worshiping Him. God has not been shy to express His disgust with His people when they sing one thing and live another thing. "These people acknowledge me with their lips but their hearts are far from me[2] . . . I hate, I despise your religious feasts; I cannot stand your assemblies . . . Away with the noise of your songs! I will not listen to the music of your harps.[3]" Just because we don't sing songs about our cars, our bodies, our abilities, our clothing, and our culture of cool doesn't mean that we aren't worshiping those things.

[2] Matt 15:8.
[3] Amos 5:21, 23.

Reflect on the above paragraph and write down what God is showing you.

_____

_____

_____

_____

"A cultural revolution occurs when the releasing or remissive symbolic grows more compelling than the controlling one; then it is that the inherent tensions reach a breaking point."[4] Currently there is no tension in our culture because the Church has conceded and worships the symbols of our culture found in our shopping malls right along with the rest of the public. The symbols of our culture stand unchallenged, unquestioned, and un-criticized. In our culture, the Church means very little symbolically. Her members are largely the same as non-members. Ronald Sider catalogs these alarming similarities between those who profess to be the Church and those who do not. My intention is not to judge or point fingers. I want to take responsibility for our condition. It's easy to look at a statistic on divorce or abortion and point fingers at the individuals involved. But what about the individuals that were *not* involved in the months and years leading up to such an event? What is our response when a young girl becomes pregnant? Are we quick to lecture her about the evil of abortion or are we quick to offer whatever support is required in order for her to have her baby. It's easy to lecture. It's not easy to make sacrifices so that she can make a better decision. Are we willing to own up, not just to our own character, but to the character of Christ's body? Here is a glimpse . . .

- Conservative Protestants are more likely to divorce than the general population.
- In Oklahoma, where 70% of the population attends a church service weekly, the divorce rate is 50% higher than the national average.
- If every Christian in America gave away 10% of their income, there would be $143 billion on hand for ministry.
- On average we spend seven times more time watching TV than we spend in Bible reading, prayer, and worship.
- Between 13 and 19% of Christians believe that adultery is morally acceptable.
- Between 11 and 20% of white Christians object to having an African American neighbor.
- Husbands who attend conservative protestant churches or hold conservative theological views are no less likely to engage in domestic abuse than others.[5]

---

[4] Rieff, *The Triumph*, 205.
[5] Sider, *The Scandal*, 18–28.

It's alarming to me that we are fast losing any sort of identity that is distinctive and distinguishable from the surrounding culture aside from weekly attendance to a religious service.

Recovering the art of becoming a community that worships a God who is the most powerful and compelling Person in the universe is crucial for our times. Let us become addicted to Jesus. Let us come under His control as we marinate our hearts and minds in His truthful and present existence. In order for our community to become 'a more compelling symbol' than the controlling symbols of our culture, we must identify the symbols that are controlling us, renounce them, and help one another see God. This is how God will gain control over our lives. This is how we will become a compelling symbol for the world as God's character and work is made known to the world through us.

Identify the status symbols that give you a sense of power or significance. Ask God to give you the courage to abandon them. What would be some practical first steps away from your status symbols?

_____

_____

_____

_____

_____

Part 2: We Are Always Worshiping: Worship as Response

"Believe me, dear woman, the time is coming when it will no longer matter whether you worship the Father on this mountain or in Jerusalem. You Samaritans know very little about the one you worship, while we Jews know all about him, for salvation comes through the Jews. But the time is coming—indeed it's here now—when true worshipers will worship the Father in spirit and in truth. The Father is looking for those who will worship him that way. For God is Spirit, so those who worship him must worship in spirit and in truth." (John 4:21–24)

Read Acts 5:12–42.
What is God showing you in this story?
Write down any thoughts, questions, or promptings.

_____

_____

_____

_____

What makes Peter's and the other apostles' actions worship vs. simply a collection of good deeds?

_____

_____

God calls us to be worshipers of Him; people who are absolutely captured by, enthralled with, and dedicated to because of His beauty and perfection. Our own desire to be god is the first thing that prevents us from worshiping God.

When I was in jr. high, I wanted to be like everybody else because I felt like I had no value. The best I could hope for was to copy those around who I believed had value. If I could become like them, I would be one of them and thus worth something. People didn't want me to be like them. If I became like them, I was now a threat to their identity. At some point we've been on either the giving or receiving end of this. Someone buys the same item of clothing that you have and you vow to never wear it again. The benchwarmer brags about winning a game and the team captain shuts them up because the benchwarmer 'had nothing to do with it'. We are all clamoring to be little gods. An attractive woman walks into a room full of people socializing and every other woman looks at her in jealousy and anger because her beauty threatens their perceived standing of 'most beautiful woman in the room'. We are hard at work protecting our identity precisely because our hope is in becoming little gods of our own personal universes.

It is nothing short of a miracle that God doesn't look at us and get rid of us. We're trying on His clothes, we're trying to play His game but we can't measure up. We're a band of wannabe's but nowhere near being who God wants us to be. We are kingdom bench-warmers, all of us. Our righteousness is the equivalent of filthy (menstrual) rags. Our best efforts are worthless. In fact, our best efforts are not even neutral—they are destructive, undesirable, and are best to be thrown out with the trash. God is demanding something from us that we are unable to give. He demands perfection and He demands that our lives be fruitful. The consequence for not meeting these demands is death. It is precisely God meeting His own demands that makes Him worthy of our worship. Because of Christ's death, we are now hidden within *His* perfection. The pressure to be good is off. We can now be real and enter into good works, not as a form of repayment to God, but as recipients of His generous grace to involve us in His nature and work.

I was playing the piano for God one day and He thundered back at me, "Who do you think you are that you know the first thing about who I am?" It actually scared me and I had to wrestle with His question. Here I was a benchwarmer pretending that my King's victory somehow had something to do with my superior bench-warming skills. His question, and more specifically the answer to His question humbled me. For a brief moment I glimpsed how big God is and how small I am. The realization brought me back to the Cross—to God's grace for sinners like me. I humbly played 'Jesus Loves Me' on the piano as I saw that it was only by grace that God loves me, uses me, and is patient with my ignorance, rebellion, and self-absorption.

It's easy for us to start believing that God should feel fortunate to have us on His team. It's easy to feel entitled and deserving of all God has to offer. As long as we are the center of our universe we will remain conceited and in control. Being able to worship God is His grace that He offers to us. It is our ticket out of our long list of self-isms.

If a first century Jew wanted to experience the presence of God they went to the temple. Prior to Jesus, the temple was where God met with people. In the Old Testament, prior to the people of Israel having a geographic home, God met them in a tent-like tabernacle that went where the people went—the Tent of Meeting. Jesus changed all of this. We now live in the New Covenant. We are now the temple; the place where God comes to meet us and where we 'go' to worship Him. Because God dwells in His Church (people) and His life is expressed through those people, worship is a 24/7 vocation. Yes we gather with other believers to 'worship' God. But this does not mean that the other six days of the week and the remaining 22.5 hours of the seventh day are off limits for worshiping God. We are always worshiping *something*. What we need to come to terms within ourselves is what in fact we are worshiping the other 166.5 hours in the week.

The world trains us to be chameleons. If someone is asked in a job interview what their top priority is, chances are they will say their career is their top priority because they want the interviewer to see they are willing to sacrifice their livelihood for the company. If their spouse asked this same person what their top priority is they would say, 'you are, Honey'. And if this individual's pastor were to ask them what their top priority is they might say 'God' or 'religion' or 'the church'. My boss is only concerned for the career compartment of my life so I work to show her that this compartment has authority over all others. Your spouse may be interested in seeing that the marriage compartment has authority over all other compartments. God doesn't want us to live in different compartments. God doesn't want us to create these goofy sliding scales of priorities; 'faith, family, finances, and fun' or 'God and country' or 'first God, then me'. Our only obligation is to the Spirit of God. If we belong to Jesus, we no longer own anything—our bodies, our resources, our time—all of it is on loan to be used for the unveiling of our Father's glory. He will set the agenda for things like our families, our finances, or our careers. When we are worshiping God and God alone, we will know what it means to love our spouse or be good stewards of our resources and time.

> "Putting God first is a misunderstanding in itself. If something is first it means that something else is second, and whatever is first is just one of many others. In the New Covenant, God is first, last, and everything in between. He is the only thing. He is the all in all. There is nothing else. In Christ everything is dedicated to God and everything is used for his eternal purpose. The notion of putting God first is inferior to the New Covenant man; Christ is everything to him and everything he does is in Christ. Anything less than that has no place. When people try to put God first they end up with a lot of rules and principles for how that should be done. If they would let God be what he wants to be, the source of everything in their life, they would be free to follow the leading of the Holy Spirit without regard to any rules on how to put him first or how to be a good Christian."[6]

I was en route to my office one day. I had a long list of things to do—things that were 'a high priority'. Outside my office door sat a middle-aged woman in distress. She was missing several teeth and the ones she had were brown. She asked me if I had the time to drive her to the pharmacy so she could get her prescription filled for some pain medicine for her toothache(s). Honestly, I wanted to shove her away with all the 'important things I had to do that afternoon'. She did not fit anywhere in my list of what mattered to me. But she mattered to God and God told me that her request was also His request. I drove her to the pharmacy. She had no means of paying for her prescription but it didn't matter at this point as God began to soften my heart by showing me His own heart for her. During the hour it took to get the prescription filled she gave me a pretty vivid picture of her life. It was hopeless and depressing to say the least. Afterwards I drove her home and was immediately confronted by a large angry man who I quickly learned was her boyfriend. He angrily ordered Ronda's 'ass' into the house. Then he drilled me with questions to discover what I was doing with his girlfriend. If we create neat and controllable priorities in our lives, we will often remain blind to the Spirit's leading and awakening as often He breaks in at inconvenient and unexpected places.

Write down in the left column below the things in your life that matter (from most important to not-as-important).

[6] Narramore, *Tithing*, 21.

How would it look different to allow the Spirit of God to have authority (the right to determine what happens) over *all* that matters in your life (right column) vs. making a list of priorities from greatest to least?

Traditional Priority-making   Spirit-led Priority-making

1. _____   1. _____

2. _____

3. _____

4. _____

5. _____

6. _____

Living in the right column is important because when our choices are filtered through what matters to God and surrendered to the leading of God we are postured to lay down 'what matters to us' and step into what matters to God at that moment. When we live in the column on the left, we begin to adopt a mentality of protecting. We privatize our homes and our families to 'protect' them from the outside world. We do this believing we are rightfully 'prioritizing' family. When in fact, "sharply privatizing family is the first step toward killing it . . . Family needs purpose beyond itself and its sentimentality to survive and prosper . . . Family has been stripped of its wider and public significance and left only with intimacy and 'private' relationships as its purpose."[7] God is calling us to surrender all that He has given us; family, career, relationships—to the leading and authority of His Spirit to do with what He will. Abraham was promised that he would have descendents as numerous as the stars. Yet Abraham dared not resort to a 'family first' philosophy that would have disqualified him from receiving such a gift (See Gen 22).

When I was a Young Life leader in Ferndale, WA I frequently attended football games. Ferndale is a town that has one cow for every resident and their rival team was Lynden High School. Lynden also can boast one cow for every resident. When Ferndale and Lynden faced off, the entire county turned out for the game. I turned out as well, decked out in face paint and obnoxious blue and yellow clothing. Ferndale scored a touchdown during their first possession and I, along with several others, spontaneously ran a victory lap on the track that circumvented the football field. As we neared the Lynden stands, security blocked our path and angry fans began to scream four letter words and throw cups of soda at us. It was beautiful. The following week I was visiting some students at school when the head football coach, who was also a vice principal, grabbed me by the arm and hauled me off to his office. It was weird to be 23 years old and get busted by the vice principal in front of a hundred high school students. He asked me 'what the hell I

---

[7] Clapp, *Families*, 65.

was thinking pulling that victory lap stunt'. All I could say is that I got caught up in the moment. He sternly reminded me of my 'responsibility to be a leader'.

Have you ever been so taken by something that *God* did that you did something spontaneous and foolish because of it? Have you ever broken out in celebration upon receiving good news about something? We have a hard time celebrating in our culture. College parties are a good illustration of this fact. Everyone is going for this feeling of celebration but there really isn't much to celebrate. Because there is nothing to celebrate, no one is really having a good time until they are thoroughly intoxicated, stoned, or both. Before you know it, everyone's dancing around and cheering excitely for no reason other than the fact that they are intoxicated. Being drunk is fun because in this state we live without the limits of our fears, insecurities, and inhibitions. Social norms mean absolutely nothing. Guys are trying to kiss girls they've never met. Someone is in the corner weeping to a dozen people about having their heart broken. In short, people are doing things that they would never do in their right mind because when they are thinking straight, their behavior is determined by the norms of culture and society. Alcohol changes all that. People are free to act on impulse because image no longer matters. Nerds are hitting on models because rejection is not a concern.

How big would God need to become to you in order for you to break some norms? Think about norms in your peer groups, your workplace, your church, and your family.

_____

_____

_____

Much of what we call worship in our churches is similar to a college party. We may not be getting drunk at church but we are showing up with hopes that our emotions will be stirred by a professional worship band and motivational pastor. I want my heart to be stirred by what God has said and by what God has promised. Do we really come to God wanting to hear from Him without placing any controls or limits on His voice? God beckons us, 'Come, behold my works!'

> "Take a long scrutinizing look at what God is doing. This requires patient attentiveness and energetic concentration. Everybody else is noisier than God. The headlines and neon lights and amplifying systems of the world announce human works. But what of God's works? They are unadvertised but also inescapable, if we simply look. They are everywhere. They are marvelous. But God has no public relations strategy. He mounts no publicity campaign to get our attention. He simply invites us to look. Prayer is looking at the works of the Lord."[8]

---

[8] Peterson, *Treasure*, 78.

What do you find yourself responding or reacting to most often? (e.g. your emotions, desirable or undesirable circumstances, others' opinions, etc.)

_____

_____

_____

What is God inviting you and your community to respond to?

_____

_____

_____

_____

Have we forgotten that God has promised to glorify Himself by imparting His Spirit unto us? As wonderful as the Passion movie was, movies are not our best witnessing tool. Lives that are accessible to God are the best witnessing tools. Movies, pornography, and crystal-meth are not the biggest threat to the work of God. Unwilling children of God is the biggest threat to the work of God. Scripture promises us that there would be false prophets, false teachings, and deceptive philosophies.

> We spend all of our time and energy arguing against what is false yet we fail to embody what God's Spirit is doing in our midst.

Agree or disagree:

In Western culture, we most often worship the thing that has the ability to manipulate our senses in a desirable manner. Discuss the difference between sensory-based worship and true worship. Write down your thoughts to share with your community.

_____

_____

_____

When we are living naively and self-centeredly, we come to God and wonder if He is worthy of our attention and investment. 'Do I really want to reach out to this person? Do I really want to seek forgiveness and reconciliation with my friend who betrayed me?' We cling to our questions; 'will I be satisfied, will I be safe, will I be thought well of?' And we keep our *Plan B* close at hand. When we are worshiping God we rightly wonder if we are worthy of God's attention, investment, and trust. Clearly we are not. But God gives us his attention and investment anyhow. This is what makes Him worthy of our worship.

Part 3: We Worship What We Want: Worship as Allegiance

"We must obey God rather then men!"—The Apostle Peter

Read Acts 5:12–42.
What is God showing you in this story?
Write down any thoughts, questions, or promptings.

_____

_____

_____

_____

Meditate for a minute on how people were responding to the activity of the church. See especially vv. 13, 14, and 17. What do you notice?

_____

_____

We know what we worship by identifying who or what we are most eager to hear from. If other peoples' opinions are the most important thing in my life, than I will be quite eager to hear those opinions. If my career is the most important thing in my life, I find myself eagerly anticipating signs that I am moving up the ladder. In high school I worshiped my ability to improve on my own personal records. As a runner, I became obsessed with shaving seconds from my personal best at every race. There was tremendous gratification in the first half of my running career because there was so much room for improvement. It was not uncommon to drop 10 to 20 seconds with every race. Things were much different in the latter half because there was less room for improvement. Dropping two seconds for a three-mile race became the benchmark. My senior year I was plagued with injuries and I never improved on my best time from my junior year. It was shameful and depressing for me because I worshiped my ability to improve and I could no longer improve. My god was dead so I searched for something new to worship. Ultimately, it is our egos that we most often worship. Our task then as ego worshipers is to find the surest way of exalting our egos. In high school the surest way that I could exalt my ego was to be a runner who was always getting faster. Once I was unable to run faster, I was forced to search for new means of exalting my ego.

How have you found success in exalting your ego? If so, how? If not, how have you tried?

_____

_____

_____

Unfortunately, popular religion in America caters to our thirst for ego exaltation. "The religious voices that command the largest audiences in our society are those that are publicists for the ego—the religious ego, to be sure, but the geo all the same. The deep-rooted, me-first distortions of our humanity have been institutionalized in our economics and sanctioned by our psychologies. Now we have gotten for ourselves religions in the same style, religions that will augment our human potential and make us feel good about ourselves. We want prayers that will bring us daily benefits in the form of a higher standard of living, with occasional miracles to relieve our boredom. We come to the Bible as consumers, rummaging through texts to find something at a bargain. We come to worship as gourmets of the emotional, thinking that the numinous might provide a nice supplement to sunsets and symphonies."[9]

It's difficult to know who or what we are allegiant to apart from thoughtful reflection. Here are some things to ponder and consider.

1. *What do I most look forward to in life?*
2. *What causes me to sing, dance, or be spontaneous?*
3. *What has the power to manipulate my emotions independent of present circumstances?*
4. *What has the power to take away my fear or insecurity?*
5. *What do I continually desire?*
6. *What has the power to make me feel like I have value and count for something?*
7. *What do I believe is able to provide something that I need?*
8. *Who or what do I most pay attention to?*
9. *Who or what do I believe improves my quality of life?*
10. *When am I content?*

What does God show you as you reflect on these questions?

_____

_____

_____

There are some who believe that God wants us to be happy and how that happiness is achieved is irrelevant. Follow your dreams, indulge, spend, fornicate, read the Bible,

[9] Ibid., 39.

volunteer in a soup kitchen—whatever makes you feel good. There are also those who believe that if we are happy then we must be living in sin. The Christian is called to a life of suffering and self-denial, they say. And we simply can't live sacrificially and be happy at the same time. I believe the truth is somewhere in between these two extremes but is itself more extreme than either of these options. Answer the following questions.

> *Does God want us to be happy? (See Josh 1:8). Yes / No*
> *Does God want us to suffer? (See Rom 8:17). Yes / No*

Here's the crux. On whose terms are we seeking/avoiding happiness and on whose terms are we seeking/avoiding suffering? Are we chasing after standards and lifestyles or are we seeking God? It is simply disillusionment to seek suffering for the sake of suffering because we are called to take up our cross! And it is simply disillusionment to seek happiness because God wants us to be happy.

> *A worshiper is one who has abandoned their fear of suffering and their need for happiness and freely seeks God in all things.*

If God wills suffering; so be it. If God wills happiness, so be it. The Apostle Paul corrected the church in Galatia on this as they became swept up in rule keeping that resulted in their own self-glorified suffering. Maybe they felt like if they were suffering that they were doing the right thing. Paul seemed baffled that they were willing to endure so much suffering for nothing (See Gal 3:1–4). Odd message from a man who endured so much suffering joyfully. We have been set free from rules (doing one thing to get another). God 'gives us His Spirit and works miracles in our midst' not because of our ability to follow orders but because of our belief. Our work is to believe that God is more worship-able than all the other things that currently have our attention. The work is to believe that the things of this world are not worthy of our worship. The work is to believe that many of the things I think I need I actually don't need. *The work is to believe that God is so good that we are free to 'seek first His kingdom and His righteousness' without arranging for our own happiness.* The work is to believe that God really is *that* good. Look again at the ten reflection questions above. Imagine if 'Jesus' was your *genuine* answer to these questions. This answer feels so cliché to us precisely because we believe it to be far-fetched in the midst of our cynicism and bitterness. Heaven will be a wonderful wakeup call. Hope does not come from believing that God will bend His ear to us and grant us relief from suffering. Hope comes from believing that God is good regardless if my day holds suffering or pleasure. Remember Henri Nouwen's words?

"To be grateful for the good things that happen in our lives is easy, but to be grateful for all or our lives—the good as well as the bad, the moments of joy as well as the moments of sorrow, the successes as well as the failures, the rewards as well as the rejections—that requires hard spiritual work. Still, we are only grateful people when we can say thank you to all that has brought us to the present moment. As long as we keep dividing our lives between events and people we would like to remember and those we would rather forget, we cannot claim the fullness of our beings as a gift of God to be grateful for. Let's not be afraid to look at everything that has brought us to where we are now and trust that we will soon see in it the guiding hand of a loving God."[10]

What do gratitude and trust have to do with worshipping God?

_____

_____

_____

Imagine if you found out the most important person in your life was 'loving' you more out of duty than passion. How would this make you feel?

_____

_____

Do you 'worship' God from a platform of duty or passion? Discuss your answer with your community.

_____

_____

_____

Loving ice cream is not a duty. We don't wake up in the morning and say, 'in what way can I demonstrate my love for ice cream?' It's a no-brainer. It's fueled solely by passion and desire. God wants to move you from duty to desire. It is a journey that will last our entire lives. Our longings for significance were given to us by God so that we might seek Him. God is not interested in animals seeking His name. Animals are content to survive. We are content when we have found something that fulfills our longings for significance and purpose.

We get stuck when we believe that God is incapable of making us happy. We forget that we were created specifically to have significance *only* in Him. We seek satisfaction in the world. We experience letdown after letdown. We assume that God will be the grand cosmic letdown. We continue to chase after significance from our friends, our activities, our families, and our careers and are left bitter and empty. We then assume that longing for satisfaction or significance is from Satan so we either repress our longings or seek to fulfill them in ways that dishonor God. 'Take delight in the Lord, and He will give you your heart's desires' (Ps 37:4). When we delight in something it cannot be faked or con-

---

[10] Henri Nouwen, quoted in Manning, *Ruthless Trust*, 31.

trived. We're either having a good time or not. Delighting in God comes from seeing God rightly. *Seeing God rightly, delighting in Him, desiring what He desires and acting on those desiring is worship.* When we see God rightly, our old desires go away. God gives us new desires—His desires. We give our allegiance to that which delights us. Peter and his friends delighted in God and thus their lives were oriented towards His glory. Flogging, public ridicule, imprisonment—all of these were cause for humble celebration. What was meant to punish them rewarded them. It was with passion and expectation that Peter declared, "We must obey God rather than man!" These words were not spoken reluctantly or dutifully but with passion and eager expectation.

More nuggets from Brennan Manning...

"The basic premise of biblical trust is the conviction that God wants us to grow, to unfold, and to experience fullness of life. However, this kind of trust is acquired only gradually and most often through a series of crises and trials. Through the indescribable anguish on Mt. Moriah with his son Isaac, Abraham learned that the God who had called him to hope against hope was eminently reliable and that the only thing expected of him was unconditional trust. The great old man models the essence of trust in the Hebrew and Christian scriptures: to be convinced of the reliability of God."[11]

"In utter self forgetfulness, Jesus lived for God . . . The central theme in his personal life was the growing intimacy with, trust in, and love of His Abba. He lived securely in His Father's acceptance. 'As the Father has loved me, so have I loved you (John 15:9)' He reassures us. Jesus' inner life was centered in God. His communion with his Abba transformed his vision of reality, enabling him to perceive divine love toward sinners. Jesus did not live from himself or for himself but from the graciousness of the Other, who is incomprehensibly caring. He understood his Father's compassionate heart." I tell you most solemnly, the son can do nothing by himself, He can do only what He sees the Father doing; and whatever the Father does, the son does also John 15:19. "His single minded orientation toward his Father freed him from self consciousness. Lost in wonder and gratefulness, he taught us the true meaning of humility [and freedom]."[12]

"Following Jesus, the humble in heart waste little time in introspection, naval gazing, looking in the mirror, and being anxious about their spiritual growth. Their self-acceptance without self-concern is anchored in the acceptance of Jesus in their struggle to be faithful. They fasten their attention on God."[13]

[11] Manning, *Ruthless Trust*, 83.
[12] Ibid., 125.
[13] Ibid., 126.

Part 4: We Worship What We Are Prideful of:
Worship as Evangelism

Write down the first time you felt ashamed or embarrassed because you are a Christian.

_____

_____

_____

"Christians in the modernized Constantinian[14] situation saw their worship marginalized. Christianity, like other religions, was a private preference. What Christians did on Sunday was removed from what they did on Monday through Saturday. Worship was an opportunity to escape politics, business, and conflict. Far from being a time of intense engagement with the world, it was moved to a 'sanctuary'. Far from being an opportunity for people to wrestle with the principalities and powers—to wage the war of the Lamb—worship was decided never to be controversial, always to be comfortable and sentimental."[15]

Read Acts 5:12–42.
What is God showing you in this story?
Write down any thoughts, questions, or promptings.

_____

_____

_____

_____

If you were a bystander to all this activity, what would your conclusions be regarding God and the community of believers? Would you have wanted to join up in this movement? Why and why not?

_____

_____

_____

[14] The term 'Constantinian' refers to the era of church history to follow Emperor Constantine who legitimized Christianity as a worthy partner and friend of governments and societal institutions. This event began the illusion that Church, state, and culture can all share the same goals and methods to achieve those goals.
[15] Clapp, A Peculiar People, 94–95.

"Leave these men alone! Let them go! For if their purpose or activity is of human origin, it will fail. But if it is from God, you will not be able to stop these men; you will only find yourselves fighting against God."—Gamaliel the Pharisee

These words were spoken by a man whose mission was to silence and destroy the Church. Perhaps Gamaliel was growing suspicious that Peter and his friends were on to something and that he and his cronies were simply opposing God with their own works.

Evangelism is the joy-filled work of bringing good news to share with others. Just as we are always worshiping (someone or something) we are always evangelizing others by our deeds and words. A friend is called after the purchase of a convertible. He is more fired up than he has been in years as he describes his new love. Hours of cruising the strip on warm nights are anticipated. Promise is in the air. And so the life of owning a convertible is 'evangelized'. The message we speak with our lives is determined by what we actually consider to be 'good news'. A new convertible may be our good news. A newly purchased pair of shoes may be our good news. News that we truly believe is good, we share spontaneously, eagerly, passionately, humorously, seriously, convincingly. We tell this news in the form of a story and then we describe how we were changed or impacted from the event. I am guilty of failing to see that the life and message of Jesus is good news. Usually this happens when I forget that God is alive and much bigger than someone's opinion.

Reflect on what you share enthusiastically and freely with others. Based on this, what is the good news you bring to those around you?

_____

_____

_____

Often we 'evangelize' others out of obligation and guilt. Or maybe we picture evangelism as that awkward and forced conversation about abstract spiritual laws with people who are justifiably uninterested in our spiritual laws. We share our 'faith' in this manner because we do not understand the gospel as news and further we don't believe that we are sharing something that is inherently good, not just for us but also for all people. We have been told that good Christians win converts so we had better get our butts out there and save some souls.

News that is only abstract is not really news. News is concrete happenings that cause other concrete chain reactions of events, emotions, and outcomes. The gospel, when received, causes a limitless series of concrete chain reactions in our lives. We worship a God who involves Himself in our concrete existence (See Ps 103).

The gospel becomes good news for us when we allow God to involve Himself in our lives. It is good because God is good and it is news because God did and is doing something that is creating new realities, outcomes, possibilities, and hope.

If God is separated from the reality of our daily affairs then we really don't have a reason to worship Him aside from fear due to an abstract belief that there are bad abstract consequences for not abstractly worshiping Him.

The flogging the apostles received (v. 40) was the same flogging Jesus received before His crucifixion. It was 40 lashes minus 1. It was believed that 40 lashes would result in death so only 39 would be given. We go to church and afterwards we whine about the drummer having bad rhythm or complain about the song selection. These apostles went to church and were severely beaten; yet instead of whining, they rejoiced for being worthy to suffer for the Name of Jesus. Surely we should be able to suffer the fate of listening to a drummer with bad rhythm.

The Apostles didn't reason that their suffering occurred because God had abandoned them but rather they understood that they were joined to Jesus through suffering for His name.

How is it that our worship has become so self-centered and entertainment oriented? And how can your community contribute to reversing this trend? Brainstorm some creative ideas together.

_____

_____

_____

_____

_____

"The Hebrews were not an aggressively proselytizing people, but they were an intensely serious people—serious about the meaning of life, serious about covenant with God. They did not campaign to convert others to their way of life, but their faith was contagious. The peoples among whom they lived were attracted by the dazzling intensities of their worship and were drawn into the maturing pilgrimage of holiness . . . The faith of Israel had never been a popular religion, even in Israel itself where it catered to the appetite of the crowds. *It made no appeal to what the majority of people thought that they wanted in a religion* . . . The appeal was authenticity: a living God and a passionate people."[16]

Activities that are traditionally thought of as 'worship' are simply intentional ways to open our hearts to the goodness of God and the story He is authoring in our midst. News of this good God and His good story makes disconformities to the pattern of the world

[16] Peterson, *Treasure*, 24–25.

and the transformation of our lives through the renewing of our minds a real possibility. "Song and dance are the result of an excess of energy. When we are normal we talk, when we are dying we whisper, but when there is more in us than we can contain we sing. When we are healthy we walk, when we are decrepit we shuffle, but when we are beyond ourselves with vitality we dance."[17]

On this day, what in your life is worth singing and dancing about? (Put *your* answer—not the 'right' answer)

_____

_____

_____

The prophet Isaiah had an encounter with God that illustrates what I believe could happen when we center our hearts and minds on God (See Isa 6:1–8). In verses 1–4 Isaiah is given a vision of God majestically seated on a throne. His vision humbles him. "I am ruined!", he cries. The greatness of God gave Isaiah an accurate picture of himself. Any hint of entitlement, self-righteousness, or self-sufficiency was crushed in one sweeping blow. God then removes Isaiah's guilt and makes payment for his sin. Isaiah was brought to his knees by God's greatness and then raised to his feet in the aftermath of receiving God's grace.

We live in a culture of entitlements and 'knowing our rights'. "The problem with our society is not that democracy has not worked, but that it has, and the results are less than good. We have been freed to pursue happiness and every citizen has been granted the desired freedom and material goods in such quantity and of such quality as to guarantee in theory the achievement of happiness. In the process, however, one psychological detail has been overlooked: the constant desire to have still more things and a still better life and the struggle to obtain them imprints many Western faces with worry and even depression, though it is customary to conceal such feelings."[18]

When you take a look around the church, what is it that we as Christians believe we are rightfully entitled to?

_____

_____

_____

"A poor self-image reveals a lack of humility. Feelings of insecurity, inadequacy, inferiority, and self-hatred rivet our attention on ourselves. Humble men and women do not have a low opinion of themselves; they have no opinion of them-

[17] Ibid., 30.
[18] Hauerwas, *Community*, 75.

selves, because they so rarely think about themselves. The heart of humility lies in undivided attention to God, a fascination with his beauty revealed in creation, a contemplative presence to each person who speaks to us, and a 'de-selfing' of our plans, projects, ambitions, and soul. Humility is manifested in an indifference to our intellectual, emotional, and physical wellbeing and a carefree disregard of the image we present. No longer concerned with appearing to be good, we can move freely in the mystery of who we really are, aware of the sovereignty of God and of our absolute insufficiency and yet moved by a spirit of radical self acceptance without self concern."[19]

When we focus on 'not sinning' or trying to be humble, we wind up being self-concerned and sinfully pious. It's like telling someone 'don't think about a pink elephant'. Immediately they are thinking about a pink elephant. When Hunter, my two-year-old son sees something larger than life (usually a dump truck or tractor), his gaze says it all. His mouth opens slightly, his eyes get big and the corners of his mouth slowly begin to rise. May the world catch us gazing at God, seeing Him as larger than life (as we presently see it), taken by His beauty and uninterested in the things of the flesh that only serve as temporary substitutes. We will never cast away our substitutes until we are growing towards a fuller admiration for God and what He does on behalf of mankind. We cannot love God until we come to see Him as lovely. We cannot love our neighbor until we can begin to see her as God sees her; fearfully and wonderfully made.

I grew up being ashamed that I was a Christian because my view of Christianity was that it was a lame and cumbersome alternative to having fun. I was ashamed because I did not know God as One who is *worthy* to be worshiped.

Agree or disagree:

We have no message to share until we begin to be awe-struck by God's greatness and thus offer our bodies [plural] as a living sacrifice [singular] (Rom 12:1 definition of worship) to God. Share your thoughts with your community.

_____

_____

_____

We don't believe that the Gospel is good news because our view of God is so small. We have turned the Gospel into a religion, and an intricate system of 'if-then's'. We are called to bring the Gospel to people who already have religion and intricate if-then systems. The Gospel is intended to free them, not enslave them to new standards and ideals.

---

[19] Manning, *Ruthless Trust*, 121.

Agree or disagree:

Worship and control are completely incompatible. We either worship God at the expense of losing control or we worship control at the expense of limiting God to an illusionary cheerleader.

_____

_____

CHAPTER 7

Becoming Truthful

"Certainly there is some value in understanding biblical principles; even those who don't know God can benefit by applying them. But the church has continued to relate to God in the manner of Old Testament men, who were not born again and spiritually re-created in union with Christ. The church has exalted biblical principles to take the place of Jesus Christ because it doesn't know how to abide in Christ and live by his new nature within . . . Knowledge of biblical principles has become an idol for Christians to trust in and build their lives upon, instead of building them on the person of Christ, who lives within them. The church has been taught to depend on principles. That has kept it from knowing Jesus and entering into the glorious life in Him that is available here on earth. Jesus didn't come to earth to give us a good life based on biblical principles. He came to give us life—his own divine, self-energizing, resurrection life and nature—through a living union with Him. A way of life that is focused on laws, rules, and principles is carnal and cannot produce or experience what Jesus promised . . . Many Christians are satisfied to live like natural men: following laws, trying to please God, and seeking blessings."[1]

OVERVIEW:

Core Scripture: Acts 3:1–4:4.

The Kingdom of God is at Hand: A Christian is at core, intended to be a follower. Jesus beckons us, 'take up your cross and follow me . . . come to me all who are weary and I will give you rest; for my burden is light and my yoke is easy'. We cling to and chase not after ideals, projects, teachings, precepts, principles, laws, doctrines, or systems; for truth is not found in these. Our calling is to a Person who embodies truth. His words, teachings, actions, and relationships broadcast what truthful living looks like.

Repent: Truth is a clear understanding of abstract doctrines about the nature of God, the Bible, and Christianity. It has more to do with knowing right from wrong than being a lover. A truthful person is concerned with knowing the correct view on obscure details and controversial issues. Being truthful is the same as being right. Telling the truth is making sure that other people know that you are right and they are wrong.

Believe the Good News: Because our Father has been faithful in revealing the truth (Himself) to us in the God-man Jesus Christ, our chains have been broken and we are now free to reject lies, falsehood, and deceptive philosophies that would otherwise hold us captive.

---

[1] Narramore, *Tithing*, 46.

Therefore Go: Write down what you know and believe about God in one column and in the other column write down what has happened with God since you met Him. Compare the two columns. Pick one or two bits of knowledge or belief you wrote down and think of a way to test that knowledge or belief. For example, if you believe that God has power over death or the ability to reconcile a recent conflict, how might He demonstrate that through your life by calling you into action that directly reveals such knowledge to those around you? Pick one of these test scenarios and do it. Share what happened with your community.

Part 1: Re-thinking What It Means to Know the Truth.

"Hence today I believe that I am acting in accordance with the will of the Almighty Creator: by defending myself against the Jew, I am fighting for the work of the Lord." Adolf Hitler

"God-almighty in his infinite wisdom has dropped the atomic bomb in our lap. . .with vision and guts and plenty of atomic bombs . . . the United States can compel mankind to adopt a policy of lasting peace . . . or be burned to a crisp." Edwin Johnson, Cold War era senator.

Read Acts 3:1–4:4.
What is God showing you in this story?
Write down any thoughts, questions, or promptings.

_____

_____

_____

_____

What truth is made known in 3:1–10 and *how* is that truth made known?

_____

_____

_____

A recent report from the Barna Group disturbs me. "Backing up its reputation as a highly religious people, half of all American adults said that their life has been "greatly transformed" by their religious faith. This is one of the key results from a new survey by The Barna Group based on a nationwide telephone survey among a representative sample of more than 2000 adults. Overall, 51% of the survey respondents said they have been greatly transformed by their faith, about one-fourth (28%) said their faith has been helpful but has not produced significant transformation, and nearly one out of five (17%) claimed their faith has not made much of a difference in their life."[2] What disturbs me is not that only half of Americans say they have been transformed by their religious faith but rather I am disturbed that 51% of Americans claim that their lives *have* been transformed by a higher power.

[2] The Barna Group, Ltd. "Half of Americans Say Faith Has "Greatly Transformed" Their Life," hhtp://www.barna.org/FlexPage.aspx?Page=BarnaUpdateNarrowPreview&BarnaUpdateID=240 (accessed June 6, 2006).

In 2003, a Harris Interactive poll found that 90% of Americans profess to believe in God.[3] I am sickened that America has a 'religious reputation' yet is primarily marked by rampant material lust and unchecked violence. A friend of mine was in Atlanta, Georgia recently for a conference. Here she was in the buckle of the Bible Belt; a culture in which well over half the population attends a weekly religious service, prays before meals, and professes faith in Jesus. Yet she lamented on the phone that everyone she meets is a Christian yet none of them seem to know Jesus.

When you look around, clearly the bulk of American citizens are not being transformed into the likeness of Jesus who embodies the whole of truth. Yet the majority of American citizens professes faith in God and participates in religious services at least occasionally. It is probable that most Americans could provide truthful answers to the basic theological foundations of Christianity. Is this what Jesus had in mind when He said, 'You will know the truth and the truth will set you free'? Are Americans free? Is Jesus really the only thing that matters to 51% of U.S. citizens? If 90% of Americans believe in God, what sort of God are we believing in? Our government is quite satisfied in thinking that God is on our side, goes before us in our wars, and favors our national interests over all other nations. The name of God can be seen in our courthouses, on our currency, in our national pledge and in the speeches of our political leaders. Yet isn't the hallmark of a disciple one who *loves* their enemies? Consider America's extensive military campaigns (destroying your enemy). "There have been at least 11 documented military interventions into Mexico since 1836 and 6 interventions into Colombia since 1868. This history is part of a long, sordid record of U.S. military incursions throughout Latin America (at least 112 interventions into 23 Latin American countries since 1831), and worldwide (at least 400 interventions into the sovereignty of over 100 countries since 1798). More insidiously, the U.S. has engineered at least 6,000 major and minor covert operations throughout the world—destabilizing, overthrowing governments, assassinating, etc. The U.S. has threatened the use of nuclear weapons on more than 20 occasions, and used them at least twice." [4] In addition to military interventions, the US Government is seeking to increase its global presence of troops that already occupy 130 nations across the globe. In 2000, America spent more money on defense than the 11 closest nations behind it. [5]

And let us revisit the report by "U.S. News & World Report"[6] which found 59 per cent of Americans declaring that religion plays an important role in their lives; yet clearly illustrates that this 'religion' seems to have more to do with materialism, comfort, and selfish gain than it does truth. Both the U.S. government and her citizens acknowledge a God who they do not know. And if they know Him they know Him like they do Mickey

[3] Religion Newswriters Foundation. "Guide to Covering 'Under God' Pledge Decision," http://www.religionlink.org/tip_031003a.php (accessed December 18, 2006).

[4] S. Brian Willson. "Assimilation or Elimination: Pax Americana—Buy In or Check Out."http://www.brianwillson.com/awolassim.html (accessed December 13, 2006).

[5] Jay Bookman, "The President's Real Goal In Iraq." *The Atlanta Journal—Constitution*. (September 29, 2002), http://www.ajc.com (accessed Oct. 1, 2002).

[6] Ibid.

Mouse who hangs out in a fantasy world waving at by-passers. We know that he's there but his existence is inconsequential to real matters.

In the U.S., war is normal, greed is normal, excessive consumerism is normal. This is what Americans are interested in, live for, and will die for. The Church, by acquiescing to the American way of life, has abandoned the ethics of Jesus that are boldly proclaimed in the Sermon on the Mount and in place have adopted the ethics of America which the Church thinks originated in the Church via the founding fathers over 200 years ago[7]. Our poor remain unfed. Our enemies continue to fall at our hands. We continue to get richer and buy more. And in so doing, we have redefined what it means to be a Christian.

What are the differences and similarities between truth and knowledge?

_____

_____

_____

A person who is dying of starvation might know truthful things regarding the human body's need for nourishment, but that knowledge does not give them access to the nourishment they desperately need. In this case, the 'truth' is powerless information. Diluting gasoline with water to save money on your commute proves detrimental to your vehicle. In this case, the 'truth' could have been very beneficial. When Satan tempted Jesus in the wilderness, He took Him to a cliff and said, "If you are the Son of God, jump off! For the Scriptures say, 'He will order his angels to protect you. And they will hold you up with their hands so you won't even hurt your foot on a stone'" (Matt 4:6). Satan quoted Scripture—doesn't that make him truthful? Jesus didn't jump—does that mean He was not who He claims to be since He didn't follow Satan's 'truthful' guidance? In Sunday school, the boy who knew the most answers in Bible trivia was also the meanest boy when trivia was over. Jesus was aroused to anger most often by those who knew the most. "What sorrow awaits you teachers of religious law and you Pharisees. Hypocrites! For you are careful to tithe even the tiniest income from your herb gardens, but you ignore the more important aspects of the law—justice, mercy, and faith" (Matt 23:23). The fruit of the Spirit (what happens when God controls your life and not you) is love, joy, peace, patience, kindness, goodness, faithfulness, gentleness, and self-control (Gal 5:22–23). These words have significance only in the context of a person. We cannot know what kindness is apart from someone demonstrating kindness to us.

And this is why we cannot discuss truth without discussing authority. In a postmodern ethos, authority lies in the individual. Further, the authority of one individual

---

[7] "Many of America's founding fathers had very minimal views concerning the fall of the human race, and almost all were highly optimistic about the capacities of human reason to discover natural law unaided by revelation. Thomas Jefferson, the author of the Declaration, especially repudiated the idea of subordinating his thought to biblical principles." Noll et al., *The Search,* 130.

cannot be imposed on another individual. It can only be voluntarily accepted. We primarily submit to authorities that suit our tastes and standards. Thus Hollywood, Victoria's Secret, Ralph Lauren, athletes, and celebrities are given the most authority in our culture. Because we give them authority, we take their values, words, and actions as embodying some sort of truth. We care little about the substance. What matters is whose mouth that content is flowing from. Oprah could say just about anything and the majority of middle-aged women in America would believe it to be true. The Boomer generation equates truth with power or the opinion of the majority/institution. For these folks, if the President of the most powerful nation in the world says it, it must be so. In an attempt to give God's voice authority, the Church has wrongly tried to make Him cool or powerful *by the world's definition*.

In what ways have you seen the Church trying to dress Jesus up in 'cool' so that you or others would be drawn to Him?

_____

_____

_____

We reason that if we can get a professional athlete to tell kids about God that kids will be drawn to God just because a professional athlete supposedly is. This is evidence that we are way off course. *We are believing that God has no authority when we scramble for a messenger who already has their own authority.* Even *Jesus* refused to speak by His own authority. The gospel liberates us precisely because it *introduces a new authority*. Slapping a Jesus sticker on existing authorities, whether they are governments or cultural forces, only enslaves us further because doing so creates an *illusion* of freedom. Our vision of God is so small and lifeless that we are turning to professional athletes and celebrities to give Him credibility and sex appeal. It's no wonder that Americans don't give a hoot about our God. We are offering them nothing new. We are just giving them a hoop to jump through as they continue on their own paths. No one is interested in another hoop to jump through.

We have given authority to the people or things that we allow to exercise some degree of control over us. Sometimes we don't have a choice. A tsunami has authority regardless if you give it authority or not. Paul uses the language of slavery, which is difficult for us in the U.S. to grasp since overt[8] slavery does not exist in the U.S. A friend of mine has a motorcycle. One time he took me riding. I was a bit apprehensive because I knew how he typically drove his motorcycle (fast and dangerous). At first he drove modestly and slowed down at sharp turns. After a couple of minutes, all that changed. He floored it on straight-away's and accelerated into turns. All I could do was hang on. Bailing would be suicide. My voice was inaudible through the helmet and high speeds. I couldn't reason with him.

---

[8] Slavery does still exist in various socially acceptable forms. We just don't call it slavery.

148

I simply had to go with it and hope that he knew what he was doing. All of us are trustingly sitting in a passenger seat of any number of vehicles. For most of us, that vehicle is culture. The driver is a faceless entity of *cool*. He shows up in marketing and advertising campaigns, pop music, television, Hollywood, and in our shopping malls. We willingly go where they lead; all the while believing that we are 'our own person' and enslaved to nothing or no one. If pop culture is not our master than perhaps it is a subculture associated with various genres of music such as Goth, Industrial, or Grunge. The bottom line in this is finding the lifestyle that provides the greatest sense of security, significance, and satisfaction. We falsely believe that we have rejected all forms of authority and that we are controlled by nothing. Paul seems to indicate that there are only two options: slavery to sin or slavery to Christ (See Rom 6:11–23).

Who or what controls you?

_____

_____

_____

Why would slavery to Christ be any better than slavery to the world?

_____

_____

_____

I have a friend who is from Taiwan. His English and social skills are well below par. In high school, Jerry had very few friends; he drove a really nice car, rarely spoke with other people and had no hobbies aside from Karaoke. I spent quite a bit of time with Jerry just to assure him that He wasn't alone in this universe. One summer Jerry sold knives to earn some money for college. I agreed to listen to his presentation yet assured him that I didn't have $100 to buy a knife. He was the worst salesman I had ever encountered. I went to his house and he showed me a table of various kitchen knives. Also on the table were a penny and a short piece of rope that was about two inches in diameter. He abruptly handed me a knife and said, 'cut the penny'. I sliced the penny in half like it was a carrot. Next I sawed through the rope like it was a rotten pear. By the end of the demo, I wished that I had $100 to buy one of those incredible knives.

This is a great example that illustrates the difference between advertising and demonstrating. Jerry simply allowed the knife to be the knife. He didn't try to puff it up and make it more than it was. 'Here, cut this,' was his only needed sales pitch. The knife did all the work. No celebrity endorsements, no fear tactics, no 'your life is incomplete until you own a Cutco knife' stuff. I believe that Christians are fearful to let God be God. Or maybe we lack the faith to believe that He indeed will reveal Himself and make things better. We are trying to advertise God. We recruit celebrities and athletes and work church audiences into emotional frenzies to give them the motivation and enthusiasm they need in their struggle to stop doubting.

What do you think it would look like if we simply allowed God to demonstrate Himself to us as well as those around us? And does your fear have more to do with what God would do or what God *wouldn't do* if we gave Him the opportunity to demonstrate Himself?

_____

_____

_____

Keeping in mind that in Hebrew culture to hear God or listen to God is to obey God, consider the following encounter in John 8:31–59. Jesus said to some Jews who placed their faith in Him, "If you continue in my teaching, you are really my disciples. Then you will know the truth and the truth will set you free." Later on in the conversation these people lost faith because Jesus continued to tell them truthful words. Jesus made a clear divide in the conversation. "Everyone who sins is a slave to sin . . . yet If the Son sets you free, you are free indeed . . . yet because I tell the truth, you do not believe me! . . . you are unable to hear what I say because you belong to your father, the devil, and you want to carry out your father's desire . . . He who belongs to God hears what God says. The reason you do not hear is that you do not belong to God . . . I tell you the truth, if anyone keeps my word, he will not taste death."[9] They then attempted to stone Jesus.

Dang . . . How would you feel if Jesus told you that your father is Satan?

> "The ethics of the Sermon on the Mount is not what works but rather the way God is. Cheek-turning is not advocated as what works (it usually does not), but advocated because this is the way God is—God is kind to the ungrateful and the selfish. This is not a stratagem for getting what we want but the only manner of life available, now that, in Jesus, we have seen what God wants. We seek reconciliation with the neighbor, not because we will feel so much better afterward, but because reconciliation is what God is doing in the world in the Christ."[10]

[9] This passage was translated using the NIV.
[10] Hauerwas and Willimon, *Resident Aliens*, 85–86.

According to Jesus' words in John 8:31–59, what is involved in knowing the truth? In what ways has this discussion caused you to rethink what it means to 'know the truth'?

_____

_____

_____

Part 2: True Religion Is Still A Lie

"The challenge is always for the church to be a 'contrast model' for all polities that know not God. Unlike them, we know that the story of God is the truthful account of our existence, and thus we can be a community formed on trust rather than distrust. The hallmark of such a community, unlike the power of the nation-states, is its refusal to resort to violence to secure its own existence or to insure internal obedience. For as a community convinced of the truth, we refuse to trust any other power to compel than the truth itself."[11]

Read Acts 3:1–4:4.
What is God showing you in this story?
Write down any thoughts, questions, or promptings.

_____

_____

_____

_____

_____

There is a tragic and well-known story in Exodus 32 that portrays a shockingly similar parallel to the 21ˢᵗ century Church in the U.S. Moses is on Mt. Sinai with God while the Israelites are encamped at the base of the mountain. After awhile people begin to get antsy waiting for Moses to come back so they take matters into their own hands.

"When the people realized that Moses was taking forever in coming down off the mountain, they rallied around Aaron and said, "Do something. Make gods for us who will lead us. That Moses, the man who got us out of Egypt—who knows what's happened to him?"

So Aaron told them, "Take off the gold rings from the ears of your wives and sons and daughters and bring them to me." They all did it; they removed the gold rings from their ears and brought them to Aaron. He took the gold from their hands and cast it in the form of a calf, shaping it with an engraving tool.

The people responded with enthusiasm: "These are your gods, O Israel, who brought you up from Egypt!"

Aaron, taking in the situation, built an altar before the calf.

Aaron then announced, "Tomorrow is a feast day to God!"

Early the next morning, the people got up and offered Whole-Burnt-Offerings and brought Peace-Offerings. The people sat down to eat and drink and then began to party. It turned into a wild party!

---

[11] Hauerwas, *Community*, 84–85.

God spoke to Moses, "Go! Get down there! Your people whom you brought up from the land of Egypt have fallen to pieces. In no time at all they've turned away from the way I commanded them: They made a molten calf and worshiped it. They've sacrificed to it and said, 'These are the gods, O Israel, that brought you up from the land of Egypt!'" (Exod 32:1–8, MSG).

Let me point out some misconceptions that proved devastating (See vv. 25–28) for the people of Israel.

1. *Reliance upon man vs. God.* "They rallied around Aaron and said, "Do something. Make gods for us who will lead us. That Moses, the man who got us out of Egypt— who knows what's happened to him?" The Israelites forgot that it was God who redeemed them from the hand of Pharaoh in Egypt. They falsely attributed their deliverance to the wisdom and power of man (Moses). With Moses out of the picture they 'rallied around Aaron' that he might make gods to lead them.

2. *Over-emphasis and Idolization of Human Offerings.* "These are your gods, O Israel, who brought you up from Egypt!" The people assembled all their wealth and cast it into a single image and called that image 'their gods'. I find this strikingly similar to the church's zealous pursuit of bright, talented, successful, and resourced people to 'accomplish God's purposes'. Successful people lead to successful churches. Talented people make talented churches. Healthy people make healthy churches. Happy people make happy churches. The list goes on and on . . .

3. *Man-shaped vs. God-shaped.* "He took the gold from their hands and cast it in the form of a calf, shaping it with an engraving tool." If *one* individual holds a Christian community together, it is more than likely man-shaped and not God-shaped. If the common denominator in every relationship is loyalty to a leader, the community will rise and fall on the leader. If the common denominator in every relationship is loyalty to the Spirit of God, the community will rise and never fall on the Spirit of God since only God is capable and reliable to provide what we need.

4. *False and Dishonoring Worship.* Aaron then announced, "Tomorrow is a feast day to God!" Aaron blatantly led the Israelites away from God upon their request and somehow thought that such actions would provide a pleasing context for worshiping Him. We do this when we acknowledge God in our church buildings and then deny Him by our lifestyles.

5. *Denying God Where It Matters Most.* "Early the next morning, the people got up and offered Whole-Burnt-Offerings and brought Peace-Offerings. The people sat down to eat and drink and then began to party. It turned into a wild party! (Literally, 'orgy')" We play church and live like the world. A dose of church gives us comfort that we are forgiven and not going to hell. A dose of the world satisfies the cravings of our flesh that we have not asked God to remove and replace with the cravings of His Spirit. We seem to think that 'going to church and reading our Bibles' matters most to God. James reminds us that 'true religion is caring for widows and looking after orphans'.

Can you see any ways that you have fallen into the sort of deceit discussed above?

_____

_____

_____

How can we humbly and lovingly expose this deception and allow God to correct us?

_____

_____

_____

Circle the word that seems more fitting to you when you think about the word 'truth'.

LOVING or *ARROGANT*

COMPASSIONATE or *CUT-THROAT*

SELF-RIGHTEOUS or *SERVANT*

DOGMATIC or *FORGIVING*

Read Acts 3:1–4:4.
What is God showing you in this story?
Write down any thoughts, questions, or promptings.

_____

_____

_____

_____

What warranted Peter's sermon (3:11–26)? Was there a church service going on?

_____

Death is more prevalent in the two-thirds world than it is in the U.S. Perhaps this is why Acts is a puzzling book to us in the West, particularly because the majority of our churches do not represent an accurate cross section of the marginalized and impoverished in our own backyards. We are simply unaware or fearful of really knowing. So we read accounts of people sharing their possessions. We read accounts of people being healed of various diseases. Yet when we look around at our Christian circles we are mostly at least middle class. And we all have health insurance and fine doctors. Somehow, sharing possessions seems unnecessary since we all have iPod's and new shoes, and counteracting the forces of death are taken care of by the Department of Homeland Security. *We live in a culture where self-sufficient individualism and material abundance make sharing an inconvenient option vs. a necessity.*

At a fundamental level, the truth of the gospel is the announcement of life in Jesus Christ. Prior to the gospel, our fundamental human fate is death—both our bodies and our souls. Therefore, a society of people that are not forced to depend on others and are content in the illusion of eternal youth provided by anti-aging creams, plastic surgery, synthetic vitamins, and herbal supplements will have considerable difficulty receiving such a gift. Apart from a felt or perceived need, people will not go looking for a solution to that need. Perhaps this is why evangelists grow so frustrated in America. They deliver a simple message that communicates God's invitation to receive life and no one bites. Or maybe an argument ensues about other religions. We walk away concluding that the world is hostile to God and hopelessly lost. I believe God is using this trend to wake the Church up to some important things. Here is what I see God showing us:

1. The intent of the truth is not to inform but to transform. The truth is not something that is received at conversion like a certificate or diploma that is then placed on a shelf to be ignored. We now have the capability to be sanctified (changed into the likeness of God) by it every day.
2. Truth sets us free, not when we know it in our heads, but when we break free from the power of death (no longer afraid; no longer subject to Satan's power) and take hold of the power of God (a willing vessel to be used by God as He determines).
3. Truth is embodied in a person and is not a set of rules and norms. Truth is thus independent of our control or mastering.
4. Truth is not received through careful study and examination. If we know truth we know it because God revealed Himself to us and not because we figured it out.

When Peter and John encountered the crippled beggar outside the temple, perhaps his heart and mind was closed to the 'message of Jesus'. A message of 'sight for the blind' is pretty empty unless the blind are actually receiving their sight; either now or at some point in the future. However, this crippled beggar was open to the possibility of being able to walk again. It's interesting how this man was carried to the temple *every day* to beg from people going into the temple. It paints a parallel picture of our own day. We are quick to offer others religion or access to a religious community that lacks the power to give something away that truly transforms another life. Apparently the best service a religious person could provide for a cripple was to place them outside the temple every day for the rest of their miserable life. I fear we aren't doing things any differently today. Maybe the people who carried the crippled man to his spot everyday felt good and religious for performing such a charitable act. Maybe there was a rotation that several families had worked out. 'You guys bring him on Monday's and we'll take him home on Thursday's . . .'

Perhaps one of the most difficult paradigm shifts that Jesus brought was the shift from knowing and applying rules to knowing and responding to a person. There were probably rules of charity that motivated good religious people to care for this crippled man. Peter and John, unlike the religious community around them, knew that life (truth) was found in a Person and thus hope could only be found in the words and work of *that* person. All else was futile, even 'good' deeds.

Jesus said, 'unless you eat my flesh and drink my blood, you have no life in you.' Traditionally this is the Church's explanation for taking weekly communion. Yet thousands of us are having communion week after week and sleepwalking through a sundry of religious activities while neglecting the words and works of Jesus in our midst.

What benefits could come from living a religious lifestyle?

_____

_____

_____

What harm could come from living a religious lifestyle?

_____

_____

_____

Religion make us feel like saints or sinners depending on our natural ability to comply with rules and seek the favor of others. We live in an illusion whether we are successful or unsuccessful. We will wrongly think we are saints due to our own goodness or we will conclude we are sinners because we are unlike the religious folk who perform well at good deeds. 'Truth as rules' is just another in a long line of deceptive philosophies that we have been freed from (See Col 2:8) which includes nationalism, witchcraft, capitalism, communism, democracy, totalitarianism, classism, sexism, consumerism, Marxism, revenge, individualism, competition, etc. All of these captivate us, are hollow and deceptive, and depend on human tradition and the basic principles of the world. I believe that religion is one of the greatest threats to the gift that God desires to give us because it appears to be good. Most Christians would agree that Nazism is evil yet few Christians living in Nazi Germany saw that it was evil. Few Christians would agree that religion, even religion that resembles the life of Jesus, bears potential destruction of life. Religion leaves us feeling comfortable and satisfied. A religious system is most often pieced together from the popular assumptions and goals within a community or nation. The basic idea is for the people to get what they want while at the same time performing enough good deeds to create a feeling of saintliness. Suburban churches cater programs and classes to families with small children. Gen-X churches and youth groups cater programs and classes to extreme living. Wealthy churches cater programs and classes to prosperity. Suburban parents are already interested in raising good families prior to Jesus. Gen Xer's are already seeking an adrenaline rush prior to Jesus. And the wealthy are already seeking prosperity prior to Jesus. Are we just giving people what they want and calling it 'Jesus'?

Those who carried the crippled beggar every day most likely felt good and looked good by religious standards of the day. Peter and John were interested in what *God* wanted for this crippled beggar.

What occasioned Peter's sermon to the onlookers?

_____

Most of the sermons we see in the book of Acts were given to confused onlookers in the aftermath of an event that broke all their rules and norms. Someone is healed. Someone is freed from demonic oppression. Someone is arrested for following Christ. Someone gives away all they own. Rarely do we see a sermon for the sake of giving a sermon. Demonstration preceded explanation. Perhaps what is most convicting about this pattern is the fact that our lives call for little or no explanation. For the most part we are carbon copies of everyone else around us yet 'we know the truth' and they don't.

Read Colossians 2:6–10. Take a few minutes and ask God to show you how He wants your life to be impacted by the truth (a Person) to the degree that an explanation is called for. Write down what He shows you.

_____

_____

_____

_____

_____

Part 3: Beyond True Laws

"Jesus' eschatological [what will happen in the future] teaching was an attempt to rid us of the notion that the world exists indefinitely, that we have a stake in the preservation of the world-as-is. Israel had always described the world as a story, which, like any story, has a beginning and an end. Although the 'end' here is not necessarily 'end' in the sense of finality, it is the means through which we see where the world is moving. The question, in regard to the end, is not so much when but what. To what end? We cannot journey forth until we have some indication of where we are going. By indicating the end, Jesus proclaims how God accomplishes his final purposes in the here and now. So discipleship, seen through this eschatology, becomes extended training in letting go of the ways we try to preserve and give significance to the world, ways brought to an end in Jesus, and in relying on God's definition of the direction and meaning of the world—that is, the kingdom of God. Our anxious attempts to preserve ourselves lead to violence, whether we say our self-preservation is in the name of peace-with-justice or national security. So the first step to peace is letting go of ourselves, our things, our world. The cross, of course, stands for us as the sign of one man's ultimate dispossession of this world in order to inaugurate a new world."[12]

Read Acts 3:11–4:4.
What is God showing you in this story?
Write down any thoughts, questions, or promptings.

_____

_____

_____

_____

_____

Which words better describe Peter's sermon:

STORY   or   THEOLOGY

THREE-POINT   or   ENTRY-POINT

ARGUMENT   or   DEMONSTRATION

The temple onlookers watched a story unfold in the healing of the crippled beggar. This story didn't make 'sense' in the context of the story that they believed to be true. Here was something untamed and uncontrollable. Reading about truthful things is easy as long as that truth doesn't come to life in our face. Reading about genocide in Sudan is much

---

[12] Hauerwas and Willimon, *Resident Aliens*, 89.

158

different than actually fleeing it by night through the desert. Reading about God is easy as long as He doesn't come to life. When a movie producer brought King Kong to New York City and proudly displayed him in a theater shackled to steel pillars, everyone was happy. The movie producer was getting rich and the audience was entertained by such a marvelous display of *contained greatness*. All that changed when Kong broke his own chains in a passionate rage. Once uncontained, this greatness became a force never before seen. We simply cannot experience truth and control simultaneously. If we choose one, we must forfeit the other.

There are countless Scriptures that tell us that truthful living is about dealing with an actual Person that we do not control vs. mastering a set of rules or doctrines that we can control. Consider how the following Scriptures become problematic when they are interpreted as literal ironclad rules or codes of conduct.

- "When you pray, don't babble on and on as people of other religions do. They think their prayers are answered merely by repeating their words again and again. Don't be like them, for your Father knows exactly what you need even before you ask him! Pray like this: Our Father in heaven, may your name be kept holy. May your Kingdom come soon. May your will be done on earth, as it is in heaven. . . But if you refuse to forgive others, your Father will not forgive your sins" (Matt 6:7–10,15).
- "If you want to be my disciple, you must hate everyone else by comparison—your father and mother, wife and children, brothers and sisters—yes, even your own life. Otherwise, you cannot be my disciple" (Luke 14:26).
- "We know that God doesn't listen to sinners, but he is ready to hear those who worship him and do his will" (John 9:31).
- "Jesus replied, "My mother and my brothers are all those who hear God's word and obey it" (Luke 8:21).
- "When the Spirit of truth comes, he will guide you into all truth. He will not speak on his own but will tell you what he has heard. He will tell you about the future. He will bring me glory by telling you whatever he receives from me. All that belongs to the Father is mine; this is why I said, 'The Spirit will tell you whatever he receives from me'" (John 16:13–15).
- "But if you remain in me and my words remain in you, you may ask for anything you want, and it will be granted! When you produce much fruit, you are my true disciples. This brings great glory to my Father" (John 15:7–8).
- "I am leaving you with a gift—peace of mind and heart. And the peace I give is a gift the world cannot give. . . So don't be troubled or afraid. I have told you all this so that you may have peace in me. Here on earth you will have many trials and sorrows. But take heart, because I have overcome the world" (John 14:27, 16:33).

The will of God is not a formula. Forgiveness cannot be reduced to a code of conduct; it is a matter of our hearts being enabled to do so by the presence of God. The work of the Holy Spirit (a Person) involves taking what belongs to another Person (Jesus) and making it known to us so that *another* Person (the Father) might receive glory. If we are just following true laws we have missed the truth altogether. It's the interpersonal exchanges (words, emotions, and actions) of the Trinity that the Father is drawing us into and not just good moral behavior.

What entry points does Peter give those he is addressing (3:11–26)?

_____

_____

_____

Peter gives the crowd of onlookers an invitation to reorient their lives. Based on his sermon, what does this reorientation look like?

_____

_____

_____

General knowledge of God is only the beginning. We understand His values, convictions, and desires as we read Scripture. General knowledge of God allows us to answer the question, 'what would Jesus do?' Revelation of God builds on general knowledge of God and is communicated to us by the Holy Spirit (See John 16:13). Revelation of God allows us to answer the question, 'what *is* Jesus doing?' and 'how am I to be involved in the work of the Father today?' When we rely only on general knowledge we miss the interpersonal exchange that takes place between our Father, Jesus, and the Holy Spirit. Without revelation of God, we are simply God's moral agents looking forward to making it into Heaven. God has something much more special in mind for us.

Part 4: Freedom

"We may have thought that Jesus came to make nice people even nicer, that Jesus hoped to make a democratic Caesar just a bit more democratic, to make the world a bit better place for the poor. The Sermon on the Mount, however, collides with such accommodationist thinking. It drives us back to a completely new conception of what it means for people to live with one another. That completely new conception is the church . . . made up of those who are special, different, alien, and distinctive only in the sense that they are those who have heard Jesus say 'Follow me,' and have come forth to be part of a new people, a colony formed by hearing his invitation and saying yes . . . Can we so order our life in the [Church] that the world might look at us and know that God is busy?."[13]

Read Acts 3:1–4:4.
What is God showing you in this story?
Write down any thoughts, questions, or promptings.

_____

_____

_____

_____

_____

To better understand our freedom, let us first look at our slavery. A slave does not exist apart from a person or a force that makes them a slave. Satan daily assaults our senses. This is how his slavery works. He will enslave you with pleasure (addiction) and he will enslave you with pain (fear). He will enslave you by making you think you have found life when you have not. He will enslave you with guilt. He will enslave you with empty promises. He will enslave you by remaining invisible, leading you to believe that you are in control of your own destiny. Satan wants to destroy any chance of intimacy that we might experience with our Father. It is crucial that we understand both how motivated he is and how strategic and calculated his moves are.

Scripture makes our slavery clear . . .

- "I tell you the truth, everyone who sins is a slave of sin. A slave is not a permanent member of the family, but a son is part of the family forever" (John 8:34–35).
- "And that's the way it was with us before Christ came. We were like children; we were slaves to the basic spiritual principles of this world" (Gal 4:3).

---

[13] Ibid., 92.

- "Don't you realize that you become the slave of whatever you choose to obey? You can be a slave to sin, which leads to death, or you can choose to obey God, which leads to righteous living" (Rom 6:16).
- "They promise freedom, but they themselves are slaves of sin and corruption. For you are a slave to whatever controls you" (2 Pet 2:19b).

Scripture also makes our freedom clear. For each Scripture below, write down what it is that 1, makes our freedom possible, 2, what we have been given freedom *from* and 3, what we have been given freedom *for.* (Some of these verses will not include all three elements.)

"Since we have been united with him in his death, we will also be raised to life as he was. We know that our old sinful selves were crucified with Christ so that sin might lose its power in our lives. We are no longer slaves to sin. For when we died with Christ we were set free from the power of sin" (Rom 6:5–7).

What makes freedom a possible reality:_____

Freedom from:_____

Freedom for:_____

"Sin is no longer your master, for you no longer live under the requirements of the law. Instead, you live under the freedom of God's grace. Well then, since God's grace has set us free from the law, does that mean we can go on sinning? Of course not! Don't you realize that you become the slave of whatever you choose to obey? You can be a slave to sin, which leads to death, or you can choose to obey God, which leads to righteous living. Thank God! Once you were slaves of sin, but now you wholeheartedly obey this teaching we have given you. Now you are free from your slavery to sin, and you have become slaves to righteous living. Because of the weakness of your human nature, I am using the illustration of slavery to help you understand all this. Previously, you let yourselves be slaves to impurity and lawlessness, which led ever deeper into sin. Now you must give yourselves to be slaves to righteous living so that you will become holy. When you were slaves to sin, you were free from the obligation to do right. And what was the result? You are now ashamed of the things you used to do, things that end in eternal doom. But now you are free from the power of sin and have become slaves of God. Now you do those things that lead to holiness and result in eternal life. For the wages of sin is death, but the free gift of God is eternal life through Christ Jesus our Lord" (Rom 6:14–23).

What makes freedom a possible reality:_____

Freedom from:_____

Freedom for:_____

"For all who are led by the Spirit of God are children of God. So you have not received a spirit that makes you fearful slaves. Instead, you received God's Spirit when he adopted you as his own children. Now we call him, "Abba, Father." For his Spirit joins with our spirit to affirm that we are God's children" (Rom 8:14–16).

What makes freedom a possible reality:_____

Freedom from:_____

Freedom for:_____

"Even though I am a free man with no master, I have become a slave to all people to bring many to Christ" (1 Cor 9:19).

What makes freedom a possible reality:_____

Freedom from:_____

Freedom for:_____

And that's the way it was with us before Christ came. We were like children; we were slaves to the basic spiritual principles of this world. But when the right time came, God sent his Son, born of a woman, subject to the law. God sent him to buy freedom for us who were slaves to the law, so that he could adopt us as his very own children. And because we are his children, God has sent the Spirit of his Son into our hearts, prompting us to call out, "Abba, Father." Now you are no longer a slave but God's own child. And since you are his child, God has made you his heir" (Gal 4:3–7).

What makes freedom a possible reality:_____

Freedom from:_____

Freedom for:_____

"So Christ has truly set us free. Now make sure that you stay free, and don't get tied up again in slavery to the law" (Gal 5:1).

What makes freedom a possible reality:_____

Freedom from:_____

Freedom for:_____

"Because God's children are human beings—made of flesh and blood—the Son also became flesh and blood. For only as a human being could he die, and only by dying could he break the power of the devil, who had the power of death. Only in this way could he set free all who have lived their lives as slaves to the fear of dying" (Heb 2:14–15).

What makes freedom a possible reality:_____

Freedom from:_____

Freedom for:_____

Time does *not* heal all wounds. Jesus heals all wounds and sometimes, that takes time. In high school I injured a ligament on my hamstring near the inside of my knee. Essentially, I couldn't bend my leg. I loved running and I didn't want to get out of shape so

I would run with a straight left leg. After a few weeks the injury finally began to heal. The pain decreased and as it did, I cautiously tested the degree of healing by slowly bending my leg back. Occasionally I would feel a small twinge of pain. The twinges of pain would cause me to panic so I would ice it and baby it for a while. Once I could test my range of motion without feeling any pain, it gave me faith that I could resume running. I would run light for a time and as that proved pain-free, I was soon racing as if the injury never occurred. This is a picture of what it looks like when God heals us from the effects of sin, both our own sin and others' sin. The death-dealing consequences of not listening to God cause us to fear death. Death seems to rule us. Death feels fatalistic, final, and undoable. Christ tells us that He has defeated death. So we repent from our own death-ways, seek to forgive the death-ways of others, and ask Jesus to heal the effects of death-filled living. We approach cautiously because our pain is real. We carefully test our range of motion by taking steps towards forgiveness or abstaining from our numbing agents. We want to find out if the healing that God promises is actually happening. Our restored condition slowly gives us courage that something supernatural is at work. We then begin to boldly seek reconciliation with those we have wronged; we seek the welfare of those who dislike us. In short, we can boldly risk or accept rejection from people because we have discovered complete acceptance in Jesus. His acceptance of us becomes the final word. We are no longer enslaved to pleasing people or feeling pleasure at every turn. If Jesus has set us free, we are free indeed! Having our hearts healed changes our emotions but it does much more. True heart-healing enables us to live as if we were never wounded while still being able to sympathize with the wounded. Our healing gives them hope. Our lives become a testimony that death has been defeated. Every occasion of sinfulness becomes chapter one in a story in which the final chapter is healing and restoration.

Perhaps the most difficult aspect of receiving the freedom that Christ offers is what take place between our sin chapter and God's restoration chapter. God has deep respect for the free will that He has given us. We have the choice to receive or reject what God offers. What God offers must be received on His terms. "If you forgive those who sin against you, your heavenly Father will forgive you. But if you refuse to forgive others, your Father will not forgive your sins."[14] God is not a vending machine. Healing and freedom do not come to us apart from repenting from our death-ways and submitting to God's life-ways. Yet it is God's infinite loving kindness towards us that leads us to turn from our death-ways

What are the death-ways that you need to turn from, which in turn, will allow God's life-ways to flow through your spirit?

_____

_____

[14] Matt 6:14–15.

Becoming a Free and Freeing People

"The way the church must always respond to the challenge of her own polity is to be herself. This does not involve a rejection of the world, or a withdrawal from the world; rather it is a reminder that the church must serve the world on her own terms. We must be faithful in our own way, even if the world understands such faithfulness as disloyalty. But the first task of the church is not to supply theories of governmental legitimacy or even to suggest theories for social betterment. The first task of the church is to exhibit in our common life the kind of community possible when trust, and not fear, rules our lives."[1]

OVERVIEW:

Core Scripture: Acts 8:9–24.

The Kingdom of God is at Hand: Neither God nor his people exist apart from culture and worldly structures. God has given us the ability to be discerning of the culture we live in and resist those accepted norms that we believe to be offensive to God and degrading, lessening, or harmful to people and creation. Jesus exhumed the spiritual needs of people through speech and action that spoke through their culture and pointed them towards the redemption of that culture freed from injustice, greed, and exploitation. We can now do the same. The image of our culture is intimately bound to the free and unencumbered pursuit of material gain and sexual enhancement and fulfillment. Therefore, what we look like here as disciples of Jesus, will be our clearest and most impressionable message to Western culture.

Repent: We will offer to God the leftovers from our lives. We want to fully participate in the offerings of our culture. We might not admit it but our time, energy, and resources are first directed towards acquiring the ever-changing status symbols and envious lifestyles as seen on TV. Once these things are secured, then we can squeeze God in on Sunday mornings and for a few minutes each morning as we rush off to work.

Believe the Good News: God has faithfully revealed the truth (Himself) to us in the God-man Jesus Christ. Our chains have been broken and we are now free to reject lies, falsehood, and deceptive philosophies that would otherwise hold us captive. The status symbols of our culture do not define our personhood. We are now free to store up heavenly treasures.

Therefore Go: With your community, make a list of the status symbols and cultural ideals that entice and enslave you. Maybe it's brand-name clothing or being recognized for something harmless like, being smart or cool or cute. Find a way to 'fast' from these things for one week. Be creative and share what God does throughout the week.

---

[1] Hauerwas, *Community*, 85.

Part 1: Destructive Illusions of Life and Freedom

"I am making this covenant with you so that no one among you—no man, woman, clan, or tribe—will turn away from the Lord our God to worship these gods of other nations, and so that no root among you bears bitter and poisonous fruit. Those who hear the warnings of this curse should not congratulate themselves, thinking, 'I am safe, even though I am following the desires of my own stubborn heart.' This would lead to utter ruin!" (Deut 29:18–19).

"When freedom becomes an end in itself people lose their ability to make sacrifices for worthy ends. The problem with our society is not that democracy has not worked, but that it has, and the results are less than good. We have been freed to pursue happiness and every citizen has been granted the desired freedom and material goods in such quantity and of such quality as to guarantee in theory the achievement of happiness. In the process, however, one psychological detail as been overlooked: the constant desire to have still more things and a still better life and the struggle to obtain them imprints many Western faces with worry and even depression, though it is customary to conceal such feelings. Active and tense competition permeates all human thoughts without opening a way to free spiritual development."[2]

Read Acts 8:9–24.
What is God showing you in this story?
Write down any thoughts, questions, or promptings.

_____

_____

_____

_____

_____

What do verses 18 to 23 indicate about Simon's motives for being baptized?

_____

_____

Why was Simon's path, though noble and good in appearance, actually dangerous?

_____

_____

[2] Ibid., 75.

Isn't freedom about the ability and permission to pursue everything our hearts desire? Isn't freedom about the self-appointed right to take any necessary measures to protect our hard-earned and well-deserved lifestyle? Isn't freedom about having the authority to eliminate those who threaten to take it from us? Isn't freedom about seizing the brand of 'life' that most suits our personal and consumer tastes? Isn't freedom about having unlimited choices when we go shopping?

"Our culture trains us to see ourselves and others as consisting "basically of unmet needs that can be requited by commodified goods and experiences. Accordingly, the consumer should think first and foremost of himself or herself and meeting his or her felt needs. The consumer is taught to value above all else freedom, defined as a vast array of choices. We are so trained and reinforced in understanding freedom as choice that we fail to question if many of our choices are actually significant . . . Our enormously productive economy . . . demands that we make consumption our way of life, that we convert the buying and use of goods into rituals, that we seek our spiritual satisfaction, our ego satisfaction, in consumption . . . Consumerism will exercise undue influence over Christians until we desecrate this unholy taboo and stop regarding our economic lives as an entirely private matter, finding ways to open our wallets and checkbooks in front of trusted Christians."[3]

Agree or disagree and discuss:

"The church is by definition reactive and reflexive to the surrounding culture. It completely forgets the church's own culture-forming and sustaining capabilities. It denies any real tension between the church and the world; it overlooks the biblical awareness of Christians as nomads and resident aliens who will never be completely at home in a fallen world. And it aligns the church with power, against those out of power."[4]

_____

_____

_____

When Satan deceives us we are both victims of sin and agents of sin. No Christian can shirk responsibility for their own sinfulness by simply saying, 'the devil made me do it' however, Satan *is* at your doorstep working to tempt, distract, entice, deceive, and ultimately destroy you simply because he gets off on it. The reason that a Christian cannot avoid such responsibility is due to the wonderful truth that God offers us authority to overcome all of Satan's power and abilities (Luke 10:18). We are human and thus we will fall into sin but we must see that God is offering us the authority and power to overcome sin.

[3] Clapp, *Crossings*, 145, 153.
[4] Clapp, A Peculiar People, 39.

What is the difference between trying to become a better person and living in a God-given authority to overcome the power of death?

_____

_____

_____

The only enemy that we are called to fight and make war with is Satan and his legions of demons that chaotically, strategically, multifacetedly, deceptively, blatantly, and cunningly lead human beings to prefer death over life. He wants us to recognize and reject the death-ways of the KKK so that we might blindly endorse a false hope in the hidden death-ways of our government who also opposes the KKK. He deceives us into engaging in spiritual battles with weapons of the flesh (war-making, legislating morality, etc.) He wants us to feel good about abortion being made illegal so that we think the 'problem is solved'. He wants us to feel discontent about our government so that we might continue to hope in and work for its perfection. He has no regard for you and seeks nothing more aggressively than the destruction of humanity[5], both now and for eternity. Satan destroys the God-created humanity of one so that they in turn will destroy the humanity of those around them. It's a violent cycle that only God has the power to stop and reverse the damages. Satan destroyed the humanity of Osama bin Laden and in turn is destroying the humanity of American citizens by causing us to hope for *Osama's* destruction. Satan deceives us into believing that the destruction of our human enemy is life-giving for us.

Jesus tells us that praying for our enemy and offering them peace are life-giving for us *and* them, even if our enemy kills us in the midst of our choice to be vulnerable. This sort of peace-building only makes sense in the context of a sovereign God whose story is more important and more decisive than our own story or our wishes to preserve our own life via death-filled methods like killing our enemies. God calls us to make peace, not because there is a guaranteed result of peace but because it is consistent with God's character to offer such peace. The day that the Son of God hung on a cross was not a day of 'peace'.

> "The love for our enemies takes us along the way of the cross and into fellowship with the Crucified. The more we are driven along this road, the more certain is the victory of love over the enemy's hatred. For then it is not the disciple's own love, but the love of Jesus Christ alone, who for the sake of his enemies went to the cross and prayed for them as he hung there. In the face of the cross the disciples realized that they too were his enemies, and that he had overcome them by his love. It is this that opens the disciple's eyes, and enables him to see his enemy as a brother. He knows that he owes his very life to One, who though he was his enemy, treated him as a brother and accepted him, who made him his neighbor,

[5] By humanity, I mean all that a person is intended to become because of who God is and what He has done for us on our behalf. A truthful definition of humanity can only be found in the context of the God who created us.

and drew him into fellowship with himself. The disciple can now perceive that even his enemy is the object of God's love, and that he stands like himself beneath the cross of Christ."[6]

Read Ephesians 6:12. What is the difference between resisting evil and making war with those in whom evil is manifest?

_____

_____

_____

War-making and peacemaking are passionate subjects for me. My heart breaks and I am stirred to anger when I see Christians enthusiastically endorse wars and national security interests that can only be protected by violent measures. (For a closer look at biblical submission to governments, see John H. Yoder, *The Limits of Obedience to Caesar*, available at http://www.jesusradicals.com/library/yoder.php.) Ironically, often my anger conjures up desires to do violence against those who so blindly endorse violence in the name of God or one of his various causes such as U.S. patriotism, national security, or 'the war on terror'. In such moments I have simply fallen prey to the degrading and cyclical nature of violence where the only solution to end violence is more violence in increasing measures. I can only repent and ask God to show me how to break the cyclical stranglehold that violence holds on all of our throats. We cannot solve the world's problems. America cannot solve her own or the world's problems. No government can or ever will. It is a sin-filled and fallen power structure crying out for the release of God's children (See Rom 8:18–20). *As long as we think we can do good things in this world, we will either act violently as soon as we encounter those who oppose our utopian visions of peace or we will poison our own hearts by fantasizing about such violence.* God is waiting for us to cry out to *Him*. He beckons us to abandon our efforts to solve our own problems in our way or in the ways the world around us seeks to make life better.

It is crucial that we understand that just as human beings are sinful, so are our governments, cultures, and social structures. Governments, societies, and cultures are much more than clusters of sinful people simply trying to implement an achievable, hoped-for, sinless, and perfected expression of government, culture, or human tradition. The structures of this world, be they governments, philosophies, public opinion, cultures, sub-cultures, institutions, the NFL, Rotary clubs, local churches, traditions, the evening news, pop psychology, the Bill and Melinda Gates foundation, technologies, etc. are all armed for the destruction of human life. Maybe you're wondering what is so evil about professional football and foundations that give millions of dollars to end poverty. Picture it this way. You're stranded on a desert island (never mind that such a place probably does not exist) and you stumble across a food source, like a banana tree or something. You fear leaving

[6] Bonhoeffer, *Discipleship*, 167.

it for not being able to find it again so you set up your base camp right next to it and never venture so far that it is out of sight. You conclude that this food source is your salvation as it sustains your life day after day, month after month, and year after year. Unfortunately, on the other side of the island is a pay phone by which you could have called for help.

Powers such as law, government, and human tradition were created by Jesus and for Jesus (Col 1:16). We can then assume that the sum of these things, which contribute to our culture, is not inherently evil. These Powers were in fact created for good and with God-conceived intentions. Cultures and governments will not cease to exist in eternity. However, they will be reconciled and perfected to fully promote fellowship between God and man (See I Cor 15:19 and Eph 1:10). When man fell into sin, so did these power structures. The powers (law, government, culture, human tradition) have become gods in themselves (Gal 4:8) and they no longer serve their divinely ordained office of holding us close to God. These Powers unite us socially and religiously and simultaneously alienate us from God. They are like the banana tree that sustains our 'life' and enslaves us at the same time. The powers provide a lesser form of life and keep us from drinking from the well of abundant life (John 10:10). "Powers unify men, yet separate them from God. The state, politics, class, social struggle, national interest, public opinion, accepted morality, the ideas of decency, humanity, democracy—these give unity and direction to thousands of lives. Yet precisely by giving unity and direction they separate these many lives from the true God; they let us believe that we have found the meaning of existence, whereas they really estrange us from true meaning."[7] As great as the Gates Foundation is, it does not lead the impoverished and uneducated to the true God. No foundation or human institution can. Only the Holy Spirit can lead people to the Father.

What do you think 'the government' will look like in Heaven?

_____

_____

_____

Do you think there will be entertainment venues in Heaven? If so, what will those look like and how might that picture change the way you currently participate in entertainment venues?

_____

_____

_____

Jesus' death on the cross and resurrection disarmed the powers and authorities (Col 2:15). Life here and now is ruled by the power structures mentioned above. These

[7] Berkhof, *Powers*, 32–33.

structures lead us to do evil and they hold us captive to a hope and a methodology for 'good' that does not depend on Christ but rather depends on human tradition and the basic principles of the world (See Col 2:8–10). These power structures are the dominant forces that shape life on earth. Apart from the authority that Christ gives us over these Powers, we are at their mercy and our lives will be formed by the vision, ideologies, and values that these Powers embody. Christ died so that we might live under His authority and His goodness.

Reflect on pop culture or one of the various subcultures in America. What are the values, ideologies, and goals contained in that culture?

_____

_____

_____

In what ways have the Powers shaped your life?

_____

_____

_____

Our culture cannot tell us what to do or 'make us' do things. And yet, most of us fully participate in its goals, values, and ideologies. Nobody forced you to buy the brand name clothing you are wearing. Nobody is checking up on you to make sure that your hair is perfect and your reputation intact. This fact demonstrates that our culture has an enormous amount of authority over us. How is this possible?

_____

_____

_____

Do you have a problem with 'authority'?

Rejecting authority is an oxymoron. If authority is rejected, it is rejected on the basis of a *different* authority. We tend to accept authority from someone or something that validates our significance. Remember the first time you fell in love? Remember all the ridiculous things you did at that person's request because you feared jeopardizing all those good feelings that resulted from their affection for you? *It is existentially impossible to reject authority.* Rejecting authority is itself an act of self-governed authority. When we say that we have a problem with authority what we are really saying is that we have a problem with the *source* of authority that we are suspicious of or fearful of. Our problem is not with authority but with the source of authority. Most of us are perfectly willing to govern our own lives with our own authority. A rejection of all other forms of authority is simply a commitment to self-reliance. We have come to believe that the only reliable and worthy caretaker is our own self.

Reflect on your experiences and issues with authority. Assuming that it is simply a scapegoat to say, 'I just have a problem with authority,' identify the sources of authority that you have had or have a problem with.

_____

_____

_____

_____

_____

Look over the following grid. Each box briefly describes four types of authority structures. One variable is the source of a leader's authority; the other variable is the presence or absence of relationships in the community.

	Authentic Relating	Unauthentic Relating
Man's Authority	Focus is on behavior modification via reward and punishment where the reward is being allowed to be in the 'in-crowd' and the punishment is threat or coercion of jeopardizing that social status. The leader appears submitted as they offer the followers the space to 'get with the program' or 'hit the road'. A church in this culture becomes cultish as the final word comes not from God, but from the leader and it is primarily the personality or behavior of the leader that is mimicked.	Totalitarian or dictator leadership that does not have the space for response or dialog. It sees things only in black and white, right and wrong. Followers choose between leaving or agreeing with everything the leader says and does (submitting). The leader fails to understand that God speaks to and through communities and not just individuals.
God's Authority	Leaders are listening to God and leading others to do the same. Through their relationships and conversations with others, God's truth and guidance is made known as all mutually submit to God and one another. The visible activity of the Holy Spirit in the community (not just the leader) breeds trust which makes it possible for members to submit even when there is not immediate understanding. Leaders are close enough to others to be known and imitated.	Leaders are listening to God and communicate His truth and leading before the congregation. It is unapologetic but also undemanding and beckons others only on the basis of their prayerful listening and faithful action. It invites dialog because the leader does not fear losing 'their agenda' but they are not dependent upon dialog. The leader trusts the presence of the Holy Spirit to transport the spoken words into the ears and hearts of those who would desire God's will, including their own.

Which of these structures have you experienced and which do you most often see?

_____

_____

_____

Which of these structures do you believe is the most beneficial to accomplishing what God desires to accomplish in us?

_____

_____

_____

Let's assume that it is indeed true that we are best cared for under the authority of God and all that He has planned. How have abusive and man-centered authorities caused you to fear God's authority?

_____

_____

_____

_____

Is there anyone you need to seek reconciliation with?

_____

Share these answers with a trusted friend(s) and ask God to heal you of your pain and free you from your rebellious self-reliance that you might be cared for in the loving arms of God.

Part 2: The Good Life: Good for Whom?

"Whoever has the power to project a vision of the good life and make it prevail has the most decisive power of all."[8]

"Nothing is more destructive for Christians in North America than the habits of mind we are taught in public schools. The narratives we are taught in those schools obscure the church as the teller of the tale of what it means for us to know the world as world. For example, when something called 'history' is taught in a way that the church is but one character among the nations, then Christians lose the habits of mind necessary to understand the world from a Christian perspective. When history is taught as the history of nations, it is assumed that nations determine the destiny of the world, not God in God's care of God's world through the church"[9]

Reflect on the following account that took place between Jesus and Satan.

"Then the devil took him up and revealed to him all the kingdoms of the world in a moment of time. "I will give you the glory of these kingdoms and authority over them," the devil said, "because they are mine to give to anyone I please. I will give it all to you if you will worship me." Jesus replied, "The Scriptures say, 'You must worship the Lord your God and serve only him' (Luke 4:5–8).

What are the kingdoms (ministries, programs, and plans, etc.) in your midst and are you chasing after their glory and seeking power within them?

_____

_____

_____

What voices around us project a vision of 'the good life'?

_____

_____

_____

What does 'the good life' look like to you when you look around at your culture and in our churches? And is there much of a difference between the two?

_____

_____

[8] The words of historian William Leach quoted in Clapp, *Crossings*, 143.
[9] Hauerwas and Willimon, *Where Resident Aliens Live*, 47.

Read Acts 8:9–24.
What is God showing you in this story?
Write down any thoughts, questions, or promptings.

_____

_____

_____

_____

What was the good life that Simon was pursuing for himself? Did Simon's definition of the good life change after his conversion?

_____

_____

In verse 24 Simon petitions Peter, "Pray to the Lord for me, that these terrible things you've said won't happen to me!" Reread verses 20 through 23. What are the 'terrible things' that Simon is referring to?

_____

_____

Do you think Peter prayed for Simon in the manner that Simon wanted him to? Why or why not?

_____

_____

_____

Agree or disagree and discuss:
Americans have come to know God by His products and He exists in our minds primarily in terms of the desires He satisfies.

_____

_____

_____

Those who hold the keys to what we believe will make us happy are whom we will most willingly submit to. When my son Hunter, age 2, wants a cookie and knows that only I have the power to grant him a cookie, he willingly cooperates with me. If he could access the cookie himself, apart from my assistance, he would be far less motivated to submit to my authority. In the latter situation, he possesses the authority to obtain what he wants. He needs only to submit to himself.

Galatians 4 speaks of God establishing 'guardians and trustees' for those who do not yet know Him. These guardians and trustees are more specifically 'the basic principles of the world (4:3) which are both 'weak and miserable' (v. 9). Yet, for those who do not know God, they are the only thing that keeps creation from careening into chaos and anarchy. "Since man outside of Christ is a 'minor,' unable to find his way, helpless and without direction, his life would be abandoned to dissolution if the Powers were not there, to whom men instinctively entrust themselves . . . Man outside Christ stood, thanks to God's preserving care, 'under guardians and trustees'. . . The Powers take us in trust, hold our lives within a sure enclosure, saving them for the time when preservation will be overtaken and included in the more far-reaching work of redemption. Thus in the world alienated from God the Powers have a very positive function. They keep men alive. We must hasten to say that such a 'life' is not fully worthy of the name; it is life 'improperly so-called,' a life under guardians, in slavery, within which man falls short of his destined end. Contrasted with the life of divine sonship it can scarcely bear the name 'life'. Yet in contrast to the chaos, to which our enmity toward God has condemned to us, life under the Powers is tolerable, even good."[10]

Reflect for a minute on what those 'guardians and trustees' were in your life before you knew Christ. Specifically, recall those things that gave your life a sense of order, purpose, identity, or fulfillment. What structures needed to be intact to make life worth living one more day?

_____

_____

_____

Now that you have welcomed Christ into your life, are those guardians and trustees in their proper place? (You are no longer enslaved to them and your welfare does not depend on them.) Or are you still living under their authority and provision?

_____

_____

_____

Galatians 4 verse 1 says that if we are in Christ but still acting as children, we are no different than slaves. Children are slaves to their parents because without them they could

---

[10] Berkhof, *Powers*, 33–34.

not live. If my wife and I left our three-and-a-half and two year-olds to make a life for themselves, things would not go well. Similarly, if the Powers that Christians have grown to love and rely on were suddenly to be ripped from our grasp, what would happen? If America collapsed and bombs fell on *our* soil as freely as they fall on the soil of our nation's enemies, would our hope and confidence crumble or prevail? When the global economic engine ceases to work *for us* but *against us*, will our joy crumble or prevail as our houses and cars are repossessed by the banks?

Picture those things in your life that give you significance, safety, and pleasure suddenly being taken from you. Would you see it as a gesture of God's grace or His wrath and how would you respond?

_____

_____

_____

_____

When Christianity is unpopular and illegal in our country as it is in dozens of countries around the world, will we wrongly assume that we no longer have 'the freedom to worship God' or will our shouts of praise remain and even grow louder? As whole generations of young people age to the extent that all Hollywood sex appeal is lost and unrecoverable, will Christians in these generations suffer a loss of identity with all the rest who are without Christ or will it be evident that their identity is in Jesus?

Imagine walking into a daycare facility and seeing three-dozen adults wearing diapers and waiting in line for cookies and juice before story-time. Weird picture isn't it? Maybe these fully functioning adults wanted less responsibility. Why go search for a bathroom when you can just go in your diaper and wait for someone to come and clean you up? Why earn a living when you can get cookies and juice at daycare? Most people would associate such rationalized behavior with various mental disorders.

It is an equally sad picture when Christians behave (spiritually, culturally, and relationally) like children. We have been given unlimited spiritual blessings and resources in Christ. We have been given the authority of Jesus' name that has the power to forgive sin, raise the dead, cast out demons, and heal the sick. Yet it remains uncommon or exceptional for Christians in America to actually live like this is the case! Most of us are hanging out in adult daycare centers promoting the agenda of America or ensuring our comfortable and ever-increasing socio-economic status. Why do we daydream about a bigger house and not about our neighbors coming to know Jesus? *Why can trips to the shopping mall be spontaneous occurrences while reaching out to neighbors or discussing God's Word requires intentionality, structure, and accountability?*

The Powers (culture, nation, law, government, race, social status, techno-sophistication) become gods when our hope, loyalty, purpose, devotion, or identity is found in their offerings. I see Christians whole-heartedly and enthusiastically endorsing pop culture, the American dream, militarism, the death penalty, legalism, astrology, war, capitalism, and democracy. I am urgently asking us to question why any of these could be worth the allegiance, endorsement, support, devotion, or hope of God's children. Jesus came to earth, died, and rose again to free us from these Powers that enslave us.

The Powers can be likened to a cast on a broken arm. Once the arm is healed, it would be quite foolish to continue wearing the cast thinking that it served a worthy function and purpose as it surely did when the arm was broken. Such thinking would result in a lifestyle of cumbersome slavery and inconvenience just as if the arm were still broken. Disciples of Jesus should expect to hear those who do not know God express delight, allegiance, and hope in various Powers. Indeed it is God's preserving order for them *for the time being*. But for us who now know God and are known by God, we should be alarmed when we see ourselves or our brothers and sisters in Christ expressing hope and enthusiasm for these Powers and their impotent abilities to bring life and peace.

It grieves me that I more often encounter Christians who express hope in America than Christians who express hope in Jesus. America seems to be more capable of bringing life and peace than Jesus does. For countless Christians, attaining the trappings and status symbols of pop-culture seems to be the essence of their personhood and Jesus is simply the endorser of those trappings and status symbols. I know very few Christians who sincerely question or oppose the sanctioned use of violence in times of war. Why are there so few Christians who have ever considered the possibility that upward socio-economic trends for hard working American citizens is NOT part of God's agenda for His creation!? We are plainly and simply seduced by the American Dream and as a result we are alienated from God.

Reflect on the Powers that most entice (enslave) you. Again, the Powers include such things as pop-culture (I must wear brand-name clothing or increase my standard of living every year), America (I am loyal to America's agenda at home and in the world and I do not object to the methods for fulfilling that agenda), public opinion, the media, tribalism, racism, classism, philanthropy, technology, and sexuality to name just a few prominent ones. Colossians 2:15 says that Jesus triumphed over the powers by His death on the cross and those powers are now disarmed.

Look again at our story in Acts.

Simon wanted Peter to ask God to preserve his financial wellbeing, which was *the one thing that prevented Simon from knowing God!* Yet how often we pray similar prayers. "Lord, keep me free from suffering, bring me financial security, surround me with people that are fun to be with, etc.' Simon viewed God as a newly discovered power to bring himself even greater fame and prosperity; something that already defined him as a person and sustained his wellbeing. Simon was not interested in knowing God aside from his pre-existing condition. God was simply there to give him more of what he was already chasing. Like Simon, *are we simply petitioning God to help us chase those things that defined us before we knew Christ?* Do your prayers revolve around petitioning God for what your culture has told you that you *must have*? "God, help me find a way to get those $85 jeans." Take a minute to examine your heart. Can you see variations of this sort of thinking in your own worldview and relationship with God? Write down what God shows you.

_____

_____

_____

_____

_____

_____

How might things have been different for Simon if at his baptism, he surrendered to God as the sole caretaker and authority in his life? Take a moment to confess the various Powers that you entrust your wellbeing to. If your heart is willing, repent of entrusting yourself to other sources, receive God's forgiveness, and ask Jesus for His authority that you might reject these Powers and in their place, come under God's provision and power.

_____

_____

_____

In their *fallen* state, the Powers are instruments in the hands of Satan to seduce you, control you, and ultimately keep you from realizing that God is your 'daddy' (See Gal 4:6) and you His beloved son or daughter. It is the Powers that seek to influence what we have come to call 'the good life'. Dominant theology in America teaches middle class Christians that their comfort and material prosperity is the *result* of God's favor. This is an easy pill to swallow. We believe that our material prosperity is what God had in mind when He told us that the earth is ours to inherit. We scurry about our middle class lives unaware that our prosperity comes only at the expense and sacrifice of countless others. There are not enough resources in the world to enable 6 billion people to live at the level of prosperity that the majority of Americans enjoy. Therefore, competition, not love, is the only method as we all race to the top to get a larger piece of the pie.

Is your comfort and prosperity (being able to participate in the rituals and customs of your culture) the result of God's favor or is it a hindrance to knowing God more intimately?

_____

_____

_____

"Many Christians rightly consider themselves loving persons and cultivate virtue in interpersonal relationships, but they lack awareness of how their participation in various economic and political structures promotes destructive policies, institutions and social practices. Character ethics desperately needs critical social theory or it can misuse people to turn them into virtuous supporters of an unjust society."[11]

What are some of the 'good' things we enjoy that inflict violence or hardship on whole masses of invisible populations?

_____

_____

_____

I believe the greatest seduction among America's popular churches today is middle class narcissism and escapism. In such a worldview the focal concerns of Christians revolve around personal comfort and pleasure along with a denial or retreat from reality. Church activities become the icing on top of all this fun. Entire masses of Christians believe that God is quite pleased with all the happiness. Our churches encourage such thinking simply by ignoring it or even endorsing it from the pulpit. This Power, which I will call *Suburban Comfort*, stands unchecked, unhindered, and seemingly unnoticed. God has warned those commissioned to leadership in the Church through the prophet Ezekiel:

"I will raise my fist against all the prophets who see false visions and make lying predictions, and they will be banished from the community of Israel. I will blot their names from Israel's record books, and they will never again set foot in their own land. Then you will know that I am the Sovereign Lord. This will happen because these evil prophets deceive my people by saying, 'All is peaceful' when there is no peace at all! It's as if the people have built a flimsy wall, and these prophets are trying to reinforce it by covering it with whitewash! Tell these whitewashers that their wall will soon fall down. A heavy rainstorm will undermine it; great hailstones and mighty winds will knock it down. And when the wall falls, the people will cry out, 'What happened to your whitewash?' Therefore, this is what the Sovereign Lord says: I will sweep away your whitewashed wall with a storm of

---

[11] Stassen and Gushee, *Kingdom Ethics*, 74.

indignation, with a great flood of anger, and with hailstones of fury. I will break down your wall right to its foundation, and when it falls, it will crush you. Then you will know that I am the Lord" (Ezek 13:9–14).

Write down how you have seen the seduction of *Suburban Comfort* deceive and distract you away from the wonderful yet terrifying work that God is doing.

_____

_____

_____

Part 3: Jesus, Our Personal Assistant

"Following Christ is too often trivialized to little more than a devotional lubricant to keep us from stripping our gears as we charge up the mountain, trying to get ahead in our careers [and activities]. In this dualistic discipleship model, following Christ is for too many of us reduced to little more than fifteen minutes in the morning and two hours on Sunday. In this model we wind up with a highly privatized and spiritualized piety that is often largely disconnected from the rest of our lives."[12]

Read Acts 8:9–24.
What is God showing you in this story?
Write down any thoughts, questions, or promptings.

_____

_____

_____

_____

_____

What does Simon fundamentally want from Jesus?

_____

What do *you* want from Jesus?

_____

_____

_____

Why didn't Jesus give Simon what he wanted?

_____

_____

I used to think that Jesus was my very own personal assistant. He was available 24/7 to help my life run smoothly and ensure that all things fell neatly into place as I pursued my goals and projects to bring fulfillment and happiness to my life. I naively fell into the guardians that were most heavily marketed to me. First I thought violence was the best guardian. If somebody threatens you, take them out. And if your cause is noble, Jesus will

[12] Sine, *Mustard Seed*, 155.

183

help you take them out. Later in life I felt that personal happiness was the proper guardian. My relationship with God then became a rollercoaster as I viewed my happiness as coming from Him while unhappiness signified that either He was not pleased with me or that perhaps those who opposed my happiness were picking a fight with God Himself.

Think for a minute . . . God existed infinitely before He created the world. For billions and billions of years it was simply God in all His glory, splendor, and might surrounded by tens of thousands of angels worshiping Him. In a moment, God creates. His creation is small and measly as it is needy, bound by time and space, and subjected to decay. So here we are, destined to walk on this planet for 85 years or so. Somehow, we have come to think that God is consumed with us. Somehow we have come to think that planet earth is the focal point of God's existence, purpose, and significance. He lives and dies for our betterment. Apart from us, He is nothing and has little to look forward to. We have come to think that the God of the universe, who existed infinitely before He even created that universe, is somehow obsessed with our troubles and happiness. Imagine if someone called you up and shared their distress over a colony of ants outside a remote village in Belize that was in danger of dying. Would you drop everything and book a flight to Central America? Hardly. In the grand scheme of your life, a dying ant colony in Belize is unable to move you to compassion, sympathy, or the slightest bit of concern. No one in his or her right mind should be concerned about this. Similarly, the Triune God that existed before the universe *was*, the Creator that created that universe from nothing, and this King that now rules over it, has no logical reason to concern Himself with our plight. It is simply selfish to feel that God owes us anything or is consumed by us (See Ps 90). What we need to find humbling is that God's character demands that He extend Himself to us.

Your life adds nothing to God and your death takes nothing from Him.

God remains the glorious King of eternity whether we are around to see it or not. If none of us were around to witness such splendor, God would feel no sense of abandonment, rejection, or loneliness. The party awaiting all those who choose salvation will be no less celebratory even if *none choose salvation.* The party will happen with or without us. If all of creation were cast into hell, God would be no less complete and no less joyful in the aftermath.

In a culture obsessed with human-centered existentialism, these are hard words to receive. We feel that all we can know is life perceived through our own set of eyeballs. We need to become God-centered existentialists.

Some examples of how this lens leads us to subtle yet profoundly false conclusions:

Jesus died . . .
- *Man-centered Conclusion*: because he couldn't imagine life without me.
- *God-centered Conclusion*: because the Father is glorified in my redemption.

God wants me to reach out to my neighbors . . .
- *Man-centered Conclusion*: because He needs me to.
- *God-centered Conclusion*: because He wants to display His infinite capabilities to perform miracles through sinful people like my neighbor and me.

God wants to glorify Himself in us. Therefore . . .
- *Man-centered Conclusion*: He wants me to do my best.
- *God-centered Conclusion*: He wants to show me His best.

God wants me to find life in Him so that . . .
- *Man-centered Conclusion*: I am happy and satisfied.
- *God-centered Conclusion*: my satisfaction in Him will give Him glory as the Life-giver.

Jesus' death makes me feel . . .
- *Man-centered Conclusion*: sad and guilty that He had to suffer so much for my sake.
- *God-centered Conclusion*: humbled that He was obedient to His Father even when it meant suffering and death.

Can you think of other examples of how a human-centered lens leads us to false conclusions about God and ourselves?

_____

_____

_____

We cannot compare the glory of man that withers like a flower and falls to the ground to the eternal, unwavering, and unmatched glory of God. We arrogantly receive God's mercy and grace, not in humility and awe, but in a spirit of self-centered entitlement. Our consumer culture has given us this predisposition. We are brought up to believe we *deserve* nothing less than the best. We refuse God's grace, not because we are hung up on not deserving it but because God is not catering to our need for immediate felt happiness. If we can correct our thinking on this one thing, I believe marvelous things await a creation that is groaning all around us as it awaits the release of God's children (See Rom 8:18–23).

It is important for us to recognize both our self-absorption and the Powers' endorsement and facilitation of our self-absorption. One morning I was praying in my truck while parked in a busy parking lot. There was a boy sitting on a bench about 15 feet from me. He was casually fiddling with his skateboard under his feet as he stared blankly at the sky. My window was rolled down. As I prayed silently, God prompted me to pray out loud. Immediately objections rose up within me and I began arguing with God as I envisioned a 15 year-old boy thinking I was either a loony or a Jesus Freak. My stubbornness indicated that I didn't want to be known as either. Reluctantly I began to pray out loud but softly so as not to be heard. Kind of defeats the purpose doesn't it? Here I sat, more concerned about one person's opinion of me than I was about honoring the rightful position that God holds in the universe and for all eternity. Pathetic. Moments like these make me grateful that I am saved by grace and not merit. Yet these moments also grieve me as they remind me of my slavery. Let us cry out together for God to free us from our captivity to the cultural forces that spur us on in such futile directions.

That God inclines His ear to hear our cries; that God scandalously came to earth in Jesus Christ, fully unveiling the glory of God; that God generously gives His Spirit to us without limit; that God is faithful to complete in us what He began—this should cause us not to marvel at how important we must be to God but rather to rightly see the generosity, grace, and flabbergasting love of this God who otherwise does not owe us the time of day. The redeeming work of Jesus' death on the cross was rooted, not in our loveliness, but in God's commitment to be faithful to His own character.

Part 4: Seeking the Prosperity of the World with Purposed Hearts

"That first community of disciples was known as those 'who turned the world upside down'. They were constantly challenging the dominant values of their culture and paying the price. The contemporary church often is one of the strongest apologists for protecting the dominant values of modern culture and is uncomfortable with those who challenge these values. We not only have settled for a model of discipleship that ignores cultural transformation but also have accepted a model of the church that has too often chosen to silently sanction all the values of the dominant culture, unless they are blatantly immoral. [The Church] is rather called to be a countercultural community that is called to unmask the values of the dominant culture, rather than sanctifying them." [13]

With your community, discuss the dominant values that you see in your culture as well as your nation/government. Write your observations below.

_____

_____

_____

_____

_____

Read Acts 8:9–24.
What is God showing you in this story?
Write down any thoughts, questions, or promptings.

_____

_____

_____

_____

As Christians, we are not culturally neutral—it doesn't make sense to not be a cultural Christian. It would be like a car suddenly ceasing to be mechanical or a light bulb no longer being electrical. God created us to have life and to live it to the full. That life includes our cultural values—not just what we say 'yes' to but also what we say 'no' to. The mission

[13] Ibid., 164.

of God is to impart life. The life that God imparts is indeed 'the good life' yet we must allow God to determine the character and the shape of the life He is generously giving us. The good life is not gaining all that my culture has to offer and living for Jesus on the side. Are you buying in to portions of the world's vision for the good life? Are you doubtful that *all* of what God desires to lead you towards is good for you?

Take a close look.

- Are we aware of our own susceptibility to the normative influences of our culture? Are we resisting? Are we confronting the vision and values of popular culture with those of the Kingdom of God? "People of faith living amid overweening consumerism have a responsibility to resist where they can, to cultivate the good life as it is understood in the Christian tradition. So we are impelled both theologically and strategically to devote attention to the peculiarly and explicitly Christian formation of character, to building a Christian way of life or, if you will, culture."[14]
- Our 'Christian' heritage is littered with accounts that demonstrate our vulnerability to the power and normalcy of our culture. Surely there is something monumental that we must wake up to that we are currently blind to or failing to resist. The following list was not only considered normal or tolerable by Christians at the time of occurrence, but many of the following were *set in motion and sponsored* by Christians:

    1. The Roman gladiator games.
    2. The systematic slaughtering of Muslims in Jerusalem.
    3. The systematic slaughtering of Native Americans.
    4. The enslavement of Africans in America and throughout the world.
    5. Disallowing women to vote.
    6. Men receiving higher pay than women for the same work.

- Are we aware of where our felt wants and needs come from? Who tells you what you want and what you need? Let's not forget that the goal of advertising is to teach us that we have 'needs' which can only be met by purchasing the commodities and services being advertised.

God's character demands that we at times be countercultural. Look over the following scriptures and make a note of some cultural practices and rituals that might better be abandoned.

- Romans 12:1–2
- 1 Peter 2:9–11
- Matthew 10:34–35
- 1 John 2:15–17
- 1 Corinthians 10:23–24

---

[14] Clapp, *Crossings*, 148.

- 1 Corinthians 2:12
- James 4:4
- Matthew 6:19–21
- Proverbs 3:6

Write down any reflections from the above Scriptures.

_____

_____

_____

_____

_____

_____

There are two stories that I want to briefly reflect on.

In the year 586 B.C. the Israelites were carried off into exile at the hands of the Babylonians. The Japanese containment camps of WWII on U.S. soil are perhaps a close example of this sort of thing taking place in the last 100 years. Japanese Americans all across the U.S. were rounded up in masses and locked up in prison camps, forced to wait out the war under meager and degrading living conditions. The prophet Jeremiah sent these Jerusalem exiles the following words: "This is what the Lord of Heaven's Armies, the God of Israel, says to all the captives he has exiled to Babylon from Jerusalem: "Build homes, and plan to stay. Plant gardens, and eat the food they produce. Marry and have children. Then find spouses for them so that you may have many grandchildren. Multiply! Do not dwindle away! And work for the peace and prosperity of the city where I sent you into exile. Pray to the Lord for it, for its welfare will determine your welfare" (Jer 29:4–7).

Some 20 years earlier, King Nebuchadnezzar also took the prophet Daniel into exile. Read the account of Daniel's first days in exile:

"Then the king ordered Ashpenaz, his chief of staff, to bring to the palace some of the young men of Judah's royal family and other noble families, who had been brought to Babylon as captives. "Select only strong, healthy, and good-looking young men," he said. "Make sure they are well versed in every branch of learning, are gifted with knowledge and good judgment, and are suited to serve in the royal palace. Train these young men in the language and literature of Babylon." The king assigned them a daily ration of food and wine from his own kitchens. They were to be trained for three years, and then they would enter the royal service. Daniel, Hananiah, Mishael, and Azariah were four of the young men chosen, all from the tribe of Judah. The chief of staff renamed them with these Babylonian names: Daniel was called Belteshazzar. Hananiah was called Shadrach. Mishael was called Meshach. Azariah was called Abednego. But Daniel was determined not to defile himself by eating the food and wine given to them by the king. He asked the chief of staff for permission not to eat these unacceptable foods. Now God had given the chief of staff both respect and affection for Daniel. But he responded, "I am afraid of my lord the king, who has ordered that you eat this food and wine. If you become pale and thin compared to the other youths your age, I am afraid the king will have me beheaded." Daniel spoke with the attendant who had been appointed by the chief of staff to look after Daniel, Hananiah, Mishael, and Azariah. "Please test us for ten days on a diet of vegetables and water," Daniel said. "At the end of the ten days, see how we look compared to the other young men who are eating the king's food. Then make your decision in light of what you see." The attendant agreed to Daniel's suggestion and tested them for ten days. At the end of the ten days, Daniel and his three friends looked healthier and better nourished than the young men who had been eating the food assigned by the king. So after that, the attendant fed them only vegetables instead of the food and wine provided for the others. God gave these four young men an unusual aptitude for understanding every aspect of literature and wisdom. And God gave Daniel the special ability to interpret the meanings of visions and dreams" (Dan 1:3–17).

These stories bring to light a tension that can only be navigated in the power and leading of the Holy Spirit. Daniel and his three furnace friends refused to defile themselves by partaking of the royal amenities. As a result they prospered. Daniel and his friends found a way to be immersed in their culture yet abstain from those practices that would have led to their defilement. Their abstinence yielded prosperity; not Babylonian prosperity, but godly prosperity. Shortly after, God exalted Himself greatly through their countercultural obedience by delivering Daniel from the mouths of hungry lions and Abednego, Shadrach, and Meshach from the flames of a fiery furnace. It all began with 'a purposed heart' to abstain from a defiling culture.

Jeremiah exhorted the Israelites to set up camp in a foreign land while seeking the prosperity of that land. We are seeking prosperity but we have allowed Babylon to define 'prosperity'.

What is the prosperity that God has in mind for twenty-first century America?

_____

_____

_____

In what ways do we need to purpose our hearts as we go about our lives in 21ˢᵗ century America?

_____

_____

_____

CHAPTER 9

Disciple Making: It Takes One
(or more) to Make One

"Welcome to the living Stone, the source of life. The workmen took one look and threw it out; God set it in the place of honor. Present yourselves as building stones for the construction of a sanctuary vibrant with life, in which you'll serve as holy priests offering Christ-approved lives up to God . . . You are the ones chosen by God, chosen for the high calling of priestly work, chosen to be a holy people, God's instruments to do his work and speak out for him, to tell others of the night-and-day difference he made for you—from nothing to something, from rejected to accepted. Friends, this world is not your home, so don't make yourselves cozy in it . . . Live an exemplary life among the natives so that your actions will refute their prejudices. Then they'll be won over to God's side and be there to join in the celebration when he arrives" (I Peter 2:4–5, 9–12, MSG).

Overview:

Core Scripture: Acts 17:1–9 and I Thessalonians 1:4–10 and 2:13–15.

The Kingdom of God is at Hand: God's loyalty, in respect to His creation, is to reconcile all things to Himself through the death and resurrection of His Son, Jesus Christ. Every breath we take rests on God's commitment to forgive and redeem us vs. destroying us. God is on a mission of calling all men and women to Himself; to receive His forgiveness, and to know His love. He has sent His Church to be a sign of His kingdom. Like the hors d'oeuvres before the main course, we are sent to give the world an appetite for spending eternity with God. God did not have to involve us in His mission. He did not create us to be passive recipients of His grace but active recipients.

Repent: The most effective way to reach people for Christ is to sponsor the most hip local church that can offer the most attractive programs and boast a pastor with dynamic sermon-giving abilities. As a normal churchgoer, the best contribution that you have to offer is your attendance, your tithe, and your sponsorship of your lead pastor. After all, he or she is the one doing the real ministry; your job is to support their ministry and calling. A congregation that is doing things well, will hit the 80/20 principle square in the nose: 20% of the people doing 80% of the work and the other 80% of the people doing the remaining 20% of the work. We look to 'our church' to do the work of reaching our neighbors. It is 'our church' that is supposed to welcome sinners (once per week on Sunday morning) and it is our pastor's job to encourage, spur, and speak truth to the person sitting next to us.

Believe the Good News: God has given gifts to all of His people; let us discover the freedom in presenting ourselves as an offering to God and a gift to the world. Let us not just be warm bodies but active bodies; active because God has equipped us for ministry to the Church and to our neighbors. Let us, as David did towards Goliath, run fast to the enemy line, confident that we are called, not because of our own abilities, but because God invites us to live an impossible life.

Therefore Go: Take some time to meditate on Ephesians 4:7,11–14; Galatians 5:22–23; and 1 Corinthians 12:4–11. Ask God to show you how He has made you and gifted you to take part in building His Church. Share these conclusions with your community and help one another grow up into the work that God is generously laying before you.

Part 1: Rethinking Our Division of Labor

Read Acts 17:1–9.
What is God showing you in this story?
Write down any thoughts, questions, or promptings.

_____

_____

_____

_____

_____

The church I grew up in would often host itinerant or traveling preachers. They would come for a couple of weeks, preach a couple of sermons and be on their way to the next town. One time we hosted one of these preachers in our home. All of my memories of this are pleasant. I don't recall my family being hauled out onto the street and brought down to the police station. It felt cool to have a stranger in our house who was also the talk of the church for a brief period of time. In some weird way it made me feel more important. Paul was on a similar journey. Thessalonica was one of many stops for him throughout the eastern and northern Mediterranean. Paul spent three weeks in Thessalonica during which time he stayed with a man named Jason. Our text records Paul preaching only three sermons. During those three weeks Paul stirred up enough trouble, simply by talking about Jesus, to land Jason and several others in court.

Read I Thessalonians 1:4–10 and 2:13–15.

The church I grew up in also supported a missionary in Mexico who would come and preach to us once a year. He was a fiery Norwegian who had no qualms about letting it fly from the pulpit. I could see his frustration year after year. He would look out at us from the pulpit and he seemed to have a look on his face that said, 'wasn't I just here preaching to the same people?' The point is that we were the same. There was no transformation happening. The point is that he needed to come back year after year and preach the same message because no one was getting it. Paul enthusiastically told the Thessalonians (remember that He was only with them for three weeks), "And now the word of the Lord is ringing out from you to people everywhere, even beyond Macedonia and Achaia, for wherever we go we find people telling us about your faith in God. We don't need to tell them about it, for they keep talking about the wonderful welcome you gave us and how you turned away from idols to serve the living and true God" (1 Thess 1:8–9).

Some of the Jews and non-Jews in the first century were stuck on nationality, gender, heritage, ritual cleansing, and social status. Paul aggressively confronted such thinking which limited the power of Christ in their lives. He boldly proclaimed to those in Galatia, "For you are all children of God through faith in Christ Jesus. And all who have been united with Christ in baptism have put on Christ, like putting on new clothes. There is no longer Jew or Gentile, slave or free, male and female. For you are all one in Christ Jesus" (Gal 3:26–28). And "Now that you know God (or should I say, now that God knows you), why do you want to go back again and become slaves once more to the weak and useless spiritual principles of this world? You are trying to earn favor with God by observing certain days or months or seasons or years. I fear for you. Perhaps all my hard work with you was for nothing" (Gal 4:9–11).

The Church in America is suffering from a pandemic of spiritual infancy. A healthy body derives its health from a combination of appropriate levels of nutritious food and adequate exercise. Some of our churches are overfed. The amount of spiritual calories being consumed is simply being deposited as spiritual fat into a body that is not exercising. Other churches are performing high levels of exercise on an inadequate food supply. It is here that the earthworm becomes our teacher. Buried in the dirt, they must eat to move and move to eat. Eating and moving are one and the same thing. Our churches are not set up this way. Our churches are primarily set up for eating. We're all about sermons, lessons, memorization, singing uplifting music, reading, quiet times, and Sunday mornings; but no real action on the street. Even our 'service projects' are often based not on genuine needs in our communities; but have been cleverly turned into a commodified form of recreation.

"To *each one of us* grace has been given as Christ apportioned it . . . He gave some to be apostles, some to be prophets, some to be evangelists, and some to be pastors and teachers, to prepare God's people for works of service, so that the body of Christ may be built up until we all reach unity in the faith and in the knowledge of the Son of God and become mature, attaining to the whole measure of the fullness of Christ. Then we will no longer be infants, tossed back and forth by the waves" (Eph 4:7,11–14, NIV).

Have you ever thought of yourself as a pastor? How about an apostle or a prophet? I have met pastors that didn't know the first thing about pastoring (shepherding God's people and feeding them with His Word). They were simply pastors because they were 'in charge' of a local church and paid to do it. Have you ever considered that being called to teach or pastor is in fact *a gift*? Or would it be difficult to see it as anything more than a burden or a job or an expectation to live up to?

Most of our churches and ministry organizations are structured in mercenary fashion. They function by procuring resources from large masses of people so that a handful of qualified professionals can be hired and paid to fulfill all the tasks required to complete the stated mission. God's mission is to involve *all of us* in His work in ways that transform us and require us to change our habits and priorities. Vocational pastors are not called to do the work that God is calling a congregation to do. And mission organizations are not called to acquire sponsorship from local churches but rather are called to lead local churches into the work of mission.

Do you believe that God has given you gifts for the purpose of 'preparing God's people for works of service'? Ask the Holy Spirit to show you how you have been created and gifted. Write down anything that comes to mind.

_____

_____

_____

_____

Paul lists four giftings in the above Scripture. Statistically, we might say that in a room filled with 100 people, 25 are pastor/teachers, 25 are evangelists, 25 are apostles, and 25 are prophets. It's a picture that is difficult to see. We've been trained to see this: In a room filled with 100 Christians, 1 is the pastor and teacher, 1 is the evangelist (missions pastor), the apostle lives in the next town, 98 show up to listen to the pastor preach, and what's a prophet? Why is it so difficult to fathom that *all are gifted*? Why do we resist the possibility that 1 out of 4 of us could be 'pastors'? Not pastors on paid church staff but individuals who have been gifted to care for and teach the Word of God to those in our midst. On top of these gifts that are empowered and executed by the Holy Spirit, we also receive the fruits of the Spirit, which include love, joy, peace, patience, kindness, goodness, faithfulness, gentleness, and self-control (See Gal 5:22–23).

Every person who has been baptized in Jesus Christ could write a résumé of sorts that has nothing to do with them and everything to do with the grace of God. Therefore it is not self-boasting but boasting in the generosity of God. Mine might look something like this:

> *"Because of God's generosity to include me in his mission of reconciling all of creation, God has graciously created me with a knack for shepherding those in my midst and establishing His Church. He enables me to do so in a manner that elicits joy, peace, and love in my heart. Further, He equips me to do this in a manner that is loving, kind, gentle, consistent with truth, patient, faithful, and self-controlled. As if that wasn't enough, God further manifests Himself within me as the Holy Spirit gives me wisdom, knowledge, prophecies, and faith to share with those around me."*

Take a few minutes to reflect on who God has made you to become. Meditate on Ephesians 4:7,11–14; Galatians 5:22–23; and 1 Corinthians 12:4–11. A chocolate chip cookie is not a chocolate chip cookie without flour, or salt, or chocolate chips. Similarly, the gifts and fruits listed in these Scriptures are the ingredients of humanity (the image of God) and the substance of what makes the Church a moving organism. And you have been given a measure and combination of these gifts 'just as Christ has determined' (I Cor 12:11). Write down your résumé below as I did, based on what God shows you about yourself. When your community gathers, share what you wrote and wrestle through the emotions of false humility and awkwardness together. Maybe you could write similar statements for one another to affirm that God has gifted *all* of you to share in God's mission of reconciling the world to Himself.

_____

_____

_____

_____

_____

_____

Can you see that God has gifted us in ways that has nothing to do with our own abilities or the accepted limits of human potential?

God's model almost feels top heavy; like a software company hiring 100 CEO's with impressive degrees and ridiculous abilities. Or maybe it looks like 23 firefighters putting out a small campfire with four ladder trucks each pumping 50 gallons of water per second. Is God really *that* generous? Would He really share *that much* of Himself with His people? We know that God can do the impossible but do we know that He is waiting for us to realize that He has chosen to fulfill those impossibilities through us? We know that Jesus has defeated Satan but do we know that He has *completely crushed him* and that all authority belongs to Jesus; making us free to 'make disciples of all nations' (Matt 28:18–19)?

Imagine if you were stranded in a remote place with 100 other Christians (none of which were formally 'in ministry'). No one has a copy of the Bible. How would you organize yourselves? Who would be the pastor? Who would have spiritual authority? Who would head up the children's programs? Who would teach Sunday School? Who would comfort people when they were distressed? Who would gather food? Would you 'name' your church? What denomination would you belong to? How would you resolve conflicts? And who is going to perform the ceremony for that couple that is engaged to be married?

It seems more natural to listen to and obey the Spirit in situations of crisis or difficulty. We throw our hands in the air and beg God to show us what to do. All other times we are just falling into our predetermined role. In the situation described above, wouldn't those who had been gifted to care for others do so? Wouldn't those who had knowledge of God's Word share that knowledge with the community? Wouldn't all the adults unite to raise and instruct the children in the community? Wouldn't talk about denominational affiliation be fruitless and hilarious in a time of crisis? Urgency has an amazing ability to create unity and cooperation. There just isn't the time or energy to manage large egos and fruitless agendas.

In your opinion, have we lost sight of the urgent nature of our calling? And has this lack of urgency made room for our preoccupations with and squabbling over secondary doctrinal matters and man–made structures of authority?

_____

_____

_____

_____

Envision a community that understands God's generous gifting to all people for the advancement of His own agenda and purposes. Because their eyes are on Christ, this community also embodies God's instructions to mutually submit to one another (Eph 5:21). Competition and power plays occasionally creep up but the community's attentiveness to the voice of God always brings them back to reverence for Christ. Members stray occasionally but they are quickly brought back to God and His wishes for their life. When you picture this community, do you see a necessity to retain pre-existing cultural codes of conduct (limited roles for women, only powerful and influential people can be effective witnesses of God, etc)? Do you see a need for man-made authority structures in a community like this? Or can we trust the authority of God to shape us 'as He determines'? Why or why not?

_____

_____

_____

_____

And why is this sort of community so rare?

_____

_____

_____

_____

Read Ephesians 6:10–20. Paul instructs us to 'put on' the armor of God. Take some time to meditate on these verses. Consider that each piece of armor is a discipline or practice. Write down what it would look like to *practice* each piece of God's armor. Discuss your findings with your community.

_____

_____

_____

_____

_____

_____

Part 2: Rethinking Hospitality:
Not Owning or Controlling the Result

"You didn't think, did you, that just by pointing your finger at others you would distract God from seeing all your misdoings and from coming down on you hard? Or did you think that because he's such a nice God, he'd let you off the hook? Better think this one through from the beginning. God is kind, but he's not soft. In kindness he takes us firmly by the hand and leads us into a radical life-change" (Rom 2:3–4, MSG).

"There can only be two basic loves, the love of God unto the forgetfulness of self, or the love of self unto the forgetfulness and denial of God." Saint Augustine

Read Acts 17:1–9 and I Thessalonians 1:4–10 and 2:13–15.
What is God showing you in this story?
Write down any thoughts, questions, or promptings.

_____

_____

_____

_____

_____

I love how Jesus went to the homes of others. He wasn't sitting around at His house waiting for some folks to show up and ask Him questions. He invites Himself to lunch at the home of Zacchaeus and hangs with Matthew and his carousing cronies. I believe this was the physical manifestation of God's constant search for vessels in which His Spirit could dwell. Hospitality begins with our willingness to welcome God without seeking to control, manipulate, or deceive Him. I often wonder what the scene looked like at Matthew's place. I don't picture Matthew and company on their best behavior. Matthew simply followed a mysterious man claiming to be the Messiah to his own house. Odd. Have you followed Jesus back to your own house? Have you given Him a good look around the place, uninhibited without trying to make things look better than they are? It's probably the one place we would rather not venture with God; home. At home is where we are our ugliest. Home is where we unlock our secrets because usually there is no one watching. And when someone comes over for dinner we hide these secrets safely behind lock and key.

God has unfathomable patience and self-control to allow us to be *us*. Have you ever had an encounter with someone who could look right through you and see that you were hard at work protecting wounds and keeping secrets? Scary, isn't it? Maybe we need to remind ourselves that God sees through all of our efforts to be good, likable, presentable, and acceptable. He knows our secrets and fortunately He is not ill-equipped to deal with those dirty secrets. In fact, He offers healing in response to our confession. He offers forgiveness in response to our repentance. And He offers the indwelling of His Spirit for those who 'keep asking' for it. God wants to put you on the road towards healing, forgiveness, and the indwelling of His Spirit. Indeed, His desire is that we would be restored by His love, empowered by His forgiveness, and transformed by His Spirit. The starting point for these things is vulnerability with God. If we want to look at offering hospitality to strangers in our midst, we must first become hospitable to the Spirit of God—confessing, repenting, and petitioning. We cannot offer hospitality to our neighbors until we have begun to be vulnerable and unpretentious with God.

Picture yourself walking into a coffee shop. God is at one of the tables in the corner: the Father in one chair, Jesus in another, and the Spirit in another. They are each seated in big soft chairs and as you enter they rise to their feet and embrace you in a way that causes you to truly believe that your presence has been anticipated and longed for. Afterward they sit down and offer you the remaining empty seat. "Please, join us!", declares the Spirit. A rosewood coffee table displays an array of tasty treats. In a matter of seconds, you are convinced that in no way are you intruding on or interrupting a prior agenda. Somehow, you are unaware of what is expected of you so you feel an amazing freedom to speak freely and refrain from being bashful about the tempting treats spread before you. It's all grins as you settle into your chair recapping your day in between mouthfuls of pastries. You spend an amazing two or three hours with God. The conversation was rich and you are left with a deep sense of awe and reverence for how it could possibly be so good being with these Three. At no point were you self-conscious and paralyzed by fears of rejection or ridicule. The expressions of delight on their faces were simply too convincing. Then the Father gets a sincere but warm expression on His face, puts His hand on your knee and gently says, 'we want you to know,' as He looks around at His Son and the Spirit, 'we know everything'. And before you can respond, He scoops you up in a bear hug that for a moment takes your breath away. Tears emerge from the corners of your eyes because your heart is overwhelmed by His love and sincerity and your mind knows that He has just told you the truth. The two realities feel frighteningly contradictory, as if you can only choose one and reject the other. His embrace does not let up and after a time Jesus and the Holy Spirit join the family hug. You wonder how they could know everything and yet embrace you like none of it mattered. You are now completely encircled in the love of God. Your mind races for an explanation; a defense, an apology, a verbal commitment to try harder next time—but you are unable to speak as your heart is washed with this embrace of healing, redemption, restoration, reconciliation, and love.

Journal any reflections from picturing yourself in this scene.

_____

_____

_____

_____

_____

_____

_____

As we learn to allow our hearts to be a hospitable environment for God (no pretending, no hiding, and no rebelling), God is able to make our hearts (and our homes) a place of hospitality for others. Jesus said that when we love Him, as demonstrated by our obedience, He and His Dad would come to us and make their dwelling place with us (See John 14:23). That sounds a lot like good hospitality. God made His heart public in Jesus Christ and He invites us to do the same by making our own hearts public to our neighbors, friends, and enemies. Popular understandings of hospitality seem to be based around glossy veneers, performance anxieties, and self-consciousness. Does my table look as good as Martha Stewart's? Do the colors in my living room elicit pleasant moods from those who walk in the door? Let's assume that hospitality has more to do with the condition of our hearts than the condition of our casseroles and furniture. That being said, let's take a look into the heart of God to see the ways that He welcomes us and other strangers.

1. *God has made His heart known to all humanity.* Ultimately, it was this endeavor that put Jesus on the cross. Our greatest fear is that our offering to our neighbor will be rejected. So we either refuse an offering or ensure that our offering is exactly what they want. Jesus willingly inhabited the same space with others without hiding His heart and purest motives towards them. He suffered rejection and death as a result.

Are we willing to be rejected by our neighbors simply because we have shown them the heart of God?

2. *God is a respecter of personhood.* In the Trinity we see three distinct and unique Persons. None of them is trying to be the other and none are competing for power, position, leadership, popularity, or favor with the others. There is mutual and unconditional love that flows freely between and among them. Jesus displayed this by freely accepting others without coercing or manipulating them into moral behavior.

What would it look like to welcome someone and have no expectations of how you must be treated, thanked, or thought of in return?

3. *Jesus was other-centered and surrendered to the Father; He felt no need to prove Himself or defend and protect his mission to redeem humanity.* Jesus was not out to *convince* the world of truth by His own authority and power. He trusted the Father's ability to draw others to Him. He trusted the Spirit's ability to fill the hearts of men and women in His wake. Jesus faithfully revealed the grace and truth of God, which consequently revealed longings and questions to which God could be the only answer. To some this truth was liberating but to others it was a stumbling block. Jesus seemed okay with this and was thus able to freely love people without expecting their allegiance in response.

What if we could lay aside our goals for our neighbor's conversion and our church's growth and simply love people? Why do we search for proof that we are accomplishing something?

4. *God truly meets us where we are.* Transformation happens when one can begin to see his or her own story intersecting, clashing, or merging with God's story. If the gospel is always in a parallel universe that never crosses over into ours, it will not become real and transformational in our lives. Hospitality is displaying the love of God without pressure or coercion whereby giving others the freedom to lay aside personal grandstanding and figure out their *real* story (seeing the true condition of their own hearts). It is here that God's story breaks into our neighbors' lives as we love and accept them with no strings attached.

What if we could meet our neighbors and be open about where we truly are? What if we could courageously take our mask off so that our neighbors might be more inclined to be real?

5. *God is vulnerable yet not self-conscious.* Jesus risked and faced rejection because He was secure in the love He shared with the Father and the Spirit. His identity was not in the successful implementation of proven strategies for dynamic and effective ministries. He lived to please His Dad and thus was free to do exactly what His Dad asked of Him.

What if our identities rested secure in the love we find in the Trinity? Might we be freed from our endless clamoring for attention and approval from those around us?

6. *God values love and relationship over being right and winning.* When we take a posture of defending or enforcing our ideas against the ideas of another, we immediately create a wall between the other and ourselves. Most of us have formulated ideas in an attempt to make sense of the painful things in our lives that we are struggling to accept. Behind our ideas are fears, pain, isolation, and a desire to be known and understood. When we attack the other's ideas we are invalidating both their experience as well as the existential crisis that they find themselves in. Being right and winning arguments are futile objectives. There are existential and theological questions that we must flat out admit we cannot answer or explain. When we have brought our own pain to God and have experienced His healing touch, we are postured to love our neighbor versus correcting our neighbor.

What if we thoughtfully examined our need to be right and allowed God to replace it with a desire to be loved and to love? Can we lay aside our agendas to convert others to our point of view and trust that God desires to heal and lead us as well as our neighbors?

7. *Our understanding of personhood and community are derived from the Trinity.* The Trinity is the relational matrix by which we understand what good relationships look like. Within the community of the Trinity we see mutual love, acceptance, admiration, and other-centeredness. Each Person of the Trinity is constituted by the presence of the other two persons. Each Person in the Trinity, Father, Son, and Spirit retain particularity and distinctiveness because of the separate space they inhabit. In other words, the expressive presence of One does not diminish or overpower the expressive presence of the Other Two. Similarly, we allow the person across the table from us to be who they are without lessening our own presence. Yet our attention is on them. We seek to be aware of them and not ourselves. We listen to understand in order that they might articulate their story and thus find unity in our friendship and acceptance. We feel no need to defend our beliefs. We are not threatened and thus feel no need to control or dominate. We are free to be vulnerable, real, and authentic because we are secure and loved in the community of the Trinity.

What if God's acceptance of us could give us new strength to step into relationships as He does? What if we were healed from our own painful experiences of rejection and thus empowered to welcome others as they are? What if we had the strength to respond to hate and bitterness with the same level of confidence and tenderness that God has responded to our own hate and bitterness?

8. *When we are in relationship with God we lack nothing.* We approach people as free persons and through our contentedness in the loving community of the Trinity, we are free to welcome persons into this community with a posture of unconditional giving because we do not need that person as a possession. This is an implication that will take a lifetime to work out. Unfortunately none of us will be fully united to God until Christ returns so we journey towards contentedness in God and thus

towards our capacity to love unconditionally. It is only when we seek to echo the communal life of the Trinity that we are able to honor one another with the space to be free persons yet also allow us to participate in the other's personhood resulting in the reconciliation of creation.

What disciplines would be required in order for you to begin your days conscious of God's intimate embrace?

9. *God's personhood is constituted by the way in which God relates with Himself. Therefore, our personhood is constituted by the way in which God relates to Himself and us as persons created in His image. Our personhood is not defined by some prior universal definition or cultural construct based on individualism or self-actualization. The surest reality in all the universe is the relational giving and receiving that goes on between Father, Son, and Holy Spirit. As persons, we derive our being and particularity from relationships that we have with those around us. If we are in relationship with God, we will relate to others in His image. If we are not in relationship with God, we will relate to others in some other image. Our personhood is at the mercy of who and what we choose to associate with and in what manner.*

What might it look like if our self-image and identity rested not on our individuality or our cultural context but on the way that God relates to Himself?

Made in God's Image:

Maybe hospitality is as simple as a willingness to be transformed into the image of God *in the presence of others.*

The image of our Trinitarian God:
- Our Father: The *Giver* (of His Son and His Spirit)
- Jesus, our Brother: The *Revealer* (of our Father's heart)
- The Spirit: The *Transformer* (of darkness into light)

To be human then is to:
- From our Father, *receive* the gifts of His Son and His Spirit.
- *See* the heart of our Father in the gift of His Son.
- *Be transformed* from darkness into light by the Spirit.

Whereby we:
- *Give generously* unto others what we have generously been given.
- *Show* the heart of our Father as we continually prepare our hearts to be the dwelling place of God's Spirit.
- *Transform* creation as God's light shines through us

To be human is to first be hospitable to God—to unpretentiously step into His presence and allow His kindness towards us to lead us to both repentance and worship (obedience). In being hospitable to God, we discover that as we are conformed by God to the image of Jesus, we become a place of hospitality to others that enables them to receive and see the things of God and be transformed by His presence in us.

Part 3: Rethinking Evangelism: Having and Telling a Story

Read Acts 17:1–9 and I Thessalonians 1:4–10 and 2:13–15.
What is God showing you in this story?
Write down any thoughts, questions, or promptings.

_____

_____

_____

_____

_____

Note some things in the verses in Thessalonians that were *done* (by God and the Thessalonians) or some things that *happened* as a consequence of someone's actions. Look for verbs.

_____

_____

_____

Note some things that were spoken.

_____

_____

_____

Western civilization is held intact by clever wordsmithing and pop philosophy. Due to our endless options for entertainment and escape, we are highly disconnected from the actual story that is being written by our choices and beliefs.

> *Our obsessions with games, sporting events, celebrities, technology, TV, and many other tantalizing forms of entertainment venues indicate that we are more interested in made-up stories than real stories.*

We would rather be happy in a fantasy than uncomfortable with real and consequential things. So what is real? God is real, what God has done, is doing, and promises to do is real. What God will do in 8,424 years is more real than which team in the NFL won the super bowl last season. It happened but it is inconsequential. God's kingdom is real. The life that God offers us is real. And death is real. These things are all concrete happenings that every person will be forced to reckon with some day. From these realities flow real stories. David defeats Goliath. Ezekiel speaks the words of God. Moses parts the Red Sea with his staff. Water flows from a rock in the middle of a hot dry desert. Jesus is executed, pronounced dead, but shows up three days later. Peter heals a crippled beggar. Jesus offers forgiveness to a prostitute. Jesus pronounces blessings on those who sit on the edge of the Brooklyn Bridge ready to jump to their death.

When Paul showed up in Thessalonica, he told stories. "He opened up the texts so they understood what they'd been reading all their lives: that the Messiah absolutely had to be put to death and raised from the dead—there were no other options—and that "this Jesus I'm introducing you to is that Messiah" (Acts 17:2–3, MSG).

Paul's first letter to the Thessalonians gives us a great picture of evangelism in action. It almost seems unintentional or accidental, simply a consequence of a changed community. "Do you know that all over the provinces of both Macedonia and Achaia believers look up to you? The word has gotten around. Your lives are echoing the Master's Word, not only in the provinces but all over the place. The news of your faith in God is out. We don't even have to say anything anymore—you're the message! People come up and tell us how you received us with open arms, how you deserted the dead idols of your old life so you could embrace and serve God, the true God. They marvel at how expectantly you await the arrival of his Son, whom he raised from the dead—Jesus, who rescued us from certain doom" (1:7–10, MSG).

Traditionally in the West, we have thought of evangelism as information: statements of 'belief,' acquired and spoken knowledge, and philosophical maxims and utterances. The one thing that these all have in common is language. Philosophers can sit in a room and talk philosophy for seven years and the only guaranteed outcome after those seven years is the exchange and debate of words. Similarly, Christians can meet weekly for seven years and all that will have happened is the exchange and debate of words. A scientist can lecture to a classroom of students for hours and all that will have happened is the sharing of scientific knowledge. Words.

Eugene Peterson does a great job of helping us understand language. He identifies three classifications of language. Language I is primal: the cry of an infant, a cry for help in a dark alley, uncontrollable laughter, or cries of grief in the wake of tragedy. It is the spontaneous language of pain, fear, joy, and delight. "Language I is the elemental language we always use when our life, our well-being, and deepest interests—identity, health, love, guilt, trust—are at stake. There is no mere information about God here. There is no program implemented for God here. This is a cry for survival that develops into the shout of the saved."[1] Language II is information: we attach words to objects and processes to describe the physical world around us. Language III is motivation: we learn how to use words to get what we want by moving ourselves or moving others in the direction we desire. Our culture operates in languages II and III. Language I is embarrassing and shameful in our culture so we learn to suppress joy, excitement, pain, fear, disappointment, and despair.

[1] Peterson, *Answering God*, 42.

We learn to communicate around these things and in so doing our hearts grow distant and cold. For who can bear grief and sadness in complete isolation? Or how diminished is joy when it must be contained and managed? Language I embodies the bulk of the substance and story of our lives. A good story is good because it contains elements such as pain, sorrow, joy, fear, suspense, and celebration. We tend to only speak in Language I when things are really bad or really good. It's okay to cry at a funeral but not on a Wednesday afternoon at the office. It's okay for men to embrace after a touchdown is scored but not simply for the sake of their brotherly love for one another.

We have brought the language of our culture (II and III) into our churches and continue to use it in our prayers, our speech with one another, and in our witness to the world. Our language lacks connection to the concrete world. Our religious speech is attached, not to stories that have happened and are happening, but to doctrines, philosophies, and knowledge that is *never tested in the real world.* I am not opposing philosophical language, doctrines, or knowledge. I am calling us to recognize that our philosophies, doctrines, and knowledge is derived from story; specifically the story of Jesus of Nazareth, who lived, died, and rose again thereby forever destroying the power of death. This is good *news* and not just sound and dusty doctrine! If our doctrines and knowledge lose all connection with story, the only story left is the recitation and proselytizing of those doctrines and knowledge.

Most Americans have the ability to buy their way out of feeling the sting of their own impending death. But God has a plan for all of this. For those who are unable to feel the sting of death, I believe He is sending you to those that feel it daily. On a recent trip to Africa, I met mother's who *daily* needed to choose between selling their bodies to HIV infected strangers or watching their children starve. Do these women need a Savior? I need a Savior because I spend most of my time thinking about me. Perhaps God wants to show me, through the desperation of others, that He died not just for me and many other individuals, but that He died to redeem the manner in which we all relate to or ignore one another. Paul tells us that when we share one another's burdens, we are fulfilling the law of Christ. Spiritual laws, even all four of them, would mean little to a mother dying of AIDS and watching her children starve.

Try this. When you gather with some fellow believers, make statements of prayer, worship, or conversation *only when they can be traced to a story that warranted the knowledge or conclusion you are sharing.* For example, don't say, "I learned this week that God loves me because I read it in the Bible." Rather, "I realized this week that God loves me because just as Jesus ate in Matthew's house with sinners, He proceeds towards me even when I am bitter and rebellious like I was the other day when I . . ." (And if you're brave, share what you are bitter about and the manner in which you are rebelling.) And only say what you can really mean in your heart. If you can't say anything like this and mean it, then say just *that.*

Evangelism is all about telling God's stories and explaining the implications of those stories. Our lack of and misunderstanding of evangelism indicates that we ourselves have missed the point and we need to repent in light of this. We have no story to tell (of a living and adventurous relationship with God that challenges us, humbles us, and leaves us in awe of a true and living God) so our conversations revolve around discussing doctrines or forecasting the same lofty and noble plans that we have been waffling about for months or years. Here is the great thing about God; as He has repeatedly done throughout history, He patiently waits and promises that when we confess our sin, He heals us and transforms us into His image.

There is a road on a steep hill by my house that is over one mile long. There is a trail towards this road and while on it, nearly the entire one-mile stretch of road is in view. One time I was walking on this trail with my family. Suddenly our attention was diverted to a honking car towards the bottom of the hill. The road has an un-crossable median and most cars travel between 50 and 60 mph in both directions. To our horror, we realized that a car was traveling up the hill on the left side of the road. The driver couldn't decide if they should floor it, go slowly, or just stop altogether. We helplessly stood there and watched while dozens of cars locked up their brakes and swerved going down that hill. The scene was fantastic and miraculously, there was not one single accident. I shared this story in every conversation for about a week. People's reactions were always the same, eyeballs like saucers waiting to hear the conclusion. Things would have been much different in these conversations if I would have skipped the story and simply said, 'Hey, just so you guys know, don't drive on the wrong side of the road, it could get ugly. You'd be crazy to do it.' Surely they would be left wondering why I felt compelled to share such information with them.

Perhaps evangelism is so tough for us because our society is so fearful of relevant matters. It's just so much easier to gossip about inconsequential matters and recap sporting events or what we found at the mall last week. Or maybe we struggle to see the relevance of Christianity in our own lives so we feel foolish talking to others when we ourselves don't really have it all figured out. Or maybe our Christianity is just information; information that does get us into Heaven no less. Maybe we don't have a personal testimony; we just don't have any stories to share about God showing up and changing the course of our lives. So we get guilted into doing the work of evangelism. We hand out tracts, we memorize the four spiritual laws for the purpose of explaining the mysteries of the universe to non-believers, and we formulate clever arguments to counter atheists, Hindus, Muslims, and Buddhists. We abandon our heart's cry to be involved in a real story and we settle for mastering information and doctrines. At least this way we have the gratification of winning theological debates with pagans.

What if our starting point for evangelism with our neighbors was the page of the story we are actually on? "Why am I joyful? Because God revealed His goodness to me today when He . . . " or "Yeah I'm a Christian but sometimes I feel like God isn't there or that I just can't connect with Him." Could that possibly open up a door to a conversation with an atheist that gave up on God because they felt the same way but were scolded by the church for having weak faith? Do we have faith that God is able to accomplish His work without needing us to have polished and rehearsed lives? God has a habit of meeting people in the midst of their doubt, rebellion, fear, despair, or cowardice. He came to Adam and Eve after they ate of the Tree of Knowledge. He met Matthew at his tax collector's booth while he was ripping people off. Jesus met Zacchaeus when he simply wanted to *see* Jesus from a safe distance. Interestingly, Jesus did not declare his salvation until his choices began to reflect God's kingdom (a new story rooted in the character and activity of God and not Zacchaeus). After He was resurrected from death, Jesus met Thomas, whose heart could not believe the other disciples' testimonies, and graciously offered him the scars in His own hands, feet, and side.

I believe God is extending us outward to various people groups in the world as well as to the people in our own backyards that daily taste the sting of death. I believe He is doing this because He is restoring the manner in which we relate and the degree to which we are willing to share one another's burdens. I believe that through this extending, we will recover our primal language. We will learn to cry more freely, to mourn over not just our losses, but our neighbor's losses as well. We will be able to laugh like children do when they are reunited with their daddy when he walks in the door from work. We will spontaneously and un-self-consciously clap our hands in public as our hearts are filled with the joy of the Holy Spirit. I believe that our cold hearts will be made warm and free when we can say to our unbelieving neighbor, (who sees by our aloofness that our heart is cold and uncaring), 'My heart is cold and I am asking my God to make it warm and new.' I believe our prayers will become much more than telling God information He already knows. I believe our conversations will grow beyond clarifying and refining our doctrinal positions. I believe our conversations with strangers will lead us to honest friendships. I believe that when we embrace the truth of where we stand and invite God to meet us, He will. I believe that until God enables us to live this honestly, we have nothing worth saying to our neighbors. Our greatest and only testimony is what we can truthfully and honestly tell one another. Thomas got this. On page 253 of his story he adamantly and honestly proclaimed his doubt, "Unless I see the nail marks in his hands and put my finger where the nails were, and put my hand into his side, I will not believe [that Jesus is alive]." One week later on page 264, Jesus appears to Thomas and he humbly responds, "My Lord and my God!" For all of our criticizing of him as 'the doubter,' at least he was not a poser pretending to believe something that his life was not reflecting. In other words, Thomas was not pretending to be on page 264 when his heart was painfully stuck on page 253. He honestly acknowledged his doubt to his friends

Several years ago I was one of four track coaches at a middle school. My experience is in long distance but I was delegated to coach hurdles, which I have never done. For weeks I coached drawing simply on my knowledge drawn from watching the Olympics every four years. One day a student asked me to demonstrate a technique I was trying to teach. 'No that's okay,' I said. More students gathered around and suddenly it dawned on them that I had never actually been seen going over a hurdle, not even once. They took it to the wire and eventually I had to tell them that I had never competed or practiced hurdles in my entire life. Hurdles just can't be faked. In a fraction of a second, I lost all credibility as a coach, and rightfully so. I believe this is where many of us sit. We are trying to be Jesus coaches to the world, discussing matters that we ourselves have never internalized or discovered to be the case through face to face encounters with God in the real world. We are simply recycling information, hoping that people will just buy it so we can fulfill our evangelism quota for the year. What we need to do is sit at the feet of Jesus, repent for our dishonesty, and ask Him to fill our hearts with His grace for sinners like us. Then we need to go get real with our neighbors.

Let's go tell our neighbors why *we* need a Savior and leave it for God to show them why *they* need a Savior.

What emotions do you feel when you envision this conversation with a neighbor?

_____

_____

_____

_____

_____

Reflect on your story. Where are you honestly at? Think about what you are hoping for. Reflect on circumstances that have made you sad in the last month. Reflect on God's story. Think about what *He* wants to see happen in the world and what circumstances have likely brought *Him* sadness in the last month. Write down any thoughts you have.

_____

_____

_____

_____

_____

_____

_____

DOXA

What is the most honest thing you could say to your neighbor as it pertains to being a Christian?

_____

_____

_____

_____

_____

Are you prepared to begin here?

_____

_____

_____

Part 4: Rethinking Our Programs:
Turning Off Autopilot

"Prove by the way you live that you have repented of your sins and turned to God. Don't just say to each other, 'We're safe, for we are descendants of Abraham.' That means nothing, for I tell you, God can create children of Abraham from these very stones. Even now the ax of God's judgment is poised, ready to sever the roots of the trees. Yes, every tree that does not produce good fruit will be chopped down and thrown into the fire" John the Baptizer (Luke 3:8–9).

Read Acts 17:1–9 and I Thessalonians 1:4–10 and 2:13–15.
What is God showing you in this story?
Write down any thoughts, questions, or promptings.

_____

_____

_____

_____

_____

John's audience, convicted by this truth, frantically asked him what they should then do. "The man with two coats should share with him who has none, and the one who has food should do the same. And if you've ripped anyone off, stop it!" Imagine if a congregation of 1,000 adopted this as the only program for one year? No mock amusement parks in the church parking lot, no food drives, no door-to-door tract giving. Simply find those in your community that lack life's most basic physical necessities and share what God has given you. Then watch and listen for the Spirit of God to lead, transform, convict, and illuminate His own presence.

The church I grew up in had a small pantry of food in the office that was available for those in need. I remember going to the church office one time with my mom when I was six or seven. As we were going in, an anxious-looking woman was on her way out with a sack of groceries in her arms. It seemed odd to me. Why was it necessary for the church office to be the 'middle man'? Because in fact, the food *did* come from the pantries of churchgoers. Did anyone at the church know this woman? Did she know any of us? Maybe we don't know our neighbors well enough to know their needs? Or is it just too awkward for us to interface so directly and uncomfortably in others' lives? Maybe it just feels better to show up at church and glad-hand the pastor as we deposit our donated food items. And why do we have soup kitchens in church buildings but not in our own neighborhoods, in our own houses and apartments? Why is it considered 'tithing' when we write checks to a church that is a registered 501(c)3 and not when we buy groceries for our neighbor in need? Is it because the former shows up on our tax return and the other doesn't?

Read I Thessalonians 1:4–10 and 2:13–15.
What 'programs' do you think the Thessalonian Christians created?

_____

_____

Who was in charge of these programs? Who was involved in them? Where did these programs take place?

_____

_____

To whom does God give His authority and for what purpose? (To make it interesting, look at Rev 2:26, I Thess 4:8, and John 8:28.)

_____

_____

_____

_____

Read Acts 26:6–11. Does the pastor of a smaller church have less authority than the pastor of a larger church? Does a paid pastor have more authority than a person who has been given a pastoring gift but is not paid to use it? How big was Jesus' church in 33AD? How big is it now? Does Jesus have more authority now than He did when most people had deserted Him while He hung on a cross? Was Jesus a paid pastor or a volunteer pastor? Was Jesus a pastor or a 'ministry leader'? Does a 'ministry leader' have a different or lesser kind of authority than a 'pastor' does? Who had authority over Jesus? Who told Him what to do and when to do it? Who had authority over Paul or Peter? Who told the Christians in Thessalonica what to do and when to do it? (See especially I Thessalonians 2:13.) Who should be telling us what to do and when to do it?

Reflect on the above questions and write down any thoughts or reflections.

_____

_____

_____

_____

_____

_____

_____

_____

I believe that God is bringing a refreshing to His church. I see God manifesting Himself today as He did in 1st Century communities of Christ followers. The physical epicenters of spirituality in the 1st Century shifted from a few prominent halls of ceremony and tradition into the dwellings of common people. I see God doing this today. We have made our church buildings places of exclusion and performance. Most of our icons and symbols have been robbed, cheapened, or stripped of their meaning. I guess you could say that God is removing all of our scapegoats, substitutes, and imitations of what He most desires to accomplish through us today. I think we could all agree that wearing a cross around our necks is not necessarily a testimony of faith in Jesus. I think we could also say that attending a church on Sunday morning is not necessarily a testimony of faith in Jesus. Fifty years ago, maybe a neighborhood church was a sign of hope or security to those within walking distance of it. Today, a neighborhood church is often at best a relic of irrelevance and at worst a symbol of exclusivity.

I was embarrassed about my church when I was growing up. There was no way I was going to bring someone without thorough briefing and excessive apologizing for the strange looks and oddities they would be subjected to endure. I was not embarrassed to hang out with my friends elsewhere though. Yet I was never empowered to see that 'hanging out with my friends' didn't have to be a whole lot different from 'church'. Isn't a church (architecturally speaking) simply the physical location where believers gather to be strengthened, equipped, and sent? *Doesn't God call His people to gather for the purpose of gaining strength, wisdom, and courage to go hang out with our neighbors and friends (as well as our enemies and those we would rather avoid or ignore) in a way that glorifies and honors God?*

Church programs "seek to involve large numbers of lay people in the name of the mission of the Church in the world, whereas in fact such programs divert laymen from the mission in the world, that is, from a full involvement in secular affairs because of the attrition resulting from participation in churchly activity and discussion about secular affairs. The Christian social witness is achieved only insofar as Christians are deeply implicated in the real life of society—in unions and political clubs and citizen groups and the like; it is not made by Christian people gathering off by themselves in a [church] to study and discuss social issues."[2]

---

[2] Stringfellow, *Faith*, 53–54.

Often church activities revolve around a facility or the giftedness of paid church or ministry staff. Perhaps the existence of a facility and its various functions limit the scope and creativity of the ministry that God is giving us that will never find expression in such a facility. Because our neighbors 'don't come to church with us,' we assume they have no interest in spiritual matters. Or maybe we have bought into the false notion that our primary goal with our neighbors should be getting them to our church to hear our pastors preach.

How might our 'Christian activities' actually distract us and prevent us from the work God is doing?

_____

_____

_____

_____

Which is easier and safer, meeting homeless people in your community face-to-face and learning their needs through a conversation or volunteering at a soup kitchen that is a considerable drive from your residence? Which option would be more transformational (for you and them)?

_____

_____

_____

_____

Are our programs set up in a way that they stifle authenticity in our relationships with other believers as well as with our neighbors at large?

_____

_____

_____

_____

How do our programs contribute to the stifling of creativity and work of the Holy Spirit?

_____

_____

_____

_____

With your community, make a list of all the needs that you are aware of. These could be large structural needs like homelessness or high concentrations of strung-out meth heads or these needs could be more relational in nature (my friend lost their job, my dad is high all the time, my next-door neighbor does not know Jesus, etc). If you're having trouble thinking of some needs, ask yourself why that might be. Compile the list and as a community, prayerfully decide how you will either communally and/or personally pursue meeting those needs identified.

_____

_____

_____

_____

_____

_____

_____

_____

_____

_____

CHAPTER 10

Becoming and Going

"And since we are his children, we are his heirs. In fact, together with Christ we are heirs of God's glory. But if we are to share his glory, we must also share his suffering. Yet what we suffer now is nothing compared to the glory he will reveal to us later. For all creation is waiting eagerly for that future day when God will reveal who his children really are. Against its will, all creation was subjected to God's curse. But with eager hope, the creation looks forward to the day when it will join God's children in glorious freedom from death and decay" (Rom 8:17–21).

OVERVIEW:

Core Scripture: Acts 19:11–20.

The Kingdom of God is at Hand: Jesus is on a mission and we follow in His footsteps of bringing the future that God has in mind to the city where we dwell. In our community we encourage each other towards living dangerously close to Jesus, knowing that our hope is grounded not in our abilities, resources, and visible outcomes but in Jesus' promise to make Himself known through hearts and hands that are loyal to Him. In our community, we surrender our personal and corporate agendas so that Jesus might be free to lead us into His agenda.

Repent: We will direct our efforts towards a weekly church service. Engaging with people in a spiritual context will happen only at prescribed times and places. We will rely on slick marketing and savvy programs to grow our church or ministry. And we will participate in only those things that we are good at and comfortable with. We will seek to get people involved and well managed in programs at the church so the pastor doesn't have to do everything.

Believe the Good News: God is up to something in your community that is far beyond your scope and capabilities. God is revealing these things to you! He delights in working through ordinary and common vessels like you and me so that He is glorified in all of creation. God sends us, not to church, but into the world so that we might join Him in His work of reconciling creation back to Himself.

Therefore Go: With your community, complete the exercise at the end of the chapter and put together a plan to be intentional with each other and intentional on the streets of your community (this might require a few meetings). Put it into practice and support and encourage one another as you journey together. God speed.

Part 1: Non-relational, Un-experienced Knowledge of God.

Read Acts 19:11–20.
What is God showing you in this story?
Write down any thoughts, questions, or promptings.

_____

_____

_____

_____

What do you think was motivating the seven sons of Sceva to cast out demons 'in the name of Jesus, whom Paul preaches'?

_____

_____

Do you think they knew Jesus in the way that Paul did? How did they know Jesus?

_____

_____

_____

I've never seen a demon give someone a nosebleed and strip them of their clothing. I'm guessing it's a sobering sight. It certainly was for those in Ephesus that day. "The name of the Lord was held in high honor." Previously it must not have been. People now came forward and confessed their sins and destroyed their articles of witchcraft, which were worth about 136 years' wages. That's a lot of money going up in smoke. But it didn't matter. The name of Jesus suddenly took precedence. Seven men see from a distance that the name of Jesus has power, but they missed something. Power for *what*? Authority to accomplish *what*? These are the questions we must examine. Jesus went about His Father's work. That is what He was given authority to do.

> Jesus didn't give Himself license or authority to do anything beyond what His Father said and taught.

What is God doing in your community? If you don't know, stop pretending and get on your knees. Jesus promised us that we would be shown what the Father is doing and that these works would be greater than the works performed in Jesus Himself. Are we listening? Or are we pretending our way through the motions? Do you know Jesus because you heard someone preach about Him? Or do you know Jesus because you've *seen* Him?

Second-hand knowledge of Jesus is powerless and ineffectual if it stops there. The seven sons of Sceva found out the hard way. Those who witnessed this beating found out the easy way and quickly came out of their dark hiding places. Jesus' name was held in high honor. The cosmic magician, who does miracles to make earthlings happy, was now properly viewed as the only One who can spare us from death and Satan. The community is sobered. Flirtations with evil that previously seemed harmful are now seen as destructive and infectious.

Why are we driven to pretend our way through things as Christians? What is the source of our fearful pretending?

_____

_____

_____

_____

All of our posing and pretending is completely unnecessary. I don't think it results from not *believing* in God. I think it is the result of not *knowing* God. We can only believe what we have come to know or test in a real and life-threatening way. I won't fully appreciate a parachute until I jump out of an airplane and trust the parachute to safely land me on the ground with all of my bones and organs intact. We have a small view of God because we do not know Him or rely on Him. Our small picture of God leads us to rely on ourselves. In the midst of our attempts to rely on ourselves, we see how weak we are so we inflate our egos and mask our ugliness. And thus a life of pretending begins. If we can fool those around us, maybe we can fool ourselves too. This is why vulnerability is so important for us. When we see that it's necessary and okay to be weak, we can embrace our weakness and begin to reach for God's strength and rely on His capabilities, His promises, and His wisdom and leadership.

Take as much time as you need and reflect on the following Scriptures. Note those promises that are difficult to receive due to fears or insecurities. Envision those new possibilities because these words are indeed true. Colossians 1 has been written in the form of a declaration to emphasize the vast implications of the promises contained in this text. The Scriptures from John and Ephesians have been written as if spoken by the Father to help us understand both the relational and Trinitarian nature in which God calls us, loves us, equips us, and sends us.

"You may live a life worthy of Jesus Christ.

You may please Jesus in every way possible as you bear fruit in every good work and grow in the knowledge of God.

You may be strengthened with all power according to the glorious might of your Dad. In this, you may have great endurance and patience and thankfulness.

Your Dad has qualified you to share in the inheritance of the saints in God's kingdom. For you have been rescued from the kingdom of darkness and have been brought into the glorious kingdom of Jesus, our Dad's beloved Son. The Kingdom of Jesus is no ordinary kingdom. For all things were created by Jesus and for Jesus. All things are held together because of Him. This Creator and King is your king. His word is the first word and the last word and over you He has spoken love and redemption. He has preeminence over all things. He silences all who oppose His rule of love and truth. His suffering and death has destroyed the power of death.

You now have access to this King and his kingdom of love, grace, truth, and peace, which was made possible because of his own death. His death presents you holy and without fault before God. No one has grounds or authority to accuse you or diminish who this King created you to be.

You may now live by faith that what your Dad has done and spoken is true, final, and eternal.

You may now live in hope, as death no longer has power or authority in your life" (Col 1:10–28, adapted from the NIV).

"I, your Dad, am blessed! And what a blessing I am! I am the Dad of your Master, Jesus Christ, who takes you to the high places of blessing in him. Long before I laid down earth's foundations, I had you all in mind, had settled on you as the focus of my love, to be made whole and holy by my love. Long, long ago I decided to adopt you into my family through my Son, Jesus Christ. (What pleasure I took in planning this!) I wanted you all to enter into the celebration of my lavish gift-giving by the hand of my beloved Son, Jesus. Because of the sacrifice of my Son, the Messiah, his blood poured out on the altar of the Cross, you're a free people—free of penalties and punishments chalked up by all your misdeeds. And not just barely free, either. Abundantly free! I thought of everything, provided for everything you could possibly need, letting you in on the plans I took such delight in making. I set it all out before you in my Son, a long-range plan in which everything would be brought together and summed up in my Son, everything in deepest heaven, everything on planet earth. It's in my Son that you find out who you are and what you are living for. Long before you first heard of my Son and got your hopes up, I had my eye on you, had designs for you for glorious living, part of the overall purpose I am working out in everything and everyone. It's in my Son that you, once you heard the truth and believed it (this Message of your salvation), found yourselves home free—signed, sealed, and delivered by the Holy Spirit. This signet from me, your Dad, is the first installment on what's coming, a reminder that we'll get everything I have planned for you, a praising and glorious life" (Eph 1:3–14, adapted from the MSG).

"Don't let this throw you. You trust Me, your Dad, don't you? Trust my Son. There is plenty of room for you in my home. If that weren't so, would my Son have told you that He's on His way to get a room ready for you? And if He's on His way to get your room ready, He'll come back and get you so you can live where He lives. My Son is the Road, also the Truth, also the Life. No one gets to Me apart from Him. If you really knew Him, you would know Me as well. From now on, you do know Me. You've even seen Me! To see my Son is to see Me. So how can you ask, 'Where are you, Dad?' Don't you believe that my Son is in His Dad, and I am in Him? The words that my Son speaks to you aren't mere words. He doesn't just make them up on His own. I craft each word into a divine act. Believe my Son: He is in Me and I am in Him. If you can't believe His words, believe what you see—His works. The person who trusts Him will not only do what He is doing but even greater things, because He is on His way to Me, and is giving you the same work to do that He's been doing. You can count on it. From now on, whatever you request along the lines of who He is and what He is doing, He'll do it. That's how I will be seen for who I am in my Son. He means it. Whatever you request from Him in this way, He'll do. If you love my Son, show it by doing what He's told you. He will talk to me, and I'll provide you another Friend so that you will always have someone with you. This Friend is the Spirit of Truth. The godless world can't take Him in because it doesn't have eyes to see Him, doesn't know what to look for. But you know Him already because He has been staying with you, and will even be in you! The person who knows my Son's commandments and keeps them, that's who loves Him. And the person who loves Him will be loved by Me; and my Son will love him and make Himself plain to him. If anyone loves my Son, He will carefully keep His word and I will love him—my Son and I, we'll move right into the neighborhood! Not loving Him means not keeping His words. The message you are hearing isn't my Son's. It's my message, from His Dad who sent Him. The Friend, the Holy Spirit whom I will send at my Son's request, will make everything plain to you. He will remind you of all the things my Son has told you. My Son doesn't leave you the way you're used to being left—feeling abandoned, bereft. So don't be upset. Don't be distraught. You've heard Him tell you, 'I'm going away, and I'm coming back.' If you love my Son, you would be glad that He's on His way to Me because I am the goal and purpose of His life" (John 14:1–4; 6–7; 9–17; 21, 23–28, adapted from the MSG).

Write down what God shows you about His promises and His desire to involve you in great things.

_____

_____

_____

_____

_____

_____

_____

_____

One day the mission will be over. Eternity will be the life that the Trinity shared before creation, now fully extended unto and shared freely with us. Days will be filled with endless joy and celebration, just as it was before creation. It is difficult for me to fathom that there can be such joy in *a Person*. No ambitious projects to tackle; no activities to keep busy with; no achieved goals; no gadgets or possessions; simply a victorious King with His people living in delight and celebration.

It is this victorious King that takes us by the hand and leads us as sheep among wolves into a hostile land of worldly kings and impossible giants.

From God's perspective (who has no beginning and no end), the story of His creation (from 'in the beginning' to Jesus returning) is the blinking of an eye. We are not the focal point of God's existence. God and His matchless glory is the focal point of God's existence. God's act of creating, your existence, is all His doing and for His glory.

What do you think God did for billions and billions of years before He created? Did He get bored? How did He spend His time?

_____

_____

_____

_____

Part 2: Why Do You 'Go To Church' There?

"He expected a crop of justice, but instead he found oppression. He expected to find righteousness, but instead he heard cries of violence" (Isa 5:7).

Read Acts 19:11–20.
What is God showing you in this story?
Write down any thoughts, questions, or promptings.

_____

_____

_____

_____

_____

For the past year I have been 'planting a church' which has been an odd experience. As in most ministries, I was given direction and advice on how to boost numbers at a weekly gig. This was also the standard by which my church was measured. Lots of people at a weekly gig was a sure sign of a good ministry. Only a small handful of people at a weekly gig meant something was off a bit. These things drive me insane. By these standards, the ministries of the Old Testament prophets, Jesus, and the apostles were well below par. None of them seemed too concerned with the attendance at weekly gigs. Rather they seemed adamant about unity, character, and truthful living. Sometimes these things kill the weekly gig. Sometimes they grow the weekly gig. Can we just remove our eyes from the weekly gig and focus on what matters?

As a church planter, I refuse to plant 'my own church'. Instead, I will follow in the tradition of the prophets, Jesus, and the apostles of the New Testament. If a weekly gig is a by-product of that, so be it. If it is not, so be it. This conviction has given me immense freedom to advance God's kingdom. I no longer need to view every person I meet as a potential tither at my church. I can reach out to my Christian neighbors and work for unity without secretly hoping that they 'join *my* church'. I can love my next-door neighbors who were wounded by the church without needing their membership at my church as a sign of affirmation or success. I can simply and freely listen to God and trust His hand at work around me, in me, and through me. God determines the result.

I'm calling us to put an end to methodology that puts visible results before the Spirit of God. Let's ditch the iPod lotteries to attract people to our program venues. Let's stop publicly marketing those things about us that we believe set us apart from those other churches. These ungodly practices cause us to no longer seek God's authority and leadership and instead, coerce us to assert our own authority with methods that simply dishonor God and undermine our own character. We stop seeking what God wants and we begin shaping our ministries to the tastes of consumer Christians and anxious donors. In doing so, we also *create* consumer Christians and man-centered ministries. We tell people that it's not Jesus they need but a more hip or more comfortable church to call home. We abandon the Spirit of God and in His place erect the idol of a self-actualized congregation. We feel 'relevant' because we sit in couches instead of pews. We equate success with fast numerical growth. Dwindling numbers or slow growth indicates a need for structural reorganization. We pat ourselves on the back when we 'achieve our objectives ahead of schedule'.

I've given up my pursuit to 'plant *a* church' and in place of this I will now take part in building a Church surrendered to and worthy of our Father's kingdom. I have neighbors that spend three to four hours commuting to church each week. In fact, I don't know one Christian in my neighborhood that goes to church in my city. Everyone commutes to a different city to attend church once or twice a week. I don't get that.[1]

Here are some questions that I feel we need to honestly examine.
1. How can we become intentional about our own communities when we gather as believers in everyone else's communities?
2. How can we create transformational friendships with other believers when the only time we associate is once per week with the majority of that time spent listening to one person talk?
3. How can we effectively reach out to those in our sphere of influence if we're not intentionally and strategically working with fellow believers within that same sphere? (I believe that my neighbors who don't know Jesus will know Him when those of us who do believe in Him, come together to ask God to reveal Himself to them.)
4. Have we lost the point of gathering in the first place? Have we made it all about us? Do we attend a church because the pastor gives a good sermon or the worship band is really great or the people are really friendly? For whose sake do we attend church every week?
5. If our primary gatherings are with people that we would never otherwise see (in our neighborhoods, at the grocery store, or at work), how would we possibly collaborate to advance God's kingdom in our respective spheres?
6. Is there a better way to do church?

Reread Acts 2:44–47.

I see a community of free-flowing relationships. If a believer hosted a meal, I'm guessing other believers in the immediate vicinity joined despite prior associations or lack of association. When meetings were held in the temple courts, people probably walked to-

---

[1] The one exception to this would be the church that utilizes its facilities and leadership solely for the purpose of equipping its members to be salt and light in their own respective communities. In this model, the members' homes become the hearts of their communities as they work for unity with local fellow believers and lead the way in reaching out to their communities. The weekly gathering at 'church' is neither the epicenter of relationships nor ministry. Relationships and ministry happen on the streets. The litmus test for such a church would not be the size or attractiveness of its weekly gig but the character and fruitfulness of its attendees the other six days of the week.

gether and dispersed afterwards into local gatherings for further prayer and celebration. When more were added to their number each day, the fellowship was probably local. If I lead my neighbor to Christ and I attend a church 30 miles from my home, do I encourage my neighbor to commute with me? Or do I recommend a closer church that I have no ties to? Why wouldn't I just invite them over to my own home to build relationship, open the Scriptures, and seek the face of God together? Is this just too abnormal and uncomfortable?

Our compartmentalized and sterile church life breeds complacency and pretending. Our church life is in a vacuum that never rubs or confronts our day-to-day living. It is simply the weekly battery charge so we go to the venue that offers the best charge. We wind up going to church to be fed or because it's comfortable. If my church is on the other side of town, it does not have the capacity to intentionally lead me towards a missional lifestyle in my own community. I live under the illusion that I am being led as I listen to and agree with my pastor talking about the Great Commission but my actions in my own community are not becoming missional. Further, it does not occur to us to collaborate with believers in the places we live and work because 'we do that at church'. *How has a system so ineffectual for the advancement of God's kingdom and deafening to our own ears become so accepted, normal, sought-after, and idolized?*

How many miles do you travel to church each week?

_____

If your church is not in your community, why are you there? What does your answer reveal about your motives?

_____

_____

_____

_____

If your current church gathered four blocks from your residence, how would possibilities to strategically reach your neighborhood increase?

_____

_____

_____

_____

_____

I have this dream of one day compiling every church directory in my city. I would plug every name and address into one database and mail out to every household a list of all those on their block or in their apartment building that were currently attending a church. I would then encourage these people to begin gathering (somewhere on their block) and praying for the rest of the block that did not yet know Jesus. I would encourage them to learn the needs of one another and the needs of others and find creative and visible ways to meet those needs. I think amazing things would happen. I think members of churches would become the Church as they allowed Christ to transcend doctrinal differences and as they participated together in the uncomfortable work of reaching out to their neighbors.

What do you think would happen if you rounded up all your neighbors who are believers and proposed meeting once per week or once per month to build relationships, pray, and seek God's heart and will for the neighborhood? Discuss with your community how you could prayerfully and creatively overcome resistance that you might encounter.

_____

_____

_____

_____

_____

Agree or disagree:
When a church grows to the extent that people can join without being known or actively participating, that church is too big and should divide or de-centralize. Why or why not?

_____

_____

Paul did not publicly hail himself to be a relevant and motivational speaker or a representative of a 'warm and friendly' community. He didn't even have a worship band to boast about. Instead, on Paul's business card it might have read, 'Chief of All Sinners' or 'A Fool'. His qualifications included such things as 'weak and proud of it, worst in my class,' or 'confronts situations with fear and trembling'. Paul knew that in order for the power of God to be displayed in his life, he had to stop relying on his own strength to accomplish a God-sized mission[2]. The Church participates in the things of God when we embrace

[2] Sometimes we forget that each task, decision, and moment towards this mission is also God-sized. Even the little things that seem removed from 'the big picture' require the same amount of intervention from God. A conversation with one person is God-sized because God wants to perform His work through it. It's easy to look at Moses parting the Red Sea and recognize that he couldn't have done that without God. Our challenge is to look past our status quo ways of living and listen for the impossible things that God is doing in the midst of our normal everyday existence. A conversation is not *just* a conversation. An outing

our weakness and begin living in the strength that God provides. When we model our churches after successful Fortune 500 companies and succeed in our imitation of their goal-setting and managerial practices, we will hardly feel weak. When we are more focused on growing our own ministry than caring for the world in our midst, we have idolized the strength and power of men and have lost sight of the heart of God. The Parable of the Good Samaritan illustrates well this tendency of our flesh. The heart of God was that the man left for dead be cared for. Perhaps God is warning us that our religious leaders and their associates would be likely to prioritize their religious duties over the needs of those in their midst. I believe that when we build big churches we hurt communities. We encourage and entice disciples to become commuter Christians by drawing them away from their own communities. Further, that church becomes focused on maintaining its size and stature at a cost of neglecting their own neighbors. When we are more concerned about the reputation and image of our ministry than we are the needs in our own backyards, we have wrapped our identity into the outcomes we believe *our* ministry should produce. The King and His kingdom take a back seat. There is simply no evidence in the Bible that God is looking for a collection of strong and smart people to create glamorous ministries. Rather His method seems to be to use those parts of us that are weak and shameful in the eyes of the world.

Is your church or ministry weak and shameful or strong and successful in the eyes of the world? Which image is it striving towards and why?

_____

_____

_____

_____

_____

God's method is to work through the weak. Specifically He uses:

➤ Those who are foolish by human standards, non-influential, poor, fearful, and rely completely on the message of Christ and Him crucified. (1 Cor 1:18—2:5)
➤ Those who are thought to be fools by the standards of the day. (1 Cor 3:18)
➤ Those who are weakest in the church; they are actually indispensable (1 Cor 12:22).
➤ Those who are the 'least and thus receive grace' (1 Cor 15:8–9).
➤ Those who are led into circumstances of suffering and hardship to the degree that death is felt resulting in complete reliance upon God. Paul speaks of God's comfort to those who are suffering but the context here is suffering for the sake of the Gospel and not suffering due to personal disappointment in a quest for comfort

to the grocery store is not *just* another outing. Our Dad is always about His work.

and happiness. The comfort spoken of here is the comfort that intersects suffering that parallels the sufferings of Christ (2 Cor 1:8–10).

➤ Those who, because they have modeled their lives after Jesus, are hard-pressed, helpless, struck down, mentally at a loss, and persecuted. Those likened to an unassuming, unattractive, cheap clay jar (2 Cor 4:7–12).

➤ Those who are being given over to death in their weakness as Jesus was given over to crucifixion in weakness and who now live by God's power and not their own (2 Cor 13:4).

Jesus helps Himself through those that cannot help anything . . .

➤ Jesus turns the whole order of power upside down by bestowing upon the tax collector, the slave, and the foreigner His gracious indwelling presence.

➤ Fruitfulness in the kingdom hinges on our ability to depend on Christ's remaining in us. This implies recognition of our weakness and denial of utilizing our power for the sake of the Gospel (John 15).

➤ Jesus commissions Peter in spite of his glaring weaknesses. Jesus grants us His authority, not because we're relevant or friendly, but because we are learning to rely on Him as our only option and our only hope.

What encourages you and disturbs you about God's method to use the weak, helpless, and powerless?

_____

_____

_____

_____

_____

_____

This isn't exactly the picture of the hip 20-something church where everyone is confidently and coolly waxing Jesus over java. And it's not the suburban family-centered church where everyone is happily munching on a donut and making friendly conversation. It looks more like boot camp. It looks more like a triage and less like a country club. These Scriptures, and countless others, give me the sense that a war is being waged and if we're not getting injured, it might be because we're not fighting.

Reflect on your community for a minute. What do you think it would look like if you all agreed to embrace your weakness as portrayed in the Scriptures above? Discuss with each other what you think the risk is as well as the possibilities. Write your thoughts below.

_____

_____

_____

_____

_____

_____

God has more need for our weakness (which requires our consent to subject ourselves to the way of Christ and forfeit the power structures that we can operate and succeed in) than He does our strength and gifting.

How is being weak an act of intentionality?

_____

_____

_____

When the New Testament speaks of the church, it doesn't speak of 'going'. It rather speaks of becoming. Churches and ministries are hard at work trying to get people to go or come to church. Everything seems to be focused around 'going to church'? Staff meetings are spent brainstorming 'how to get more people to church next week.' Attendees are exhorted to bring friends. Flyers are mailed out to every other household within five miles of the church. The bad guitar player is given soundboard duty. Maybe a celebrity is brought in to boost attendance.

Is it possible that God is redirecting our attention towards *becoming the church* and away from *going to church*? What is the difference?

_____

_____

_____

I am not suggesting that we stop gathering regularly for corporate worship, prayer, encouragement, equipping, and collaboration. I'm actually suggesting that we do it more often. Can we only discuss things that are on God's heart at appointed times and places? Why is a gathering of my Christian neighbors in my house not considered 'church'? Why is a conversation between four Christian friends over dinner not considered 'church'?

God calls believers together so that we might be shaped, equipped, filled, and sent out with His Word and by His Spirit. The Spirit of God is available seven days per week. We can open his Word any time we choose. Why don't we? Why do we wait until Sunday morning?

I had a friend in elementary school whose room looked like Toys 'R' Us. But he never played with his toys. And he would get really nervous if anyone else did. "Put that back!" he would say. "It's fragile." He kept them all obsessively organized. He knew where each one was at all times. Some of them he kept in the original box for safer keeping. This same spirit is in the church. We've got a good thing going and we don't want to introduce any foreign elements that would disrupt such success. When I was on Young Life staff I was leading a ministry that had about double attendance compared with other ministries. I thought it was pretty cool that my ministry had become the poster ministry. I thought I had a pretty good thing going. Then God diverted my attention to some of the more invisible populations of students. So we changed course. We spent time with 'the losers' and the nobody's. They started showing up to our programs and after about a month, attendance at our program dropped by about 60%. Yet we knew we were doing exactly what God wanted. Cooperating with God's game plan meant that we had to take on the appearance of failure. And that was okay.

The parable of the sower in Matthew 13 is interesting. The crowd who heard this parable was so large that Jesus was literally pushed off dry ground. So He preached from a boat near the shore of the lake. The main point of His parable — 'most of you aren't going to get this. Maybe 1 out of 4 of you will. You think you know me but you really don't.' It seems like this is the sort of parable you'd tell one or two in private. But Jesus drops it on one of His largest audiences. Perhaps the most disturbing part of this scene is that Jesus is preaching to a *religious* audience that doesn't get it. He delivered His message as an illustrative story because they wouldn't get it and the meaning of His story was that they don't get it. Let's just ponder for a minute that *Jesus was preaching to a crowd of religious folk—insiders*. He was delivering a message to a crowd that came to Him. This account would be much easier to take if Jesus gave this message to a group of unrefined, irreligious and disinterested riffraff. The crowd that day fulfilled the words of the prophet Isaiah:

"Listen carefully, but do not understand. Watch closely, but learn nothing. Harden the hearts of these people. Plug their ears and shut their eyes. That way, they will not see with their eyes, nor hear with their ears, nor understand with their hearts and turn to me for healing" (Isa 6:9-10).

I fear that there is lots of hearing going on in our churches today. We hear great messages from great preachers. We hear good worship music. But what are we *doing*? Blessed are those who hear *and* do—and just what is the 'do' that Jesus is talking about? I suspect it had nothing to do with 'going to church' as we have come to know it.

The only worthwhile asset the church has is God.

The minute we put stock in our abilities, our budgets, our numbers, our buildings, we are off course. Sure, God will use these things but they must be used in a manner that He determines. When will we stop marketing ourselves and begin sharing Jesus with the world?

To some there is little question that the consensus of the Church in America is to live in the lifestyle of her choosing patterned after the world's lust for power, possession and fame. Deed speaks louder than creed. Our deeds and not our creeds reveal who we are. The spiritualization of worldly comfort is disgusting to God. The resounding and repetitious cries of the prophets were for justice translated as caring for the poor and oppressed and not for larger and more prominent assemblies.

As the church continues to pattern her goal-setting after the business community (seeking the bottom line at any cost or means necessary), we are boxed into a mindset that leads us to 'count' only those things which can be clearly measured and boasted of in annual reports and board meetings: increases in attendance or involvement in our programs, seating capacity in our buildings, revenue, press coverage and good PR. Jesus sought to bring down the church as it was in first century Palestine. I can't help but believe that He is seeking to bring down the church in America as it is today so that He might be able to rebuild her in His image (If you're feeling brave, read Isaiah 5). Jesus was more about living and doing in a manner that glorified the Father than He was about likely desired outcomes from what He practiced. He entrusted the outcomes to His Father and the future work of the Holy Spirit. We need to do the same. Telling the truth and loving outcasts led Jesus to a near alien status, social isolation, unpopularity, death threats, and eventually crucifixion. I want to see a Church that is willing to be led to this place. Jesus made people furious by His truth-telling and scandalous love for terrorists and people confused about their sexuality. Sure Jesus could draw a crowd but most of the time these scenes ended in majority disapproval.

I heard about an underground church leader from China who spoke at a conference in America. He began his address by shouting the name of Jesus over and over. The audience of pastors grew restless. He explained that he had never been able to do this before. He then scolded his audience for measuring their worship by the quality of music and number gathered. He then lifted his shirt to reveal a torso that was scarred by beatings and whippings for his refusal to renounce his King. I fear that our idolatry is so normal, 'biblically' justified, and God forbid—*blessed* by the institutional church that we are completely deaf to the Spirit's conviction. The church has transformed itself into one of the many cogs that promotes and fosters the American way of life. When we abandon the truthful way of life as modeled and revealed in Jesus Christ, we are imposters and tools of the enemy.

Let us remember that it was the established religious order that put Jesus on the cross. The religious order had become a tool for evil instead of a surrendered and lifeless instrument in the hand of a powerful and life-giving God. Jesus did not align Himself with either the religious or governmental systems. He did not establish an opposing party.

He did not represent, defend, or champion any programs. He was suspected and disliked by people from all of these various religious sects and governments. He questioned all principle-driven programs. And perhaps most importantly, He did not introduce a new and better system.[3]

So what *is* Jesus calling us to participate in? And is it possible to remain faithful to *this* without giving in to 'the system'?

_____

_____

_____

_____

_____

_____

What must happen in order for you and your spiritual community to become people whom God has captured? How must we adjust ourselves so that we can rightly and willingly understand Jesus' call to worship (*something we generally understand to be private*) in spirit (*something we generally understand to be inward and invisible*) and truth (*something we generally understand to be informational or doctrinal*) as a call to *live* in spirit (*supernaturally*) and truth (*aligned with the character and story of God*)?

_____

_____

_____

_____

_____

[3] Dawn, *Powers*, 27–28.

Part 3: Going to Church Versus Becoming the Church

Church[4] is where we become; the world is where we go.

Read Acts 19:11–20.
What is God showing you in this story?
Write down any thoughts, questions, or promptings.

_____

_____

_____

_____

_____

The seven sons of Sceva were not empowered to go out into the world. At least they did though; that's more than we can say for many of us. Yet when they went, they got fisted and laughed at by a demon.

Does your association and involvement with your church equip you to go into the world or does it distract you from the world and detract you from having a presence there? And how can you tell?

_____

_____

_____

_____

_____

Spiritual warfare in the U. S. is not as blatant as we see in the book of Acts. It's easy to forget that there's even a battle. We live our lives much like those did in Pearl Harbor before the Japanese attacked it (as portrayed in the movie anyway). We have our uniforms on, we've all been through basic training, but we spend most of our time napping and listening to the radio. In a time of 'peace,' preparations for war seem silly. Over time we learn to simply go through the motions leaving us unprepared for battle. Church marketing gimmicks seem to scream of a spiritual peace. "All is well but come to our church and

---

[4] I prefer not to call our weekly gatherings 'church' because the Church is Jesus and His people and not a building or weekly event. When we gather with believers and Jesus is in our midst, this is when we begin to see and become who God is shaping us to be.

things will be even better! Motivational 'talks'!. . .warm and friendly people . . . comfortable and casual atmospheres . . . professional full-band music!. . . fun for the kids . . . free coffee and donuts . . . and a chance to win an iPod!"

What would an honest church flyer announce (assuming we should even be doing this in the first place)?

_____

_____

_____

_____

_____

Are you seeking to be faithful to God or relevant to your culture? Are you trying to please God or are you trying to be the answer to the desires of men? And how can you tell?

_____

_____

_____

_____

_____

_____

_____

Being faithful to God is the most relevant contribution we can make to our culture.

In living to please God, we will become either the desires of men or the object of man's hostility. God appointed Joshua to lead Israel into the land that He promised to give them. He told them to go into the land and take possession of it and that they were not to fear. I love how they entered on the wings of a miracle; God held the waters of the Jordan River at bay and they walked across the dry riverbed. Once the Jordan was crossed, there ensued battle after battle; Jericho, Ai, the Amorites, Makkedah, Libnah, Gezer, and many more. Joshua conquered 31 kings in all. The battles were bloody and not without Israelite causalities. God's will has a personal cost yet for the sake of God's glory, it is worth it. As long as we are caught up in weighing the personal cost, we will shy away from His call. Hebrews 11, after cataloging ordinary people with faith in a heroic God, concludes by saying, 'All these people earned a good reputation because of their faith, yet none of them received all that God had promised. For God had something better in mind for us, so that *they would not reach perfection without us.*' (Heb 11:39–40) There's a lot of mystery in these verses but one thing I see is that God's Kingdom is not a distant 'other world' but rather it advances within the very fabric of history. The obedience of godly men and women who walked planet earth 3,000 years ago is made complete through our obedience and the obedience of those 500 years from now. I am thankful that God has a bigger picture that far exceeds my lifespan.

Let us be reminded that God will not compromise His glory. And let us be reminded that He has chosen to glorify Himself in and through us. Yet how often do we question God's ability to glorify Himself? As long as our eyes are on ourselves and what we feel we can accomplish, we will indeed fail. If our self-estimation is correct we will be sheepish and filled with doubt. If our self-estimation is exaggerated we will go in the confidence of our flesh, something that Paul equated with 'poop'.

God lives to see Himself glorified and it is not our place to question His capability to do this. By His grace, He has chosen to perform these supernatural works through us, His Church, in view of all of creation. The work that He calls us into is a deep and sincere expression of His grace. It is work that we are powerless to do—only God can do it so by grace, He breathes life into us and reveals His plans and sets us on course for things that are humanly impossible. As we go, we literally become the hands and feet of the God who created the universe.

Before creation, God created something special for this moment. There is something that God wants to do right now that we ourselves cannot do. God is extending His grace—He wants to show us and empower us for something right now; healing, transformation, or an act of love or service. Beforehand it may appear mundane and normal. "Moses, raise your staff over the water . . . and I will part the sea." "Go to the pool and wash your eyes . . . and your sight will return to you."

> *What matters is not the action that we are being asked to do but rather what God is going to do through that act of obedience.*

Anyone can hold a stick over the sea. Anyone can wash his or her eyes in a basin of water. But only God can create dry land on the seafloor and give sight to the blind.

There's this bizarre moment in Luke 11 where Jesus is talking about the proper way to cast out a demon and He is interrupted as a woman in the crowd calls out, 'Blessed is the mother who gave you birth and nursed you.' And Jesus has an interesting reply. 'Blessed rather are those who hear the word of God and obey it" (Luke 11:27–28). I think Jesus was still referring to His mother when He spoke these words. But I think He wanted the crowd to see that the blessing that Mary received in being the mother of Jesus was made possible because she *obeyed.* She found joy in the scandal because it was a scandal ordained by God. "I am the Lord's servant. May it be to me as you have said", was Mary's response to the angel. She then continued her praise in song, "My soul glorifies the Lord . . . my spirit rejoices . . . the Mighty One has done great things for me . . . His mercy extends to those who fear him" (Luke 1:46–55).

Some of us are going because we feel that it is our duty. We are driven by guilt, a desire to please our pastor, or simply to feel good about ourselves. The works of God are vastly different. Impregnating a virgin in a culture that stoned women for adultery or choosing the weak to upset the order of the strong is not exactly our picture of 'doing our good deed for the day'.

Some of us are not going because our eyes are on us. We feel inadequate. We're scared out of our minds. It's just easier to go to church and forget about the world.

The work God is calling you to is already a created entity. It has already been conceived of, prepared, and created in the heart of God (Eph 2:10). I picture a big warehouse somewhere that is filled with millions and millions of 'good works' that God has created for each moment and each person. The work that we're called to step into is not our own work by our own effort in our own strength and contingent upon our talent, ability, and effort. The work is completely of God and can only be accomplished from, in, by, and for Christ. Let's allow this truth to draw us away from the works of man that glorify man (idolatry) and towards the works of God that glorify God . . .

> ➤ "Don't put your trust in mere humans. They are as frail as breath. What good are they?" (Isa 2:22).
> ➤ "Cursed are those who put their trust in mere humans, who rely on human strength and turn their hearts away from the Lord" (Jer 17:5).
> ➤ "For all the nations of the world are but a drop in the bucket. They are nothing more than dust on the scales. He picks up the whole earth as though it were a grain of sand. All the wood in Lebanon's forests and all Lebanon's animals would not be enough to make a burnt offering worthy of our God. The nations of the world are worth nothing to him. In his eyes they count for less than nothing—mere emptiness and froth" (Isa 40:15–17).
> ➤ "But whatever I am now, it is all because God poured out his special favor on me—and not without results. For I have worked harder than any of the other apostles; yet it was not I but God who was working through me by his grace" (1 Cor 15:10).
> ➤ "I dare not boast about anything except what Christ has done through me, bringing the Gentiles to God by my message and by the way I worked among them" (Rom 15:18).
> ➤ "Some nations boast of their chariots and horses, but we boast in the name of the Lord our God" (Ps 20:7).
> ➤ "We now have this light shining in our hearts, but we ourselves are like fragile clay jars containing this great treasure. This makes it clear that our great power is from God, not from ourselves" (2 Cor 4:7).

We need to stop doing things for God. We need to start submitting to God so that He might do things for us. We need to stop trying to pay Him back believing that somehow we have something worthy and helpful to offer Him. The only thing we have to offer

God is what He has already given us. "Workmen get no gifts. They get their due. If we would have the gift of justification, we dare not work. God is the workman in the affair. And what he gets is the glory of being the benefactor of grace, not the beneficiary of service . . . Nor should we think that after justification our labor for God begins. Those who make a work out of sanctification demean the glory of God. Jesus Christ is our righteousness and sanctification (I Cor.1:30). 'Did you receive the Spirit by works of the law or by hearing with faith? Are you so foolish? Having begun with the Spirit, are you now being perfected by the flesh?' (Gal.3:2–3). God was the workman in our justification and he will be the workman in our sanctification."[5]

Because we are stepping into the works of God and not performing our works for Him, It would be impossible to formulate a generic standard for obedience. Yes, the 10 Commandments are a glorious display of God's character, which we are called to love and imitate. But God wants to lead us into specific supernatural works for specific times that marvelously display such character. God told Moses to raise his staff over the waters because God wanted to part the Red Sea and by His grace, He used Moses to do it. If Moses was our standard, should we all go find a stick and hold it over the nearest body of water? The man with a withered hand was commanded to stretch out his hand because Jesus was going to heal it. Blessed are those who hear and do. Are we listening or just hearing?

> "The New Covenant doesn't operate by generic standards like the tithe. It is administrated by the Holy Spirit in a way that is unique to each person and situation. Jesus told the rich young ruler to sell everything, give the money to the poor, and come follow him (Matt. 19:16–30, Luke 18:18–30). Those instructions were unique to him. A tithe would not have been sufficient. In First Timothy 6:17–18 the rich are not commanded to give everything away like the rich young ruler was. They are instructed how they should use their wealth. When Peter asked Jesus what would be required of John, he was told that it was none of his business (John 21:20–22). God deals with each person and situation individually. There are many ways that faith can be expressed; however, they will all be uniquely inspired by the Holy Spirit for the specific situation. Faith is what God is looking for now, not [generic standards]."[6]

God is summoning His church to fight. Hebrews 5 tells us that Jesus learned obedience *because of* His sufferings. Suffering was not a consequence of obedience; it was a necessary ingredient to *produce* obedience. If *Jesus* had to learn obedience through suffering then clearly obedience is not just going to spontaneously happen for us. For Jesus, every day was a test to trust in His Abba; who sent Him in love yet willed Him to suffer for His glory. The goal of all of our learning and being together as Church is that we could move forward in trust and obedience, which we are *assured* will require suffering. Scripture beckons us to *press forward* while forgetting what is behind (Phil 3); to *run hard* as to cross the finish line first (1 Cor 9:24); to *hunger and thirst* for deeds of love, justice, and service

---

[5] Piper, *Brothers*, 41–42.

[6] Narramore, *Tithing*, 40.

(Matt 5), to *seek above all other things* God's kingdom (Matt 6:33), to *ask*, to *seek*, to *knock* (Matt 7:7), and to enter through the narrow gate which requires *arduous searching* (Matt 7:13). This is hardly the life of happy-go-lucky weekly church attendance. We live in times of war. And yet, we do not do this in our own strength. "Are you tired? Worn out? Burned out on religion? Come to me. Get away with me and you'll recover your life. I'll show you how to take a real rest. Walk with me and work with me—watch how I do it. Learn the unforced rhythms of grace. I won't lay anything heavy or ill-fitting on you. Keep company with me and you'll learn to live freely and lightly" (Matt 11:29–30, MSG).

Ponder the following Scriptures and note the verbs used in these verses. Write down any observations or reflections.

- Hebrews 5:14
- 2 Corinthians 4:8–12
- Philippians 3:8–11,14
- Colossians 1:29
- I Timothy 4:10)
- Hebrews 10:32)
- Hebrews 12:4)
- 2 Corinthians 10:3
- 2 Timothy 4:7
- Ephesians 6:11–13
- 1 Peter 2:11
- 1 Peter 4:12–13

In your opinion, is this the sort of vision that we are courageously announcing to the public around us? Why or why not?

_____

_____

_____

_____

_____

> Jesus said we could ask for anything *in* His name—not *anything by way* of His name. Therefore, we are only able to ask for what would be found in Christ—all other things will not be given and thus should not be asked for.

God's agenda with His creation is to glorify Himself through it and to display that glory for all to see. His glory is displayed when His character and joy incarnates through His people. Our agenda then becomes living in such a way that His character and joy becomes evident in our lives.

Part 4: The Church in Submission to the King and His Kingdom

"You see, we don't go around preaching about ourselves. We preach that Jesus Christ is Lord, and we ourselves are your servants for Jesus' sake . . . So we live in the face of death, but this has resulted in eternal life for you . . . All of this is for your benefit. And as God's grace reaches more and more people, there will be great thanksgiving, and God will receive more and more glory . . . That is why we never give up. Though our bodies are dying, our spirits are being renewed every day. For our present troubles are small and won't last very long. Yet they produce for us a glory that vastly outweighs them and will last forever!" (2 Cor 4:5, 12, 15–17).

"Not to us, O Lord, not to us, but to your name goes all the glory for your unfailing love and faithfulness. Why let the nations say, "Where is their God?" Our God is in the heavens, and he does as he wishes. Their idols are merely things of silver and gold, shaped by human hands" (Ps 115:1–4).

"If we want publicity in the eyes of men we have our reward. In other words, it is immaterial whether the publicity we want is the grosser kind, which all can see, or the more subtle variety which we can only see ourselves. If the left hand knows what the right hand is doing, if we become conscious of our hidden virtue, we are forging our own reward, instead of that which God had intended to give us in his own good time. But if we are content to carry on with our life hidden from our eyes, we shall receive our reward openly from God."[7]

Read Acts 19:11–20.
What is God showing you in this story?
Write down any thoughts, questions, or promptings.

_____

_____

_____

_____

Picture a 'successful' church or ministry. What does it look like? How many people attend? How fast is it growing? Why is it growing? Why do people go there? Why do people give their time and resources to it? What motivates the leaders of that ministry?

_____

_____

[7] Bonhoeffer, *Discipleship*, 178.

_____

_____

Jesus repeatedly warned those who held the highest positions of religious authority (man-centered). "What sorrow awaits you teachers of religious law and you Pharisees. Hypocrites! For you are so careful to clean the outside of the cup and the dish, but inside you are filthy—full of greed and self-indulgence! You blind Pharisee! First wash the inside of the cup and the dish, and then the outside will become clean, too" (Matt 23:25–26). The Pharisees, like us, were simply trying to achieve an image that validated their sense of self-worth. So they spent their time polishing their religious image. We have fallen into the same trap. In what ways do we polish our image as a church or ministry? (To earn respect and authority perhaps?) What is it we believe matters in order to maintain this identity to maintain our status?

_____

_____

_____

_____

_____

When I was directing a youth ministry, I started a program at an alternative high school. Immediately objections rose up from my committee. Some of them quit and refused to give funding. One of these committee members parting words were, "I don't know those kids, why would we have a ministry there?" 'Alternative school kids' are invisible in their communities. They are the kids that most people don't want to think about or would rather pretend don't exist in the first place. The ministry at the alternative school looked different than our ministries in mainstream schools. We didn't have any glitzy programs and we weren't doing anything that would attract donors with lots of dollars. I simply recruited a handful of adults to volunteer their time in a classroom to tutor and offer guidance to students as they attempted to figure out a career path beyond high school. We didn't do the usual weekly program because we were fairly certain that students who were living in their cars or were their family's primary breadwinner wouldn't have much interest in our skits and games. So we faithfully loved them in ways that were largely unnoticed by the community and the organization I was employed by.

When a church or ministry becomes idolized due to its own 'success,' the energy of the leaders will be directed towards maintaining that ministry's standing as an idol. If leaders are idolizing their work because of its growth, than growth will be achieved at all cost and by any available method. Congregants and volunteers in turn will be exhorted to direct their time and resources in ways that maximize the organizations potential to grow.

As we look outward at the world, there are two important things we must consider.

1. We do not build churches or ministries on the hoped-for success of that particular ministry but on a platform of (King)dom advancement in the strength, timing and methodology that God Himself provides. In this way, God receives the glory and not our ministry. (Gideon is a great example of this.)

2. Jesus sent His disciples out as sheep among wolves. If we are being faithful, we should expect to get beat up, opposed, and kicked out. Apart from intimacy with God, we will not survive these beatings and will find alternative places of refuge (perhaps an affair or worse, a successful ministry that dishonors God).

God sends us in His intimate embrace—our Dad, our brother, Jesus and the Holy Spirit. We never go alone. God sends us so that we might discover that we do in fact need Him. If we have ambitions of doing missional things for God apart from intimacy with Him, we will fall flat on our faces. So let's begin here. Take a few minutes to meditate on the four points below.

Intimacy with God is:

➤ Merging into an eternal conversation between the Father, Son and Holy Spirit that had no beginning and will have no end.

➤ Discovering that the Father, Son and Holy Spirit are equally as delighted to have *us* at the table, as they are to have *each other* at the table.

➤ Discovering that we are *no less welcomed* into this divine Community than Jesus is. We are never in jeopardy of being kicked out.

➤ Discovering that it is God's nature to enjoy others without needing them; He enjoys you even when you're not intrinsically enjoyable.

God's covenant with us is unilateral meaning He offers a gift (eternal relationship) for which there is no ability for the receiving party to repay, match, or fulfill. We are accustomed to bilateral covenantal agreements in which two equal parties have equal offerings (mutual sharing of personhood, resources, etc.). The covenant God offers to us is unilateral. Only He can provide what He is asking of us. We cannot repay Him for what He's done. If we think we can, we are making ourselves equal with God by assuming that we also hold the keys to life and goodness. *Our first and only action in covenantal relationship with God is receiving.* Intimacy with God begins by seeing how deeply God is committed to us. Intimacy with God is built as we receive what He is generously giving us and reciprocate this Gift to those around us as sheep among wolves.

What is God committed to?

Committed to giving generously without getting anything in return from us.

> "When we were utterly helpless, Christ came at just the right time and died for us sinners. Now, most people would not be willing to die for an upright person, though someone might perhaps be willing to die for a person who is especially good. But God showed his great love for us by sending Christ to die for us while we were still sinners" (Rom 5:6–8).

> "One of the criminals who hung there hurled insults at him: "Aren't you the Christ? Save yourself and us!" (Luke 23:39).

Committed to being faithful yet appearing foolish.

> "For Christ didn't send me to baptize, but to preach the Good News—and not with clever speech, for fear that the cross of Christ would lose its power. The message of the cross is foolish to those who are headed for destruction! But we who are being saved know it is the very power of God" (1 Cor 1:17–18).

> "Then Pilate had Jesus flogged with a lead-tipped whip. The soldiers wove a crown of thorns and put it on his head, and they put a purple robe on him. "Hail! King of the Jews!" they mocked, as they slapped him across the face" (John 19:1–3).

Committed to injuring us for our benefit.

> "We think you ought to know, dear brothers and sisters, about the trouble we went through in the province of Asia. We were crushed and overwhelmed beyond our ability to endure, and we thought we would never live through it. In fact, we expected to die. But as a result, we stopped relying on ourselves and learned to rely only on God, who raises the dead. And he did rescue us from mortal danger, and he will rescue us again. We have placed our confidence in him, and he will continue to rescue us" (2 Cor 1:8–10).

> "Jesus turned around and looked at his disciples, then reprimanded Peter. "Get away from me, Satan!" he said. "You are seeing things merely from a human point of view, not from God's" (Mark 8:33).

Committed to sacrificing what He has so we can receive what we don't yet have.

> "Jesus gave his life for our sins, just as God our Father planned, in order to rescue us from this evil world in which we live. All glory to God forever and ever! Amen" (Gal 1:4–5).

> "About three o'clock Jesus cried out with a loud voice, "Eli, Eli, lema sabachthani?", which means, "My God, my God, why have you forsaken me?" (Matt 27:46).

Committed to being associated with us.

> "Even before he made the world, God loved us and chose us in Christ to be holy and without fault in his eyes. God decided in advance to adopt us into his own family by bringing us to himself through Jesus Christ. This is what he wanted to

do, and it gave him great pleasure. So we praise God for the glorious grace he has poured out on us who belong to his dear Son" (Eph 1:4–6).

➤ "Later, Matthew invited Jesus and his disciples to his home as dinner guests, along with many tax collectors and other disreputable sinners. But when the Pharisees saw this, they asked his disciples, "Why does your teacher eat with such scum?" (Matt 9:10–11).

Committed to forfeiting His status, rights, and privileges for our benefit.

➤ "Though he was God, he did not think of equality with God as something to cling to. Instead, he gave up his divine privileges; he took the humble position of a slave and was born as a human being. When he appeared in human form, he humbled himself in obedience to God and died a criminal's death on a cross. Therefore, God elevated him to the place of highest honor and gave him the name above all other names, that at the name of Jesus every knee should bow, in heaven and on earth and under the earth, and every tongue confess that Jesus Christ is Lord, to the glory of God the Father" (Phil 2:6–11).

➤ "So he got up from the table, took off his robe, wrapped a towel around his waist, and poured water into a basin. Then he began to wash the disciples' feet, drying them with the towel he had around him" (John 13:4–5).

Committed to exercising power without needing to be right or in control.

➤ "You were dead because of your sins and because your sinful nature was not yet cut away. Then God made you alive with Christ, for he forgave all our sins. He canceled the record of the charges against us and took it away by nailing it to the cross" (Col 2:13–14).

➤ "Jesus answered, "My Kingdom is not an earthly kingdom. If it were, my followers would fight to keep me from being handed over to the Jewish leaders. But my Kingdom is not of this world . . . You would have no power over me at all unless it were given to you from above" (John 18:36; 19:11a).

Committed to displaying His glory in us.

➤ "I tell you the truth, when you were young, you were able to do as you liked; you dressed yourself and went wherever you wanted to go. But when you are old, you will stretch out your hands, and others will dress you and take you where you don't want to go." Jesus said this to let him know by what kind of death he would glorify God. Then Jesus told him, "Follow me" (John 21:18–19).

➤ "But whenever someone turns to the Lord, the veil is taken away. For the Lord is the Spirit, and wherever the Spirit of the Lord is, there is freedom. So all of us who have had that veil removed can see and reflect the glory of the Lord. And the Lord—who is the Spirit—makes us more and more like him as we are changed into his glorious image" (2 Cor 3:16-18).

Reflect on the ways that God is committed to you, your community, and the world. How might these commitments, factually demonstrated by God Himself throughout human history, transform your heart and shape your commitments to those around you?

_____

_____

_____

_____

_____

_____

How do these commitments change your outlook towards those in your midst (particularly those you would rather not associate with)?

_____

_____

_____

_____

What is the risk in practicing these above commitments to those around you? And what is the risk in *not* practicing these above commitments to those around you? Take some time with your community to discuss these commitments. How can you be tangible reminders to *one another* of God's commitments? Write your thoughts for discussion below.

_____

_____

_____

_____

_____

_____

When we feel God's intimate embrace and see the depth of His love and commitment to us and our neighbors, we are then empowered and freed to extend the same degree of love and commitment to those we would rather choose to ignore or harm.

If God's commitments shape and empower our commitments to our neighbors, how will you and your community demonstrate the truthful character of God to those around you? Brainstorm some real and actual ideas below that you will do together. Write down your creative ideas and responses below.

_____

_____

_____

_____

_____

_____

_____

_____

Join with me . . .

Essentially the Church is a room of sinners that share in the transformative presence of Jesus. Sometimes this is exciting; sometimes this is terrifying. The point is not to search for or fabricate a feel-good Jesus experience for ourselves or others but to accept the grace that God is giving us in being His body in this moment and in this place with other sinful people on their way to becoming like Jesus. There is nothing 'attractional' about this to a world that is seeking an identity in pleasure and ego. Let us beware of being so quick to turn church into fun-times that appeal to hungry egos. It is not our job to try and make church look more appealing for ourselves or our neighbors. It is indeed true that we are scared of commitment. We are scared of intimate friendships because we might get hurt. We are fearful of becoming vulnerable because we might get teased or exploited. These are real concerns. However, God invites us to enter into a covenant with our brothers and sisters that requires us to face these fears. If my brother in Christ injures me, I do not have license to write him off. My covenant with him is bound, not by my degree of satisfaction with the friendship, but rather by God's degree of commitment to my brother. Jesus died, not just so that each of us might be saved, but that our *relationship* might be saved as well. God's covenant with each of us defines the terms of our covenant with one another.

As this book nears its end, your journey is just beginning. The last pages of this book is a tool that is designed to catalyze into creative action all that you have been chewing on over the past 10 weeks. Together, use this tool to creatively and prayerfully begin implementing an intentional way of being together that is both transformational and missional in your local community and abroad. Together, write up a practical, strategic, and intentional plan that might help posture you to be listeners before God and ready to respond to Him accordingly.

I was always told growing up that the best thing a Christian can do for a non-Christian is to 'invite them to church'. Well if 'church' is not a building or an event but a community of people empowered and led by Christ as their King and Savior; that certainly broadens the possibilities of what we might offer the world. Prayerfully reflect on the questions and together, retool what your gatherings and expressions of love and service to your community might look like.

I invite you to prayerfully and creatively think through this with me. What is God calling His children to give to the world? A church service? A service project? I believe it will look different yet strikingly familiar everywhere. And I believe that our habits and priorities will need to be changed. God draws us into His work to renovate our hearts. Paul tells us that we (plural) are the aroma (singular) of Christ (2 Cor 2:16). To some we are the smell of life and to others the smell of death. We are not to be concerned if people smell Christ and call it death or call it life. We are simply called to be faithful to smelling like Him and not something or someone else. Due to our attempts to be hip, cool, and relevant, we have lost the aroma of Christ. We have the aroma of our culture or our selves, but not Christ. Let us return to the rhythms of steadfastly listening and obediently responding to the Spirit of God.

The following tool is not intended to be a formula or blueprint. It is intended to catalyze and bring to light the things the Spirit of God is up to in your midst. Use it to draw attention to your neighborhood and relationships. Use it to help shape the practices and habits that *must become normal* in order for you to be equipped as a community of disciples. Use it to bring creativity and intentionality to all that you are doing together. Think of it as the 'T' in T-Ball or maybe Driver's Ed. Driver's Ed or T-Ball is not something you do for years. It simply gets you on your feet so that you are free to get on to bigger and better things. The aim of this journey has been to simply get you on the path to bigger and better things—namely, the things of God. There is a sense of safety that comes from getting absorbed in a study or a structure. But we mustn't remain there. God is calling us out into the open spaces to see the un-limits of His greatness and glory.

"So let us not speak falsely now, the hour is getting late."—Bob Dylan

"This is the kind of fasting I want:
Free those who are wrongly imprisoned;
lighten the burden of those who work for you.
Let the oppressed go free,
and remove the chains that bind people.

> Share your food with the hungry,
> and give shelter to the homeless.
> Give clothes to those who need them,
> and do not hide from relatives who need your help.
> Then your salvation will come like the dawn,
> and your wounds will quickly heal.
> Your godliness will lead you forward,
> and the glory of the Lord will protect you from behind.
> (Isaiah 58:6–8)

Creatively and Prayerfully Envision . . .

Our calling, as a living cell of God's local church, is to discover and *live* the innovative and creative ways that the Spirit is revealing our Dad's heart to reconcile the world to Himself. God determines things; we do not. It is *His* kingdom, not ours.

How will we ourselves and how will we invite others to . . .
- Allow the Spirit of God to lead in the work of the Father and to have authority over our values, decisions, relationships, and cultural practices?
- Move towards a *lifestyle* that is both mission (other-centered) and community (builds itself up in love) oriented?
  - Phase 1: I observe other Christians being Christians [*SEEN*]
  - Phase 2: I participate in a planned community or mission oriented activity [*DISCIPLINE*]
  - Phase 3: I live missionally and in community spontaneously and holistically [*LIFESTYLE*]
- Pursue whole-life discipleship as brothers and sisters in Christ; discovering and becoming fruitful in what it means to love God with everything and to love your neighbor as yourselves and maintain the disciplines necessary to wage spiritual war?

How can we creatively retool our planned gatherings so that . . .
- We can become friends who learn to pray with one another, cry with one another, and share God's Word with one another without needing an organized 'church event' to do so? How can we blur the line between 'at church' and 'not at church'?
- We can live holistically; becoming a community that values what God values in all areas of life; relationally, spiritually, and culturally?
- We can develop kingdom (other-centeredness, building each other up in love) instincts that guide us irrespective of organized 'church activities'? How can we blur the line between discipleship/fellowship and evangelism?

Creatively and Prayerfully Envision Intentional and Celebratory Gatherings For . . .
1. Practicing life in covenant with God and with our brothers and sisters in Jesus. How will we . . .
➢ Move from Sunday Christianity to daily, whole-life discipleship?
➢ Learn from God's story and help one another surrender our story to His?
➢ Give and receive healing and prophetic words?
➢ Provide a safe space to be vulnerable and raw and begin practicing a new way of life?
➢ Share our lives so that we can celebrate, shoulder each others' burdens and see the Spirit's activity in our midst?
➢ Seek God's leading in our lives through Scripture, prayer, and listening?
➢ Speak the truth in love to one another?
➢ Pray for God to restore His Church and to reach our community?

2. Sharing testimonies (factual and experiential stories) of God's promise and presence in our lives, our community, and the world with each other and our neighbors. How will we . . .
➢ Show a churched or unchurched person what it looks like to be disciples of Jesus?
➢ Deconstruct cultural paradigms of God and Church in order to introduce whole life discipleship in a *kingdom* context?
➢ Create a new 'front door' by which to welcome the world in to 'taste and see' that God is good?
➢ In a public or relational context, share stories from our own lives that illustrate God calling us out of our own story and into His story; revealing both His glory and the hardship?
➢ Quiet our hearts before God that we might see Him clearly and adore, celebrate, and revere Him?
➢ Tell God's stories by which we discover Him and become His disciples?

3. Inviting our neighbors to participate in the work of God that they might experience the heart of God. How will we . . .
➢ Demonstrate and lead others towards becoming Christians while not 'in church'?
➢ Dream up creative ways to build relationships with and serve our neighbors and unveil God's character and redemptive purposes to the community?

Bibliography

Adbusters, Jul/Aug 2003.

Allender, Dr. Dan B., and Dr. Tremper Longman III. *The Cry of the Soul*. Colorado Springs, CO: Navpress, 1994.

Arnold, Johann Cristoph, *Seeking Peace: Notes and Conversations Along the Way*. Bruderhof Foundation, 2003. http.www.bruderhof.com. (accessed August 25, 2003).

The Barna Group, Ltd. "Half of Americans Say Faith Has "Greatly Transformed" Their Life," (June 6, 2006). http://www.barna.org/FlexPage.aspx?Page=BarnaUpdateNarrowPreview&BarnaUpdateID=240 (accessed June 6, 2006).

Berkhof, Hendrik. *Christ and the Powers*. Translated by John H. Yoder. Scottdale, PA: Mennonite Publishing House, 1977.

Bonhoeffer, Dietrich. *The Cost of Discipleship*. New York: Simon and Schuster, 1959.

Bookman, Jay. "The President's Real Goal In Iraq." *The Atlanta Journal—Constitution*, (September 29, 2002). http://www.ajc.com/ (accessed Oct. 1, 2002).

Bryant, David. *Christ Is All!*, New Providence, NJ: New Providence Publishers, 1999.

Caussade, Jean-Pierre De. *Abandonment to Divine Providence*. Translated by John Beevers. New York: DoubleDay, 1975.

Chambers, Oswald. *My Utmost For His Highest*. Grand Rapids: Discovery House Publishers, 1935.

Clapp, Rodney. *A Peculiar People*. Downers Grove: InterVarsity Press, 1996.

———. *Border Crossings*. Grand Rapids: Brazos Press, 2000.

———. *Families At the Crossroads*. Downers Grove: InterVarsity Press, 1993.

Cooke, Graham. *A Divine Confrontation*. Shippensburg, PA: Destiny Image Publishers, 1999.

Crabb, Larry. *Connecting*. Nashville: Word Publishing, 1997.

———. *The Safest Place on Earth*. Nashville: Word Publishing, 1999.

Dawn, Marva. *Powers, Weakness and the Tabernacling of God*. Grand Rapids: Wm. B. Eerdmans, 2001.

———. *Unfettered Hope: A Call to Faithful Living in an Affluent Society*. Louisville: Westminster John Knox Press, 2003.

Ellul, Jaques. *False Presence of the Kingdom*. Translated by C. Edward Hopkin, New York: The Seabury Press, 1972.

Grubb, Norman. *Rees Howells Intercessor*. Fort Washington, PA: Christian Literature Crusade, 1952.

Hauerwas, Stanley, and William Willimon. *Resident Aliens*. Nashville: Abingdon Press, 1989.

———. *Where Resident Aliens Live*. Nashville: Abingdon Press, 1996.

Hauerwas, Stanley. *A Community of Character*. Indiana: University of Notre Dame, 1981.

McCoy, Kevin. "Online Gamble Pays Off for Internet Sports Books" *USA Today* (March 29, 2002). http://www.usatoday.com/money/covers/2002-03-29-online-bets.htm (accessed June 6, 2006).

Manning, Brennan. *Abba's Child: The Cry of the Heart For Intimate Belonging*. Colorado Springs: Navpress, 1994.

———. *Ruthless Trust*. San Francisco: Harper San Francisco, 2000.

McManus, Erwin. *Seizing Your Divine Moment*. Nashville: Thomas Nelson Publishers, 2002.

Maxwell, Janine. *It's Not Okay With Me*. Enumclaw, WA: Winepress Publishers, 2006.

Meyers, Bryant L. *Walking With the Poor*. New York: Orbis Press, 1999.

Narramore, Matthew. *Tithing: Low-Realm, Obsolete & Defunct*. Graham, NC: Tekoa Publishing, 2004.

Newbigin, Lesslie. *Foolishness to the Greeks*. Grand Rapids: Wm. B. Eerdmans, 1986.

———. *The Gospel in A Pluralist Society*. Grand Rapids: Wm B. Eerdmans, 1989.

Noll, Mark A., et al. *The Search For Christian America*. Colorado Springs: Helmers & Howard, 1989.

Bibliography

Peterson, Eugene, *Answering God: The Psalms As Tools For Prayer.* New York: Harper Collins, 1989.

————. *Where Your Treasure Is.* San Francisco: Harper San Francisco, 1989.

Piper, John, *Brothers, We Are Not Professionals.* Nashville: Broadman and Holman Publishers, 2002.

————. *The Passion of Jesus Christ.* Wheaton, IL: Crossway Books, 2004.

Reiff, Philip. *The Triumph of the Therapeutic: Uses of Faith after Freud.* Chicago: University of Chicago Press, 1966.

Religion Newswriters Foundation. "Guide to Covering 'Under God' Pledge Decision." (September, 2005). http://www.religionlink.org/tip_031003a.php (accessed December 18, 2006).

Sider, Ronald J. *Rich Christians In an Age of Hunger.* Downers Grove: InterVarsity Press, 1977.

————. *The Scandal of the Evangelical Conscience.* Grand Rapids: Baker Books, 2005.

Sine, Tom. *Mustard Seed Versus McWorld.* Grand Rapids: Baker Books, 1999.

Stassen, Glen, and David Gushee. *Kingdom Ethics.* Downers Grove: InterVarsity Press, 2003.

Stringfellow, William. *A Private and Public Faith.* Eugene, OR: Wipf and Stock Publishers, 1999.

Duffy, Brian. "Defining America." US News and World Report, (June 28–July 5, 2004): 36–57.

Wangerin, Walter Jr. *Whole Prayer.* Grand Rapids: Zondervan, 1998.

Willson, S. Brian. "Assimilation or Elimination: Pax Americana—Buy In or Check Out." (1999). http://www.brianwillson.com/awolassim.html (accessed December 13, 2006).